FREEDOM AND SIN

FREEDOM AND SIN

Evil in a World Created by God

ROSS McCULLOUGH

WILLIAM B. EERDMANS PUBLISHING COMPANY
GRAND RAPIDS, MICHIGAN

Wm. B. Eerdmans Publishing Co.
4035 Park East Court SE, Grand Rapids, Michigan 49546
www.eerdmans.com

28 27 26 25 24 23 22   1 2 3 4 5 6 7

ISBN 978-0-8028-8183-0

Library of Congress Cataloging-in-Publication Data

A catalog record for this book is available from the Library of
Congress.

Unless otherwise noted, Scripture quotations are taken from the
Revised Standard Version of the Bible.

CONTENTS

CONTENTS

FOREWORD

This book is a defense of the thesis that Ross McCullough calls "indeterminist compatibilism." The compatibilist part of this is that freedom is held to be compatible with God's determination of what we do. God's agency and ours are in this way not in competition with each other. God can bring about what we bring about, and we can still bring it about freely. The indeterminist part of the thesis, however, is that while God can sometimes act indefectibly, not allowing our defection, God can also sometimes act defectibly, so that we can decline to conform our will. This gives us a chance to act rightly when we could have not done so. The benefit this gives us is not freedom, because of the compatibilist part of the thesis; it is what Ross calls "self-creation." The key insight here is that our defection is a failing to act, and in the Platonist tradition that Ross endorses (with sophisticated qualifications) this does not count as an action that must be founded in the agency of a sovereign God.

There are at least three reasons to read this book. The first, and most important, is that if Ross's thesis is coherent, we have a way to hold together two ideas that have usually been held to be in deep tension with each other, but that Christians have usually wanted to assert together. The first idea is that God is against sin, and the second is that God is completely sovereign. These two ideas are central to the Christian faith, and the felt tension between them is a difficulty for the faith. Ross's account is a positive proposal for how to construe these two ideas. He does not try to show that his is the only way to do this or to show that other ways fail. But it is still a remarkable achievement if he can pull it off. Thus the first reason to read the book is to see if he can pull it off.

The second reason is that the book is beautifully written. It is clear when it needs to be clear, and it makes all sorts of original and insightful distinctions. But the book is also full of humor and poetic or even rhapsodic diction. This makes reading the book a pleasure and (unlike much philosophical theology) an edification. The Christian life is taken seriously as a difficult and worthwhile practice, and the theory is grounded in this practice and contributes to it.

The third reason is the scope of Ross's sources. He is a bridge-builder, and he brings together ideas and vocabularies from theologians and philosophers of widely different schools. The primary source for the book is the Bible, and Ross has many readings of scriptural passages that are illuminating in their own right. But beyond the Bible, he is learned in both scholastic philosophy and contemporary analytic philosophy. Within scholastic theology and philosophy, he takes ideas from both the Dominicans and the Franciscans. One of the delightful features of the book is the way in which both Scotus and Thomas appear as heroes in different sections. The project is nonpartisan in this way and is deeply refreshing for this reason. Moreover, within Thomism Ross is sensitive to the merits not just of the medieval period but of post-Tridentine and especially twentieth-century writers in that tradition. The reader comes away from the book feeling that she has tasted the fruits of many centuries of reflection about these topics that lie at the heart of the faith.

The path to Ross's constructive suggestion requires dealing with many other difficulties in understanding the faith, which we might call "theological knots." I will mention some of them in order to whet the appetite, but it is not the job of a foreword to try to be complete. Ross has a detailed discussion of voluntarism, of its various forms, and the difference between the suggestion that we can will something under the form of evil (which Ross rejects) and the suggestion that the will can suspend its own activity of willing under the form of good (which Ross accepts). This discussion involves dealing with the question of the will in the next life, in what sense (if any) the freedom of the blessed includes the possibility of defection. This in turn requires distinguishing between human freedom and God's freedom. Ross argues that humans retain the difference from God that they are creatures that are becoming, not simply being. This means that a distinction is necessary between different kinds of deification; substantial deification is something humans cannot have, but accidental deification they can have (coming to have some of God's properties).

Another theological knot is the relationship of our language to God. Ross has a richly worked out account of analogy and metaphor. This involves delving into the disagreement between Thomas and Scotus on univocity: In what sense (if any) does our language about God have the same meaning as the same words used to talk about the world? Ross shows that the disagreement is not as straightforward as interpreters have often assumed. Our verdict is going to depend upon what kind of access we think we have to understanding the kind of infinity that God has and we do not, and Ross is skeptical that Scotus can produce a non-analogical account of this access.

For a Christian, questions about the relation between God's freedom and ours will raise questions about the incarnation. How did Jesus combine the two? Ross takes the view that the incarnation was not simply a response to the Fall of human beings, but that God already (in the first creation) fashions us after the pattern of Christ's humanity. And this is not merely the generically human, but the individual excellences that are our individual goals. Here Scotus is the hero. But Christ in his humanity also gave us a pattern of self-creation, including facing suffering and death, and we can enter into this pattern, even though Christ did not have, as we have, the possibility of defection.

Here is one last example of a theological knot that Ross investigates: Are we predestined to either salvation or damnation? Ross takes the view that Paul's discussion in Romans 9 ("Has the potter no right over the clay?") is not about individuals but about Israel. God's judgment is therefore temporary, as Paul goes on to say; as Jeremiah already put it, the pot headed for destruction can be remade.

This is just a sampling of the good things in this book. There is a great deal more. This book is a model of how theology can be both learned and inspiring. The reader who goes through it carefully will end up informed, sometimes entertained, sometimes provoked, but in the end edified. A faith that is seeking understanding will get some of what it seeks.

John E. Hare

ACKNOWLEDGMENTS

This work would not have been possible without the insights, kindness, and perseverance of many people. Thanks are due in particular to Kathryn Tanner, John Hare, Jennifer Herdt, John Pittard, Denys Turner, Thomas Osborne, Stephen Ogden, Brad East, Jamie Dunn, Janna Gonwa, Ryan Darr, and the many colleagues whose advice I have benefited from, sometimes rather too much in the breach than the observance. Of the saints, besides those acknowledged variously in what follows, Saint Bonaventure and Saint Francis de Sales especially should be mentioned: the one for his emphasis on exemplarity and the noetic effects of sin, the other for his penetration of the pettifogging around predestination and its implications for the incarnation.

Above all, as Bonaventure himself notes in the prologue to his *Breviloquium*, "If anything here is found to be imperfect, obscure, superfluous, or inaccurate, let it be imputed to pressing business, insufficient time, and my own inadequate knowledge; if anything is found to be good, let the honor and glory be rendered to God alone." This is an appropriate acknowledgment for any work, but especially this one, for what follows is in a sense an attempt to specify what Bonaventure means. I would only add, what afflicts me no doubt more than Bonaventure, that much in the way of pressure, insufficiency, and inadequacy here are themselves a symptom of the slavery of sin—this slavery, too, being important in the adumbrations of Christian freedom to come—and pray the reader "remember these my fetters. Grace be with you" (Col. 4:18).

INTRODUCTION

CREATED FREEDOM

And he gave skill to human beings
that he might be glorified in his marvelous works.
By them he heals and takes away pain.

—SIRACH 38:6–7

"For from him and through him and to him are all things" (Rom. 11:36). If God is the Creator of all that is, then God is the Creator also of our acts. Indeed, God is the Creator even of our causing our acts, at least to the degree that our causing is an ontological positive and not either a defect or a mere formality or empty description, a kind of Cambridge property with no associated reality. God's creative activity is not alongside our own, as if we two were co-creators of what we bring about; God brings about our bringing about.

I will take this point as a premise for all that follows, and its attractions, briefly and broadly, are threefold. First, it better befits the majesty of God; not only is it devotionally appropriate that, all else being equal, we should exalt God more, but it is also perhaps philosophically necessary, if one takes the cosmological argument seriously, for every aspect of contingent existence to be directly rooted in the necessary being. Second, and stemming in part from this first reason, it is the view of most major figures in the Christian tradition, including Augustine, Aquinas, and Calvin. Third, setting God behind and not alongside human beings allows us to make better sense of other Christian commitments in, for instance, Christology, ecclesiology, and the inspiration of Scripture. Thus it is not clear that a human being could take on a canine nature without it implying some kind of new third nature that combined the features of humanity and caninity, for humans and dogs act, as it were, on the same plane or in the same order; but God can become man without confusion. Again, it is not clear how we could inspire the words of another without it being either mere counsel or full dictation; and yet the Holy Spirit authors the Bible in neither way. Or again with a Christian politics, broadly conceived, this high view of creation sets up God's governance not as our domination but as our empowerment: because our causal activity is not in competition with God's, not on the same plane as God's, we are not constrained or crowded out by God's involvement but the product of it. We are quite literally nothing without it.

Against all this is the fact of evil—particularly, where our acts are concerned, moral evil. If God brings about our acts, then it would seem that God brings about our sins. God's involvement may be empowering, but it often seems to empower us only to fail in our projects, to harm our friends. To put the question also in political terms: if it is a tyranny of one kind to think God governs as an external overseer, and if it is a tyranny of another to think God's interior influence is behind our evils, then how is a liberating theology to proceed?

In general, it has proceeded by emphasizing one side and remaining at a loss for the other. Thus Kathryn Tanner, from whom I have taken this dichotomy of tyranny and empowerment,[1] has provided a spirited defense of this noncompetitive view and an unyielding assertion of God's opposition to evil

1. As the subtitle to her defense of a noncompetitive relationship be-

3

while admitting that "one can offer no account of how sin actually arises that does not imply that God's creative will is directly behind such an eventuality."[2] On the other side, the black post-Christian theologian William Jones has suggested that "the choice is between (a) a black hope based on God as a white racist and (b) one based on God as functionally neutral relative to human affairs. If these are the alternatives, then the choice open to us seems clear-cut."[3] For Jones, any God who is so intimately involved in human affairs as to be able to save us from racism is, by the fact that we have not been saved, implicated in racism; better then to think that God is removed from our affairs. The same discomfort with God's influence appears, in milder form, with liberationist appeals to human freedom as a limitation on God's power—as if our free activity were a check and not a manifestation of the Creator's activity. Thus Gustavo Gutiérrez: "God wants justice indeed . . . but God cannot impose it, for the nature of created beings must be respected. God's power is limited by human freedom; for without freedom God's justice would not be present within history."[4] The assumption here is that God does not impose on our freedom, as if human freedom, both the power and its use, were not themselves creatures

tween Creator and creatures, Kathryn Tanner, *God and Creation in Christian Theology: Tyranny or Empowerment?* (Minneapolis: Fortress, 2005).

2. Kathryn Tanner, "Human Freedom, Human Sin, and God the Creator," in *The God Who Acts: Philosophical and Theological Explorations*, ed. Thomas F. Tracy (University Park: Pennsylvania State University Press, 1992), 132–33. Cf. also Karen Kilby, "Evil and the Limits of Theology," *New Blackfriars* 84 (2003): 13–29.

3. William R. Jones, *Is God a White Racist? A Preamble to Black Theology* (Boston: Beacon, 1997), 197.

4. Gustavo Gutiérrez, *On Job*, trans. Matthew O'Connell (Maryknoll, NY: Orbis Books, 1987), 77.

imposed, like all creatures must be, by the Creator. God's opposition to evil is maintained only by putting God alongside, and so into a kind of competition with, creation.

The aim of this project is to hold together God's opposition to evil and God's noncompetition with creatures: not just in tension, by a kind of equal and opposite emphasis; not contrapuntally to produce some higher harmony; not dialectically toward some sublating synthesis; but as containing no intrinsic opposition, as complements, without contradictions to be worked out over time or sounded together or juxtaposed dispositively. My argument as a whole, then, will be a kind of inverted *reductio*, designed to lead not to absurdity but to congruence: an *eductio ad armoniam*. As such, it will not primarily be concerned to show that different syntheses of similar issues are worse. It will in general take the alternatives to fail by insufficiently attending to one or the other of these classical cum liberationist premises; it will in general assume that the proponents of these alternative themselves often— though not always—appreciate that insufficiency. (Some five-point Calvinists may have eradicated all Arminian intuitions about evil, some analytic theologians may have occluded all classical notions of creation; this will come off more as a merely intellectual exercise to them.) The advantage of this approach, then, is that the bar for proof is somewhat lower, because of the dissatisfaction with the alternatives: it must minimally show that these instincts neither contradict one another nor contradict other important Christian beliefs; it must, with slightly more ambition, show how they fit together well, one to the other and both within the larger constellation of Christian thought and practice. The disadvantage of this approach, the source of its opponents' dissatisfaction, is that these premises may be irreconcilable.

Providence, in Four Prayers

If the classical and liberationist character of these two premises is insufficiently manifest or insufficiently compelling, consider instead three basic prayers.

"Deliver me from my enemies, O my God, protect me from those who rise up against me" (Ps. 59:1). Implicit in this plea for deliverance is that God has power over evil without being implicated in it. We ask God to remove evil because God is powerful enough to be able to do it and because God is good enough to be willing to do it. To say that God is not implicated in the evil of our enemies, then, is not just a point about God's guilt. What we want is a God who will overcome the evil in our lives, not just a God who can be exonerated of their evils: implacable opposition, not just innocence. God should in no way bring about evil, even where this bringing about does not inculpate God—and yet should also be able to put a stop to it. What sort of doctrine of providence is implicit in this commitment?

One possibility, going back at least as far as Origen, is to conceive providence as an overarching force bringing all things to good even in the face of particular historical evils. Providence operates at a general level to bring history and its evils to an end but not necessarily to bring an end within history to any particular evil. Evils that stem from an inviolable human freedom, for instance, cannot be avoided but only turned in the long run to good. Joseph's brothers cannot be made to treat Joseph well; at best, God can use their jealousy and Joseph's suffering for salvation. This on its own is rather weak, conceiving God's sovereignty at so general a level that particular historical evils must in general be endured with an eye toward future rewards. Providence just does not deal much with our more temporary travails.

Our hopes for a historical deliverance are still not satisfied even where God's involvement is made more granular and the ultimacy of the overcoming remains, for instance with a Barthian combination of intimate involvement and universal salvation. Here the problem is not that providence does not touch our historical problems but that it does, and that it authors them. What comfort it provides the cancerous, what exodus it works for the enslaved, is reliable only beyond history; within history, providence has in some manner brought about our sickness and our slavery—and may continue to do so.

Consider then a second prayer: "nevertheless, not my will but thine be done" (Luke 22:42). Often this is taken to be a prayer of resignation to the divine will, as if we were asking only to align our wills with God's and not finally to align the world with it; as if it pointed only to the crucifixion and not through it to the resurrection. If the first kind of prayer was "deliver us from evil," the second is "thy will be done on earth as it is in heaven"—but as the words suggest, this is about changing the earth, not just changing the one who prays, and about eradicating the evils of history, not just about their eradication in heaven. It is about resignation to God not by a retreat into passivity but by a rearrangement of all things, including one's will, including one's surroundings. Its doctrine of providence is both more implacable and more immediately involved.

Even more, this sort of prayer begins to suggest a practical ground for the idea that God can predetermine our free choices. For a great deal of the evil we seek to overcome is precisely moral evil, not least the evil choices of those who would oppress us. Nor do we ask only that their oppressive effects be taken away; we pray indeed as Christians for their conversion. "Brethren, my heart's desire and prayer to God for them is that they may be saved" (Rom. 10:1). This is the third kind of prayer, and it is at least a part of what we ask when we pray "thy kingdom come." But this is a strange request if we do not think that the Spirit can bring us freely to accept the Father through the Son—that is, if we do not think that God can effect our conversion.[5] If having real freedom means that our important choices cannot be predetermined by God, should I then not pray for the salvation of my enemies? Should I not pray for the salvation of my children, as if that were to demand a gavage of grace that chokes their very freedom? Or is my prayer perhaps only a petition for a shifting of probabilities, as if what I am asking of the omnipotent God is not so much a definite outcome as a weighting of the dice however more slightly in one direction? Certainly this is not what I think I am doing when I make such prayers. I intend rather, as the bishop said to Monica weeping over the wandering Augustine, to make it "impossible that the son of such tears should perish!"[6] On the other hand, if we think God does predetermine all these choices, does my request that my son be saved betray a lack of faith in God's goodness, as if there were any world in which God would predetermine one of his children to damnation? It seems manifestly implicit in this sort of prayer, if the implicit can indeed be manifest, that we presume both the ability of the beloved to fall away and God's ability to bring them back, both a defectibility and an indefectibility to God's work in them.

This is only a *prima facie* practical ground for what follows, and of course alternative views will have their ways of accommodating these prayers, with more or fewer epicycles;

5. Cf. Augustine, *Grace and Free Will* 5.10 and 14.29; *Admonition and Grace* 8.17.

6. Augustine, *Confessions* 3.12.21, translated by John K. Ryan, *The Confessions of Saint Augustine* (New York: Doubleday Image, 1960), 92.

but the view it immediately suggests is the one with which I began: that the God to whom we pray neither brings about our evil choices, with their long train of ill effects, nor is unable to have made them good. God can work good in us infallibly, with no possibility of our defection, but sometimes does not. The possibility of (moral) evil is rooted in the second of these, and our pleas for deliverance and conversion are rooted in the first. On this account, God is going to have some reason for sometimes allowing our defection; but these reasons will be defeasible by other considerations, and in particular by our lamentation. When we cry to God, this gives God more reason to eradicate what we decry. God's acts do make evil possible in this world, inasmuch as God chooses sometimes to act in a way that we can defect from; but God does not in any sense bring about that defection (e.g., by failing to supply the aid necessary to remain upright—though he may fail to supply the aid sufficient to remain upright), nor does God allow the possibility of defection in order that we might in fact defect (e.g., so that a greater good could be brought out of it). Rather, God makes possible our defections in order to give us a chance to act rightly when we could have not—a chance to stay true in the face of temptations, for instance. When we pray not to be led into temptation, then—a fourth prayer—the goods of this sort of possibly defective right action are not eradicated so much as instantiated in the act of prayer itself. We may no longer be credited with resisting a temptation we could have succumbed to, but the credit accrues to the petition we could have failed to make.

This is already to court confusion, and I will have much more to say about these features of God's action, but we have enough here to see that this view is going to cut across the standard philosophical ways of categorizing freedom. Anglo-American philosophy's first division of proponents of free will cleaves them into two categories: compatibilists, who think that our free choices are compatible with being determined, and libertarians, who think that our free choices cannot be determined. Libertarians are committed to thinking that we have choices that are not determined, and compatibilists tend therefore to think that we do not, that all our choices are determined. But the upshot here is a kind of compatibilist indeterminism. It is compatibilist in that these choices, even when predetermined,[7] are still ours, and still choices—still free. (I do not pray that my child might be forced to love God but freely to choose it.) It is indeterminism in that God does not predetermine all choices. A consideration of Christ and his freedom is particularly instructive here and will prove more so in chapter 4: he is perfectly good without being any less free, which means both that his human freedom does not suffer from being predetermined to goodness (our free actions *can be* predetermined) and that his divine freedom engenders no evil (our sins *were not* predetermined). God

---

7. The philosophical literature tends to treat the determination of our choices by God as basically similar to their determination by created things—by neurochemistry or the state of the universe immediately prior to our choice or whatnot. Compatibilism thus encompasses any sort of determination whatsoever. On the sort of noncompetitive account I am adopting here, however, God, as the source of all being and therefore all actions, is not the sort of "thing" whose "determination" threatens the contingency or freedom of creatures. God brings about free acts in their freedom. Following the Thomistic tradition, then, I will refer to God's infallible actions as predeterminations, to distinguish them from the determinations that hold among creatures. Also with the Thomistic tradition, as with contemporary libertarians, I will assume that our free choices are not determined by other creatures. Because our free acts will also be human acts and therefore in some way bodily acts, there will be some story to tell about the role of our biology in our choosing. But the relations of Creator and creature present enough problems without getting into the relations of body and soul—to say nothing of, for example, the freedom of separated souls—so I will not broach the latter here.

can, but does not always, predetermine our free choices. The obvious question is why: why allow the possibility of evil acts if it is not required by our freedom?

In What Sense a Theodicy?

To ask that question is to court the charge of theodicy, which has received its share of theological scorn in recent years. Even if this account does not claim to give a complete explanation of all the different evils in God's world, even if it is focused just on moral evils or perhaps a subset of moral evils, still it might seem to approach these evils in the wrong way. "At the heart of the various criticisms is the claim that theodicies tend to put both the author and the reader into the wrong kind of relationship with evil, or, more to the point, with particular evils. They try to reconcile us to evils, that is, in a way which we should not be reconciled. If one takes the long enough view, if one really gets the right perspective, the theodicists seem to say, everything is not so bad."[8] But notice a difference here: I am not asking what it is that mitigates the evils of history, what justifies them by overcoming them or integrating them into some greater good. I am asking what makes them possible. And the point of the question is not to reconcile us with these evils but to undergird our opposition

8. Kilby, "Evil," 14–15, reading Terrence W. Tilley, *The Evils of Theodicy* (Eugene, OR: Wipf & Stock, 2000), and Kenneth Surin, *Theology and the Problem of Evil* (Eugene, OR: Wipf & Stock, 2004). See also N. N. Trakakis, "Anti-Theodicy," in *The Problem of Evil: Eight Views in Dialogue*, ed. N. N. Trakakis (Oxford: Oxford University Press, 2018), 94–122. Part of these concerns are bound up with the Enlightenment character of much theodicy, but that will have to be dispelled more by the practice of this project as it unfolds, and especially by its reliance on premodern figures, than by anything I could say here.

to them—to underscore the way in which God is inveterately opposed to them and is able, from even the most horrendous, to effect our deliverance. This is the sense of theodicy that, as Sherman Jackson says, "has acquired a status among Blackamericans comparable to that of the problem of reconciling God with modern science among white Americans. . . . [N]o religious movement that fails to speak convincingly to the problem of black theodicy can hope to enjoy a durable tenure among Blackamericans."[9]

The point here is that it is not enough to assert that God is not racist if we cannot back up that assertion. David Burrell, who defends much of the metaphysical underpinning of what is to come, has emphasized that evil is not overcome through the theodicist's explanation but through a different kind of performance, including a different kind of speech performance.[10] Still, our explanations are implicated in our performances: wrong explanations hinder how we perform and right ones encourage it; or better, the right performance embodies a certain kind of explanation, one that is implicit in how one acts. Even more, as Jackson suggests without quite saying, there is a tendency sometimes to treat the marginalized as uninterested in explanation, or as at most interested in its consequences for action—as if they were so immiserated that they have lost the capacity for wonder; as if they could not ask about God simply for the sake of "growing in the knowledge of our Lord" (2 Pet. 3:18). The wrong kind of polemic against theodicy can cut off from the marginalized much of their experience, and especially the difficult parts of their experience, as any sort of source of reflection

9. Sherman A. Jackson, *Islam and the Problem of Black Suffering* (Oxford: Oxford University Press, 2014), 5.
10. David B. Burrell, *Deconstructing Theodicy: Why Job Has Nothing to Say to the Puzzle of Suffering* (Grand Rapids: Brazos, 2008), 107–22.

about their Deliverer—because their experience is taken to demotivate reflection.

Notice also that none of this requires an actual justification of God. It may be, as many of my Christian interlocutors and many of Jackson's Muslim ones hold, that God does not have any obligations toward creatures at all and therefore stands in no need of justification. Still, we can ask the question of how a particular evil accords with God's wisdom in creating the world; there is still a problem of evil, and a need for explanation, in that sense.[11]

So I will take the question of why God permits evil as one about explanation and not necessarily justification. And I will take it to be not about the actuality of evil, as it were—for example, an explanation about how God's intervention is withheld because evil is in some way, within the larger story, made good—but about the possibility of evil: why God might allow that possibility while hoping that it goes unrealized. And notice that it is this second question that can have answers within the sort of broad Christian Platonism that is Burrell's, and my, frame. For Christian Platonism holds evil itself to be a nonentity, a privation of something due, and therefore takes it to lack the kind of intelligibility that explanation is after.[12] Evil does not have causes in the way that existing things have causes, as will become important in the first two chapters; it lacks especially the sort of final cause or what-for-ness that theodicy sometimes seeks to give it. On the other hand, the possibility of evil is rooted in a kind of being—imperfect, perhaps, but not a total nonentity—and so it can make sense to ask what sort of thing it is and what

11. I take the distinction between justification and explanation from Marilyn McCord Adams, *Christ and Horrors: The Coherence of Christology* (Cambridge: Cambridge University Press, 2008), 42–43.

12. See, classically, Augustine, *City of God* 12.7.

it is for.[13] Put differently, God does not create evil, so there is no way of linking evil to that Intelligibility that underlies creation and makes possible our explanations. But God does create the possibility of evil, and we should not be surprised to find in it some vestige of the Logos.

SOME PRESUPPOSITIONS

As should be clear, this project is going to presuppose a broad Christian Platonism—above all, that God is source, exemplar, and end; that his creative agency underlies all that we do; that evil is therefore to be understood as a privation. I will also take for granted some everyday assumptions about agency: that actions are performed or caused by agents (as opposed to events), that these agents can be held responsible for their actions, that those harmed by such actions deserve restitution of some kind, that restitution and responsibility do not dissolve immediately but endure with the agent and patient across time, and so forth.[14] When pressed, the Christian Pla-

---

13. One standard example of this in the tradition is to point to the fact that we are from nothing, which makes it possible for us to fall back into nothing. Our createdness is one of the conditions that makes evil possible. Still, it is hardly a sufficient condition: Christ's humanity is from nothing and cannot do evil, the saints in beatitude are still suspended over the void but are protected from the pit, and so on.

14. One obvious set of questions here is those raised by Derek Parfit, *Reasons and Persons* (Oxford: Oxford University Press, 1984), although theologians might find more to the point Alasdair MacIntyre's criticism of the Nietzschean tradition in *Three Rival Versions of Moral Inquiry* (Notre Dame: University of Notre Dame Press, 1990), ch. 9. Analytic philosophy after Kripke is less allergic to essences on the whole, and with regard to free will in particular has become more open to substances as causes (starting at the latest with Timothy O'Connor, *Persons and Causes: The Metaphysics of Free Will* [New York: Oxford University Press, 2000]). This

tonist tradition in the West has tended to account for these assumptions in Aristotelian terms, and where necessary, especially in the first chapter's account of efficient causation, I will delve into some of those details.

As the end of chapter 1 will suggest, I am skeptical of our ability to make detailed metaphysical judgments after the fall. I will therefore be less committed than many of my interlocutors to the unfolding intricacies of the medieval Aristotelian tradition, with its early arabesques, its tedious scholia, its baroque elaborations. Still, metaphysics is unavoidable in general and especially on these issues; and the advantage of the Aristotelian tradition, precisely because of its intricacy and even tedium, is its great flexibility. The intricate ironwork of an intellectual tradition is more arbor than prison: it offers less restriction than possibilities for selection. Aristotle begins with a definition of substance as the what-it-is of things, no more,[15] and his followers do not so much give us one highly specific theory of that "what" but many, with the arguments for and against in their variety.[16] Even so, while I will assume substances and causes here, I will not be concerned with much in the way of details about classification or constitution, Aristotelian or otherwise, beyond some com-

---

cuts against the theologian David Kelsey's suspicion that a metaphysics of substance and operations is inadequate to "personal reality" (David H. Kelsey, *Eccentric Existence: A Theological Anthropology* [Louisville: Westminster John Knox, 2009], 33)—though note that I do not bring in here the hylomorphism that especially worries Kelsey. I will assume a kind of agent causation throughout, and indeed in the more Aristotelian stretches a kind of substance causation generally.

15. See, e.g., the opening of *Metaphysics* 7.

16. E.g., whether substance should be defined hylomorphically (foreclosing the possibility of immaterial substances), whether two like substances share the same form or essence (as in the nominalist debates), and on and on.

ments about the character of efficient causation in chapter 1 and a general Neoplatonic emphasis on the role of final and exemplary causation.[17]

Something similar is true about analytic philosophy: that it appears more restrictive than it is, that it is therefore more useful than theologians especially have tended to think. The vices that theologians tend to ascribe to it, even where real, are hardly ineradicable. Anglo-American philosophy could be irredeemably ahistorical only if it were itself outside of history; it could be unfixably foundationalist only if it were itself grounded on some fixed foundation; it could forever avoid knowing itself as a tradition only if it were not in fact one. But of course it is a tradition, one whose Christian branch begins in opposition to a certain kind of epistemologically enforced atheism (thus the early attention to religious epistemology and apologetics) and in continuation of a certain confidence in one's own ability to produce and assess rational argumentation and so submit the past summarily to judgment. This latter would seem to be especially dangerous when applied to theological material, which is inevitably mysterious and in practice quite obscure; which is held together less by logical implication than by relations of fittingness between the free acts of God; which therefore calls for giants standing upon giants. But here Christian philosophy has picked up, sometimes tacitly, those features of Protestantism that emphasize the Bible as the explication of the mysteries of the faith and everything after the Bible as dispensable. Scripture's are the only shoulders we need stand on in order to see. In this, it has taken the same form as certain kinds of biblical

---

17. A brief explanation of these is given in the section "Two Questions, Three Causes, Four Chapters" below, and at slightly greater length in chapter 2 (final causality) and chapter 3 (exemplary causality).

criticism—like biblical criticism, its formal Protestantism has sometimes overridden material Protestant commitments, most famously with the Dutch Reformed defense of libertarian freedom[18]—though with a confidence and academic respectability rooted more nearly in mathematics than in the empirical sciences. All of this is true; none of it is fixed. There has already, for a generation at least, been an increasing care in the attention to historical figures, matched also by an increased attention to its own history. It was probably never as foundationalist as its critics imagined, or not in the way of their imaginings. And the farther the Christian strand gets from logical positivism, the more it becomes interested in properly theological topics, and the more its peculiar form of Protestantism becomes apparent (and contestable).

Now this essay is a Catholic one, and its form is an implicit contestation on many of these points. It assumes, most notably, that these mysteries can be explored only with the aid of the Holy Spirit, and that this Spirit has not slept quiescent in her nest since the apostles but has been retrieving more and more the olive branches of Ararat that lead us into all truth. That is, it assumes that the Catholic tradition gives us a trajectory that we should follow in our reflections—through obedience to its theological dogmas, but also through respect for its general philosophical categories. (This is part of the reason for following a broad Christian Platonism: Neoplatonism did not just happen to be current when the gospel was being articulated philosophically, since nothing in history

---

18. In Alvin Plantinga, *God, Freedom, and Evil* (Grand Rapids: Eerdmans, 1978). It has also infected Catholics in ways that override traditional Catholic commitments, as for instance in Eleonore Stump's insistence that grace is not an efficient cause of our acts. See Eleonore Stump, *Aquinas* (London: Routledge, 2005), ch. 13.

just happens.) Moreover, the reliability of that tradition is confirmed in the liberating commitments it helps underpin, and this kind of argument-from-political-implication is one that analytic philosophy has been slow, though not entirely stubborn, in adopting. Against much philosophical habit, then, the resources for this project are drawn from before Frege and even before the scholastics; against present theological fashion, they are drawn also from that neglected third of Catholic history between Aquinas and Henri de Lubac. Since debates about divine and human freedom recur periodically throughout this tradition and especially during this latter period, let me say something very briefly about how they have unfolded up until now.

A Potted History of Our Possibilities for Evil

Human freedom is invoked as an explanation for evil very early in Christian history, especially in opposition to Gnosticism. Already in Irenaeus there is a clear emphasis on evil as emerging from our will and not inscribed into our nature. The diversity of creatures is due to God's creative action, as is our original immaturity, but our sins are due to our own bad choices.[19] In Origen, these choices are famously removed to some prior moment, and the multiplicity of material things, too, is explained in terms of free choice.[20] For both Origen and Irenaeus, this invocation of choice is meant to explain some outcomes as *not* due to God;[21] their chief interest in

19. Irenaeus, *Against Heresies* (*Haer.*) 4.37.
20. Origen, *First Principles* (*Prin.*) 2.9.6.
21. This is implicitly a rejection of Reginald Garrigou-Lagrange's great principle of predilection, by which all differences in creation are to be ascribed to God, a principle that occasions for him so much confusion

the voluntary as a category in contrast with the Gnostics is the way that it secures a kind of indeterminism and therefore blocks any ascription of evil to the Creator.

For Origen, this seems to mean creating a sphere of action that is purely human and in no way God's: "I do not understand this, that because the hand moves, e.g., to punish unjustly, or to commit an act of theft, the act is of God, but only that the power of motion is from God; while it is our duty to turn those movements, the power of executing which we have from God, either to purposes of good or evil."[22] Origen's view seems to be that our actions are finally a combination of two independent contributions, from God and from us—the power of motion and our use of that power—and the view of divine and human agency is basically competitive. For "if it is God's doing, it will not be our own act to live agreeably to virtue, but altogether (the result of) divine grace."[23]

Irenaeus, by contrast, thinks of our virtue or goodness as God's act within us, by which our creation is brought to completion. "For you did not make God, but God you. If, then, you are God's workmanship, await the hand of your Maker which creates everything in due time; in due time as far as you are concerned, whose creation is being carried out." We can, however, resist or reject this completion of creation in us: "But if you, being obstinately hardened, reject the operation of His skill, and show yourself ungrateful towards Him, because you were created a [mere] man, by becoming thus ungrateful to God, you have at once lost both His workman-

---

on these points. See Reginald Garrigou-Lagrange, *Predestination: The Meaning of Predestination in Scripture and the Church* (repr., Rockford, IL: TAN Books, 1998), e.g., at 35.

22. *Prin.* 3.1.19.
23. *Prin.* 3.1.15.

ship and life."[24] Although it is not fully explicit, Irenaeus's logic points to rooting the indeterminism of our choices not in independent contributions but in an ability to undo the contribution God would work in us.

The influence of this anti-Gnostic emphasis would be especially pronounced in the East, in the work of people like Basil, Nyssa, and Chrysostom, though the noncompetitive underpinnings of Irenaeus are sometimes less manifest among them, or less explicitly articulated in their relation to human freedom.[25] In the West, Augustine would pick up the anti-Gnostic, indeterminist emphasis in his rejection of Manichaeism,[26] and he would pair it with a robust account of noncompetition articulated in response to the Pelagians.[27] As Augustine's thinking develops, however, it becomes uncertain whether he finally retains the sort of indeterminism that is central to the anti-Gnostic thrust—certainly the justification of the sinner tends more and more to become an irresistible grace, though it remains less clear whether God predetermines Adam's original choice.[28]

---

24. *Haer.* 4.39.2.

25. See, e.g., Basil, *Hexaemeron: Homily* 2 n. 5 and the *Homily Explaining That God Is Not the Cause of Evil*; Gregory Nyssa, *Homily 6 on Ecclesiastes*; *Life of Moses* 2.74–75; and John Chrysostom, in his *Homilies on Romans* (*Hom. Rom.*).

26. In early works like *On the Free Choice of the Will* and *Against Fortunatus*.

27. In, e.g., *Retractations* 1.9.6; *Grace and Free Will* 8.20; *Admonition and Grace* 14.43.

28. My own view is that, from *To Simplicianus* on, Augustine is a compatibilist and predeterminist about justification, and progressively also about the perseverance of the baptized. See esp. J. Patout Burns, *The Development of Augustine's Doctrine of Operative Grace* (Paris: Études Augustiniennes, 1980). But—and this is too little remarked—even the late Augustine is an indeterminist about Adam's choice (see *Admonition and Grace* 11.31–32, which also contains a nice statement of compatibilism;

We might say schematically, then, that besides a kind of phenomenology or introspection,[29] Gnosticism and Pelagianism are the chief spurs in the development of a Christian conception of human freedom. The Christianization of Neoplatonism in some ways only extends the problem. For the Christian account of creation that emerges against emanationist schemes involves both an affirmation of God's free ability not to create, suggesting that some kind of indeterminism is ingredient in freedom, and also God's immediate presence to and creation of all that is, which makes it difficult for creatures to be undetermined by God. But the encounter with Platonism also produces the first approximation of a solution, in the adoption of a privative view of evil and Augustine's un-

see also Jesse Couenhoven, "Augustine's Rejection of the Free-Will Defence: An Overview of the Late Augustine's Theodicy," *Religious Studies* 43 [2007]: 285). So I take the late Augustine to endorse what I am calling compatibilist indeterminism—in that sense, against a certain kind of Calvinist and a certain kind of Thomist, Augustine thinks a creature undetermined by the Creator is a metaphysical possibility—while limiting the indeterminism to Adam (and perhaps the angels: see Peter King, "Augustine and Anselm on Angelic Sin," in *A Companion to Angels in Medieval Philosophy*, ed. Tobias Hoffmann [Leiden: Brill, 2012], 261–81).

This limitation creates a dilemma, however. Does grace predetermine the sinner because it is impossible to regenerate a fallen creature in a way that reintroduces the indeterminacy that Adam's choice had, or does grace predetermine simply because God decided that it should do so (as indicated, perhaps, by Scripture or experience)? The worry with the first horn is that it seems to give sin rather too much power over against God, as if it could destroy the possibility of indeterminacy in a way that even God cannot restore (as if God could not simply bring us back to Adam's condition, to "once more . . . stand / On even ground against his mortal foe"). The worry with the second horn is that whatever goods God secures by endowing Adam's choice with this contingency would seem to apply also to our choices, were they so endowed—and Scripture and experience both seem to many, including to me, to suggest that such goods are given to us (to Mary, etc.) and not just to Adam.

29. As, e.g., in *Prin.* 3.1.4.

derstanding of the sinner as a deficient, not efficient, cause. These emphases become standard in subsequent Western theology, but they leave open the question that would come to dominate the discussions: whether these deficiencies in the agents and in the acts are finally traceable to God as the one who could have supplied the assistance necessary to overcome them but did not. In a series of synods from the fifth through the ninth century, this ambiguity was expressed in eschatological terms: "that certain ones are saved, is the gift of the one who saves; that certain ones perish, however, is the fault of those who perish."[30] Did God then not try—or not try as hard—to save them? And how does this square with what these synods also affirm, that God wills that all be saved?[31]

These questions continued to trouble those in the medieval period most careful to avoid a competitive account of divine and human agency; those who endorse a more Origenist model, picturing God's concurrence with our free acts as somehow alongside and not underpinning our contribution, had an easier time disavowing any divine involvement in evil. Thus of the two greatest scholastic systematizers, John Duns Scotus weakens and possibly abandons altogether an account of divine concurrence under these pressures,[32] whereas Thomas Aquinas maintains a noncompetitive account of divine action but leaves a much-disputed legacy about God's role in evil.[33]

---

30. Council of Quiersy (853), ch. 3 (D. 318), quoting Prosper of Aquitaine. Other notable synods here are Arles (475), Orange (529), and Valence (855).

31. Quiersy, ch. 3.

32. See Gloria Frost, "John Duns Scotus on God's Knowledge of Sins: A Test-Case for God's Knowledge of Contingents," *Journal of the History of Philosophy* 48 (2010): 30–31.

33. "Les textes de saint Thomas ne sont pas toujours cohérents, ni entre eux ni avec d'autres parties de son enseignement le plus avéré." See

These issues again come to a head with the Reformation. Lutherans, Calvinists, and Catholics are each divided by similar debates in the late sixteenth and early seventeenth centuries. Among Catholics, the Franciscans of this period increasingly follow and try to make sense of Scotus on these questions, whereas the Dominicans follow Thomas's insistence on God's intimate involvement and consequently favor more predeterminist accounts, including of God's involvement in sin. Against this, and inspired by the Council of Trent's affirmation of resistible grace,[34] the newly formed Jesuit order defends a more robust indeterminism in a series of heated polemics with the Dominicans, until the pope finally calls a truce to this so-called *de auxiliis* controversy in 1607. In ways that the first chapter will make clear, both the Dominicans and Jesuits of this period begin to depart from a strictly noncompetitive view of divine and human agency; but the Jesuits, whose most able systematizer in this respect is Francisco Suárez, are more straightforwardly Origenist in restricting God's agency to one part or feature of our acts.

By the mid-seventeenth century, the Jesuit position begins to come under fire from the radical Augustinianism of the Jansenists. Though less interested in working out the metaphysics of divine and human agency, the Jansenists downplay our freedom to such an extent that they come under explicit condemnation first in the 1650s and then again in the eighteenth century. The substance of these condemnations is to reaffirm the earlier teaching that God wills that all be saved, that grace is necessary for this salvation, but that some resist or reject that grace.[35]

Jean-Hervé Nicolas, "La volonté salvifique de Dieu contrariée par le péché," *Revue Thomiste* 92 (1992): 179.

34. In the sixth session's Decree on Justification, esp. ch. 5 and canon 4.

35. See especially the bulls *Cum occasione* and *Auctorem fidei*.

The metaphysical thickets surrounding that rejection—if we need God to make an act of acceptance, then is our rejection due to God not giving us that aid?—are left unexplored in magisterial teaching, but they get taken up again in the twentieth century with scholasticism's Leonine revival. Most notable here is Jacques Maritain's defense of the claim that our rejection is not traceable to God in any way but solely to our (nonpredetermined) negation of the positive acts to which God moves us. We can do nothing positive without God, but we can do something negative; we can, that is, fail to do something positive, even where God would have us do it. Maritain is still working within the Dominican departure from strict noncompetition, but his view, when combined with the stricter observance that emerges in people like Bernard Lonergan and Herbert McCabe, provides the immediate background to the more detailed account that I will give in the first chapter.

Two Questions, Three Causes, Four Chapters

The question at the heart of this history is how a creature can depart from the plan of the Creator; the question at the end of the second section was why the Creator would allow such departures, given that divine freedom, and our imitation of divine freedom, does not require them. For the broad Christian Platonism of this tradition, these two questions can be put in terms of God's threefold causality. All things are from, in, and to God; God is the efficient, exemplary, and final cause of creation. As efficient and final cause, God moves creatures to their acts: God is both the source of their action and the Good they seek in acting. (Though I gesture at a broader account of final causality in the second chapter, all that I mean here, and all that the argument requires, is that rational agents act for reasons or perceived goods and that these goods are themselves reflections of God.) For a creature to depart from God's plan—the first question—is therefore for a creature to reject God as both source and aim of action; it is to resist both God's push and God's pull. To account for that departure is therefore to ask about God as efficient and final cause.

Chapter 1 will consequently deal with our resistance to God as efficient cause, which has also been the focus of the historical debates: can we give an account of God moving us to act in which our freedom is not threatened by divine predetermination, nor all our acts predetermined? Since the Aristotelianism of the tradition in which these questions have developed bases efficient causality on a relation of causal dependence in the effect, I will give an account of God's moving us to sinful acts in terms of these relations. Because God's knowledge is, classically, bound up with God's doing, this chapter will treat divine foreknowledge as well, leaving open the possibility of embracing the more straightforward Molinist account while also suggesting some of the attractions, and metaphysical obscurities, of a classical version of simple foreknowledge.

The second chapter will then adapt this account to how we resist God's final causality: how can we be undetermined by the goods available in some of our free choices while being predetermined by the Good in others? Because this predetermination by way of final causality occurs only in the special circumstances of the beatific vision, this will require a consideration of eschatology; it will also raise the question of why we were not created with such a vision from the beginning.

This naturally leads to the third chapter, on God's exemplary causality. Exemplary causality, in this tradition, names the way in which all created goods are contained in a pre-eminent manner in the Creator: God is the *exemplum* upon which all creatures are modeled. In the third chapter, I will indicate the roots of this position in the cosmological arguments that come out of Neoplatonism; here note only that there are important Euthyphro-type reasons for holding this view. For if some created goods are not contained in the divine nature, then either they are themselves only arbitrarily good (as if slavery could have been as good as freedom should God have so decided), or they are necessarily good, but God does not possess them (and so is less than perfect), or God possesses them by instantiating them and so is made subordinate to some higher standard of goodness.[36] Now the answer to why God does not begin us in beatitude is that there is some good made possible by the possibility of going wrong, a good that is not freedom. At the same time, the good seems to be something in the neighborhood of freedom, being often confused with it and having something to do with the indeterminism inherent in God's free ability not to create. The question of the third chapter is therefore the second of our questions above: what good is that? In particular, if all goods are imitations of God, how could our ability to do evil allow us in any way to imitate the one in whom there is no darkness at all (1 John 1:5)?

If the compatibilist indeterminism of the first two chapters is rooted in the liberating intuitions I suggested at the beginning, there is a liberating intuition in this point about exemplarity as well. For what is at stake here is accounting for the emergence of evil without in any way writing evil into the Godhead—for example, without, as a certain kind

36. Note that on this latter view, in which God is just one more good thing—no doubt the best thing—the whole noncompetitive account of causality that drives this project would have difficulty hanging together.

of twentieth-century German-inflected trinitarianism tended to do, making an ability to fail somehow essential to freedom or love or other features of the Trinitarian life. Darkness, even the possibility of darkness, is not necessary for light. Since this is a temptation one feels especially when reading Hans Urs von Balthasar, this chapter will briefly consider his account of divine freedom.

Notice that all of this cuts against accounts of the defeat of evil in which the dark episodes of our lives are organically connected to, and metaphysically required for, some larger and more luminous narrative.[37] How can the defeating good require evil if, like all goods, it is an imitation of God in whom there is no evil? Indeed, the problems that exemplarity raises for theodicy have been too little remarked, for it makes appeals both to free will and to greater goods difficult: the first because our freedom is an imitation of or participation in God's, which is impeccable; and the second, because any greater good is also an imitation of or participation in God, who does not require evil to possess it.[38] In the first chapter,

---

37. E.g., in Marilyn McCord Adams, *Horrendous Evils and the Goodness of God* (Ithaca, NY: Cornell University Press, 2000), or in Julian of Norwich's *Showings* or even in Augustine's contention that sin is required for showing forth God's punitive justice. I am not denying any kind of defeat of evil, but the defeat must be one in which the darkness of our lives becomes an occasion for God's in-breaking luminosity, not one in which the darkness is metaphysically necessary for the light. If these dark periods are in fact defeated, this defeat only approaches again that luminosity that would have been available without any darkness at all. Even Adams's more modest contention that defeated evils provide goods that are incommensurable with evil-less goods (*Horrendous Evils*, 167) is going to run into the problems of exemplarity: where are such goods in God?

38. One possibility is to deny divine impassibility, as Adams does, and so allow a kind of darkness into the Godhead that can then be the occasion for divine patience, mercy, and other goods that metaphysically require evil. The problem here is that this darkness, and so these goods,

I will suggest that traditional predeterministic Thomism has not taken the second of these problems seriously enough.[39] But I raise the issue here, in the context of the third chapter, to note that my own approach will be to focus on the exemplarity of freedom. In particular, my aim will be to develop, out of scholastic debates around the doctrine of analogy, an account of how we imitate God; and to argue that our having a role in our fragility as creatures—our having a measure of control over our avoidance of nothingness—allows us better to imitate God on these terms. The good secured by theological indeterminism will therefore be not a human freedom that imitates divine freedom but a kind of self-creation that imitates God's uncreatedness. Against the strong views of defeat, this will imply only that some kind of *fragility* is ingredient in our creaturely imitations of God, not some kind of *brokenness*.

In brief, then, my view of freedom will be compatibilist, but asymmetrically so: freedom will be compatible with predetermination to the good but not with predetermination to evil. Christ is free; the devil is not. Merit (praise- and blameworthiness) will track freedom; Christ is thus able to merit as a human being even though predetermined to the good, but the devil will not continue to incur blame in hell. Self-creation will be incompatibilist, but only with respect to predeterminate causes and not all preexisting things, like foreknowledge: our ability to have a hand in our creation is not threatened by, for example, a prophecy that we will do so, so long as that prophecy does not figure into our decision in a causally determinative way.

---

only enter in with creation; God does not possess them at first. But if God does not possess them at first, then they are not part of the divine essence, and if they are not part of the divine essence, then we are back to the Euthyphro-type problems that exemplarity is supposed to solve.

39. Chapter 1, pp. 47–48 n. 20.

One other peculiarity of my account of freedom and self-creation worth noting is that it will not be purely individual. This is the task of the fourth chapter, as a kind of sequel of the third: to show how freedom and self-creation apply not just to us but also, and in a greater degree, to Christ; and not just to Christ as an individual human being but also to Christ's mystical body, the church. If the third chapter deals with God as exemplary cause, the manner of cause traditionally appropriated to the Logos, the fourth chapter deals with the Logos's exemplary causality as human, as the pattern of the fullness of life for both individuals and the cosmos. And as the second chapter works out some of the theological implications of the more philosophical first chapter, for instance on eschatology, so the fourth chapter works out the third, for instance on ecclesiology.

Together, chapters 2 and 4 try to situate within a broader set of theological commitments some of the innovations of the first and third chapters. The second and fourth chapters, then, serve in part to allay worries that this account is too focused on evil or sin in abstraction from other Christian affirmations. They also exemplify the kind of *ad armoniam* argument I take myself to be making. And this form of argument is itself rooted in the nature of the question. Theology, like perhaps all knowledge, operates on a kind of foundherentism, mixing foundationalist and coherentist principles. One of the standard examples here is a crossword, where individual lines are filled in both on the basis of the hint itself—sometimes more, sometimes less dispositive—and on the basis of how this answer works within the larger whole. Because of academic specialization, theological arguments, both analytic and otherwise, have focused more and more on the subtleties of the individual hints on particular issues. But my operative principle here will be the opposite, that the individual hints in these questions of grace and freedom are relatively obscure and occasionally contradictory and that it is therefore at least as useful to focus on filling out, if not the whole, then at least a broad region of the crossword in order to support any given line within it. This will be made easier by the more robust traditionalism of the project—it should already be apparent that the theism I am working from here is more robustly classical than just assuming an omnipotent, omniscient, omnibenevolent God, as also it will prove to be more robustly Christian than just some gestures at the problems raised by incarnation—for each hint will not have to be answered anew so much as a tradition of debated answers adapted to the purpose. Still, particular hints must receive their due, and it is in these chapters also that the most challenging scriptural passages are addressed: in the second chapter, Jesus's strange words on the purpose of parables in Mark 4; in the fourth, Paul's account of election and predestination in Romans 9.[40]

The structure here is roughly that which the great seventeenth-century Dominican commentator John of Saint Thomas discerned in Aquinas's *Summa theologiae*: "So it is that Saint Thomas, by this threefold consideration of God as cause, namely as effective principle (Part One), as finalizing happiness (Part Two), and as redeeming Savior (Part Three), divides the whole *Summa Theologiae*."[41] Trinitarian

40. Origen identifies a number of difficult passages for his view of free will in *Prin.* 3.1. While many of these passages are just pointing to the sort of noncompetitive view that Origen denies and I affirm, as with Phil. 2:12–13, the two that remain difficult for any indeterminism are Mark 4 and Rom. 9.

41. John adds, "This is clear from the second question of the First Part." See John of Saint Thomas, *Introduction to the Summa Theologiae of Thomas Aquinas*, trans. Ralph McInerny (South Bend, IN: St. Augustine's, 2003), 11.

appropriations are tricky things, but if the movement of the will under grace in the first chapter is appropriated to the Holy Spirit, and the vision of God appropriated to the Father whom the Son reveals to those he has chosen (Matt. 11:27), then chapters 3 and 4 treat the exemplary Son, first as God and then as man. The four chapters therefore correspond in a distant way to the three persons of the divine nature and the human nature of the divine person. And while it is true that this organization requires delaying consideration of Christ until the end, I can only ask the Barthian whom this bothers whether his enthusiasm would not require him to rewrite Scripture itself to "serve the good wine first" (John 2:10), and ask again, in the words of Philip Melanchthon, "What does it matter whether I take up first or last in my compendium that which will intrude into all parts of our discussion?"[42]

42. *Loci of 1521*, "The Power of Man, Especially Free Will," in Philip Melanchthon, *Melanchthon and Bucer*, ed. Wilhelm Pauck (Philadelphia: Westminster John Knox, 2006), 25.

GOD AS EFFICIENT CAUSE
OF A SINFUL WORLD

---

*Wisdom, understanding, and knowledge of the law come
    from the Lord;
affection and the ways of good works come from him.
Error and darkness were created with sinners.*

—SIRACH 11:15–16

H ow is God a complete cause of our actions and yet not a cause of sin? How are we, who are in some way less completely than God the cause of our own acts, somehow more than God the cause of our sins? To answer these sorts of questions inevitably involves metaphysics: about what causation consists in, what makes it more or less complete, how it differs between Creator and creature in the acts that creatures perform. This chapter will therefore have a certain technical character that occasionally verges on the infelicitous; not only must it adopt a metaphysic, but it also must extend the metaphysic to cover the minutiae of sin—and since sin is a slippery thing to account for, its mysteries liable to assume excessive proportions, its explanations occasionally lost in the epicycles of our action theories, the minutiae can be very minute indeed.

While I will attempt some simplifying, it is well to keep in mind three basic points at the beginning. First, God is the complete and immediate cause of all that exists. This will imply a rejection of the two most prominent late scholastic accounts of how God causes our acts—that of the sixteenth-century Jesuit Luis de Molina and that of his Dominican contemporary Diego Báñez—in favor of a view that is more strictly Aristotelian in its metaphysics of causation. Here the twentieth-century Jesuit Bernard Lonergan is particularly helpful. This position will ground the compatibilism suggested already in the introduction: that our free acts are compatible with God's predetermination of them.

Second, evil is a privation, a nonexistent that in some cases—those of moral evil or sin—is traceable in no way to God but is initiated by the sinner.[1] This will imply a rejection of the universal infallibility of God's decrees or acts, whether these are acts of natural concurrence or acts of supernatural grace; that is, it will imply that God can predetermine our free acts but that God does not always do so. This will require an account of God's involvement in sinful acts, one indebted especially to the twentieth-century Thomist Jacques Maritain.

Third, God knows all things, possible and actual, existent and nonexistent, deprived and depraved. This will involve a discussion of divine foreknowledge—classically, a knowing that is bound up with God's making or willing—and the related, though relatively neglected, issue of how God responds to sin. The suggestions here will be somewhat more tentative, as the account required to sustain the rather odd metaphysical implications of some of the options will be more extensive than I can give. (I have here some mercy on the metaphysically disinclined.)

Together, these basic points imply a position in which God causes our acts in all their being and all their particulars, but in which we can impede these acts to make them less than, worse than, God wills them to be. These impediments are not them-

---

1. "The first cause of the absence (*defectus*) of grace is from us." Thomas Aquinas, *Summa Theologica* (*ST*) I-II.112.3ad2.

selves traceable to God withholding the necessary assistance; they are traceable rather to our resistance to God's aid.

BEYOND MOLINA AND BÁÑEZ

In what does such resistance consist? One explanation—that of the sixteenth-century Jesuit Luis de Molina and the Reformed theologian Jacobus Arminius—is that God's concurrence provides a general sort of being that is then specified or particularized by the free creature.[2] God gives being to our acts, and we determine their character; God moves us to do something, we determine what something it is. Resistance, then, is when we specify the act in a way contrary to God's will. On this view, God's action does not cause us to cause the effect but causes the effect along with us. There is only one act that both God and we cause, not two acts that work together or some such thing; still, the act can be divided into different aspects that are ascribed primarily to us (specification) or primarily to God (being). This is supposed to avoid both our contribution rendering God's superfluous (a position ascribed to the late scholastic Durandus of Saint-Pourçain) and God's contribution rendering ours superfluous (occasionalism).[3]

2. See Luis de Molina, *Concordia* pt. II, q. 14, a. 13, disp. 26 (cf. Origen, *Prin.* 3.1.19); Jacobus Arminius, *Public Disputations* 10.9 (in James Arminius, *The Works of James Arminius: The London Edition*, trans. James Nichols and William Nichols, introduction by Carl Bangs, vol. 1 [Grand Rapids: Baker, 1986]) and *Examination of Perkins' Pamphlet* (in Arminius, *Works of James Arminius*, 3:415). See also Richard Alfred Muller, *God, Creation, and Providence in the Thought of Jacob Arminius: Sources and Directions of Scholastic Protestantism in the Era of Early Orthodoxy* (Grand Rapids: Baker, 1991), 253.

3. See Alfred Freddoso's introduction to Francisco Suárez, *On Cre-*

All the same, with its desire to parcel out credit within an act here to God, here to the creature, this view fails to maintain an entirely noncompetitive account of concurrence.[4] Recall from the introduction that on a noncompetitive account, God is most active precisely in our acts. This does not render us superfluous because the act that God chooses to work is a human-caused one and therefore has essential reference to us as cause, but neither does it imply some contribution to the act on our part, like specification, that is not also worked by God. For the advocate of noncompetition, the question at the heart of concurrence is not redundancy—if God works the whole, what need is there of us?—but something more like indignity: if God gives us causal powers, why not use them? Redundancy might be a worry for an account within the creaturely plane, to avoid overdetermination, but that is no reason to apply it to the excessive God.[5] After all, the theist bases the simplicity of her explanations on the goodness of creation: a simple or nonoverdetermined creation is more elegant. But creation's goodness, far from being exhausted by simplicity, contains other goods as well, ones that might

---

ation, Conservation, and Concurrence (South Bend, IN: St. Augustine's, 2002), xcviii.

4. The same problem besets the slightly later and more sophisticated position of the Jesuit Francisco Suárez, in which God's concurrence is more determinate but, where free acts are concerned, is still "in an indifferent mode . . . [offered] not just with respect to one act but with respect to more than one act" (*Metaphysical Disputations* [*DM*] 22.4.21, translated in Suárez, *On Creation*, 227). This concurrence may offer us a number of determinate acts between which we choose, but there is still some choosing, some specification among alternatives, that is our part of the act. And significantly, the act is not actual until that specification occurs: we have a contribution that is independent of God that contributes to the actuality of the effect.

5. See, for instance, Thomas's reasons for rejecting occasionalism in *ST* I.105.5.

temper or qualify simplicity. Thus it would be a simpler, in the sense of sparser, creation in which God does everything—and worse. Indeed, strictly speaking, creatures are not needed for anything at all: God could do everything; God could be everything; and the parsimonious ontologists could rest content with no creation whatsoever—a desert ontology without even a desert. But the goodness of creation, far from being upheld, would be entirely destroyed. We should, then, not be so worried by redundancy; we should indeed be no more worried than is the God to whose goodness creatures add nothing.

The Molinist account of concurrence therefore requires modification, to put God behind our specification of the act as well as the act's general being—the specification, too, is part of the act's actuality and so also existence in the full sense. God does not just contribute an unspecified sort of existence, whether that is conceived as a "'maximally neutral' property or 'on/off switch'"[6] that is added to the Aristotelian categories (as if the merely possible things described by the categories have no commerce with being until they are made actual) or the sort of thing that is at the top of the system of categories, abstracted from all difference, awaiting our specifying activity into categorically distinguishable entities. No: God does the whole of the thing. As Lonergan says, "the transcendental notions are not abstract but comprehensive: they intend everything about everything."[7]

Obviously I am using "being" or "actuality" here in an older sense, or in several connected older senses. Roughly speaking, "being" in the first place indicates what makes something actual as opposed to merely possible; it is the exis-

6. David B. Burrell, *Freedom and Creation in Three Traditions* (Notre Dame: University of Notre Dame Press, 1993), 100.
7. Bernard Lonergan, *Method in Theology*, 2nd ed. (Toronto: University of Toronto Press, 1990), 23.

tence added to a thing's essence to make it real. In the second place, since you need fully specified properties in order to be the sort of thing that can be made actual—even God cannot create animal as such but only particular animals—the specification of a thing's properties, and especially the addition of *differentiae* by which it is essentially and not merely accidentally constituted, is a step on the way toward realization and so counts as adding being. The particular is more real, exists more in this sense, than the universal. In the third place, since some things differ from others on the basis of having positive properties that the others do not—one individual might have knowledge that another lacks; one species might have rationality where another merely has consciousness—those that contain more positive properties can be said to exist more. (This is of course dependent on an account of ontologically positive properties, to explain, for example, why knowledge counts as a thing and ignorance as a lack rather than the other way around.) To some extent, the hierarchy of being was understood in these terms, moving from the corporeal that lacks life (rocks) to the living that lacks locomotion (trees) to the locomotive animal that lacks rationality (lizards) and so on.[8] There is a special way in which this third sense of "being" combines with the first sense in order to suggest a fourth meaning of the term. For an individual might be said to exist less by lacking even extraneous properties so long as they are positive—for instance, knowledge of what happened on May 4, 1675. But there is a special sense in which an individual exists less by lacking those positive properties that contribute to its flourishing. For things pass out of existence as it were slowly before doing so all at once: the sickly oak is approaching nonexistence in a way that the healthy oak is not, not in a

8. See also chapter 3, pp. 142–43 n. 32.

temporal sense (the sick oak might recover, the healthy oak might be chopped down tomorrow) but in an ontological one. In this sense, the flourishing individual is said to exist more than the sickly: not just that it has some positive properties that the other lacks, but that these positive properties remove it further from nonexistence, from returning to the merely possible. And this idea of being as flourishing is the ground for counting evil as a privation.

One way to put the problem with Molina, then, is that his God is present only by means of an unspecified being, and his God is found only by abstraction, by filtering out what characterizes us or moving up the ladder of genera until we reach the Summit. The godlikeness of the act is its unspecified being; so also the godlikeness of us is to be found in what is unspecified. But this would be a kind of Eckhartian mistake, even if it is not finally Eckhart's; it would see godlikeness as a loss of differentiation and finally of self.

We should instead heed our Aristotelian instincts here, though the Aristotelian legacy is sometimes ambivalent on this point: specifics add being; concrete particulars are more actual, more perfect—better and more beautiful—than abstractions. The Porphyrian tree branches upward, and we are closer to the Summit at its leaf-tips than at its root. And this means that God who is the source of such being is most present precisely in the specifics of the act. Father, Son, and Holy Spirit are the measure and source of actuality in every sense: not just of the actual over against the possible but also of the particular over against the universal, of the more realized member of a kind over against the less realized (the flourishing as against the sickly oak), and of the higher on the chain of being over against the lower.

We should not follow Molina so much as his fellow Jesuit Robert Bellarmine, then, in holding that God is the source of all being (*ostendamus nihil omnino fieri sine Deo*), including specification; that some choices are not predetermined by God's concurrence; and that this is so because we are able to "introduce" defects or nonbeing into the being to which the Spirit moves us, a sort of negative determination of the will (*negativa quaedem determinatio*) that is not itself predetermined by God's provision, or not, of assistance.[9] This also happens to be the line of those doctors of the Catholic Church most directly involved in the *de auxiliis* controversy.[10] Its most extensive defenders in the twentieth century include Francisco Marín-Sola, Jacques Maritain, and William Most.[11]

9. Bellarmine, *Treatise on Grace and Free Will* 4.16.

10. Besides Bellarmine, this includes Francis de Sales, who was consulted by Paul IV during the controversy but whose correspondence has been lost—and with it the details of his position (see *Oeuvres de Saint François de Sales*, ed. Jean Joseph Navatel, Peter Paul Mackey, and Benedict Mackey [Annecy: J. Niérat, 1892], 13:326, n. 2). De Sales seems to have been quite close to Bellarmine on the question of concurrence—see especially the *Treatise on the Love of God* 4.6, which Fr. Most reads in company with some other passages (William G. Most, *Grace, Predestination, and the Salvific Will of God: New Answers to Old Questions* [Front Royal, VA: Christendom, 2004], 378–79). See also Eunan McDonnell, *The Concept of Freedom in the Writings of St Francis de Sales* (New York: Lang, 2009), esp. 70–75 and 290–97. The only other doctor to examine "the matter at length" (according to Michael Torre) is Alphonsus Liguori, writing some 150 years after the *congregatio*, who also settles on a position of the same general sort (if anything, in its rejection of Bellarmine's libertarian understanding of freedom, closer to the one presented here). See esp. Liguori, *Prayer, the Great Means of Salvation*, pt. 2, and *Del modo come opera la grazia*. For a comparison of Liguori with the indeterminist Dominican line, see Michael D. Torre, *God's Permission of Sin: Negative or Conditioned Decree? A Defense of the Doctrine of Francisco Marín-Sola, O.P., Based on the Principles of Thomas Aquinas* (Fribourg: Academic Press Fribourg, 2009), 477–79.

11. For Francisco Marín-Sola, see the texts reprinted in Michael D. Torre, *Do Not Resist the Spirit's Call: Francisco Marín-Sola on Sufficient*

The standard form of this defense appeals to physical pre-motion, which is the Banezian account of how God moves our will to act. On this view, God moves us by a created "motion" logically antecedent to our will's causing the effect. This motion represents the reception of God's movement in the creature, and as such "does not have being as a natural thing does, although it does have intentional being" or *esse viale* (a sort of via-tific being).[12] For the predeterministic Thomist, this motion infallibly causes our causing in all its particulars; it is efficacious of itself. For the nonpredeterministic Thomist, the motion can be (but is not necessarily) resistible: we can destroy or nihilate it, or some part of it, as it is received in us.

The most influential critiques of physical premotion have come not just from the Molinists but, more recently, from Lonergan and those following in his wake.[13] If the Molinist

---

Grace (Washington, DC: Catholic University of America Press, 2013). The conclusion of Torre's book (227–57) contains a more detailed account of the reception of this view in the twentieth century. For Jacques Maritain, see *Existence and the Existent* (New York: Pantheon Books, 1949); *The Sin of the Angel* (Westminster, MD: Newman, 1959); and, most maturely, *God and the Permission of Evil* (Milwaukee: Bruce, 1966). And see Most, *Salvific Will*.

12. Thomas M. Osborne Jr., "Thomist Premotion and Contemporary Philosophy of Religion," *Nova et Vetera* 4 (2006): 607–31. See Torre, *God's Permission*, 61. For prominent historical accounts of premotion, see Reginald Garrigou-Lagrange ("Prémotion Physique," in *Dictionnaire de théologie catholique*, ed. A Vacant et al. [Paris: Letouzey & Ané, 1923–1950], 13:31–77, and *Predestination: The Meaning of Predestination in Scripture and the Church* [repr., Rockford, IL: TAN Books, 1998], 233–340) and John of Saint Thomas (*Natural Philosophy* I q. 25 a. 2 [*Cursus philosophicus*, vol. 2]).

13. E.g., Suárez, *DM* 22.2, esp. 13–14; Bernard Lonergan, *Grace and Freedom: Operative Grace in the Thought of St. Thomas Aquinas*, vol. 1, ed. Frederick Crowe, SJ, and Robert Doran, SJ (Toronto: University of Toronto Press, 2000), 66–93. Of his own students, Burrell, e.g., *Freedom and Creation*, 95–140; from the Dominicans, Brian J. Shanley, "Divine

account of concurrence undermines the sense in which God is a complete cause of our acts—the cause of every aspect of their existence—the Banezian account undermines the sense in which God is their immediate cause.[14] One of the Christian adaptations of Neoplatonism was to emphasize God's direct control over every effect, not just the presence of the One felt through a cascade of mediating powers; and premotions reintroduce, in however slight or spectral a way, some shadow of those interposed gods. A premotion is not a demiurge, to be sure, but it is a hemi-demi-semi-urge, a ghost of an intermediary prompting us to act. On the Lonerganian view, by contrast, concurrence is an instance of, and not distinct from, creation; it is just the creation of our acts. We do not need some special or supplementary account of how God creates actions on top of our account of how God creates agents, and just as God's creation of agents is unmediated, so is God's cre-

---

Causation and Human Freedom in Aquinas," *American Catholic Philosophical Quarterly* 77 (1998): 116; among non-Catholics, Kathryn Tanner, *God and Creation in Christian Theology: Tyranny or Empowerment?* (Minneapolis: Fortress, 2005), 141–52. Cf. also Hugh McCann, *Creation and the Sovereignty of God* (Bloomington: Indiana University Press, 2012), chs. 4–5, and Robert Joseph Matava, *Divine Causality and Human Free Choice: Domingo Báñez, Physical Premotion and the Controversy* de Auxiliis *Revisited* (Boston: Brill, 2016), who takes this view but thinks it is not finally Lonergan's (against which, see Matthew Lamb, "The Mystery of Divine Predestination," in *Thomism and Predestination: Principles and Disputations*, ed. Steven A. Long, Roger W. Nutt, and Thomas Joseph White [Ave Maria, FL: Sapientia Press of Ave Maria University, 2017], 214–25).

14. "In Molinism, God directly produces the created effect of the human will by acting with that will's own absolutely self-originating acts. In Banezian Thomism, God directly effects the created physical premotion which brings about acts of the human will within the created order; God does not effect in the same direct manner, however, those human acts themselves. In either case, the integrity of the act of the human will is assured in a naturalistic way by granting it an independence from the direct creative will of God" (Tanner, *God and Creation*, 150).

ation of actions. God moving us to act just is God creating the action in us; there is no other entity, no premotion, besides the act itself.[15] If one problem with the Molinists is that they are too worried about redundancy (if God does all of it, then what do we do?), the problem with the Banezians is that they are not worried about it enough (why posit an extra being behind every act?).

Notice two implications of this directness, paired in a kind of paradox. The first is that, even where God is said to predetermine our acts, the predetermination is not going to meet the standard definition of theological compatibilism. The reason, as Matthews Grant has pointed out, is that there is nothing here that qualifies as a sufficient antecedent cause of our actions, a cause whose presence is antecedent to and guarantees the outcome of our choice.[16] God is not such a cause because God's presence is compatible with any number of outcomes,

---

15. If we still want to speak of a *pre*motion, we can talk as Lonergan does of God providentially arranging things to be in the right spatial relations to one another. But this should not be thought to exhaust God's role in the action, as if God only conserved the agent in being and arranged that it be in the right place to act. This is how Taylor Patrick O'Neill reads Lonergan in *Grace, Predestination, and the Permission of Sin: A Thomistic Analysis* (Washington, DC: Catholic University of America Press, 2019), 263–64. But quite clearly—as a substantive matter, putting the interpretation of Lonergan to one side—God has to create the act as well as the agent, at every moment that act and agent exist. The point of what I am calling the Lonerganian position is that this creation—this reduction of potency to act, to use the Thomistic language—need not involve a mediating premotion. God just does it. In part the disagreement here may stem from O'Neill's contention that the agent changes in the action, which Lonergan denies (see n. 23 below). O'Neill is right (and Lonergan would agree) that in the case of immanent acts, acts that occur inside the agent like forming a volition or changing one's mind, God's creation of the act will involve a change in the agent—since here the agent is also the patient.

16. W. Matthews Grant, "Divine Universal Causality and Libertarian Freedom," in *Free Will and Theism: Connections, Contingencies, and Con-*

including that outcome in which no creatures at all exist. And "God's causation of the act" is not such a cause, because God's causation of the act is not some antecedently existing reality, like a premotion, that produces the act, but just is or at least includes the act itself. So on the standard definition of the term, this will qualify as a kind of libertarianism.

The second implication of this directness is that there is no longer any motion for us to destroy or resist or nihilate. God's performing the act just is the act; if it happens, then it would seem that God did it, and if it does not, that God did not. Without premotion, we do not seem to have the ontological space to mark the difference between an infallible motion, which produces its effect without fail, and a negatable motion, whose failure is a possibility.[17] The difference cannot be on the side of God, since God is unchanging; the difference cannot be on the side of the creature, since the creature just is the act.

So we have a kind of strangeness here, that this view seems to imply both a kind of libertarianism and a kind of predetermination—whereas I have promised a kind of compatibilism and a kind of indetermination.

In part, this is a fault with our definition of libertarianism. For notice that even if God does predetermine all things, the account will still count as libertarian: there will be no sufficient antecedent causes of our action (and indeed of any creature's action, including that of a rock, supposing that God's

---

cerns, ed. Kevin Timpe and Daniel Speak (Oxford: Oxford University Press, 2016), 214–33.

17. "Parce que la motion de Dieu et le mouvement de la créature ne sont qu'une seule et meme réalité concrète, l'idée d'une motion sans mouvement est denuée de sens." See Fabio Schmitz, *Causalité divine et péché dans la théologie de saint Thomas d'Aquin* (Paris: L'Harmattan, 2016), 194; cf. 167–68. Schmitz does not reject premotion, but he does recognize that it cannot mean what Maritain and others need it to mean.

concurrence is required there as well) so long as God is not required to create. There is an indeterminism here, but its seat is God's freedom, not ours.[18] What we need to satisfy the standard libertarian intuition, beyond just this standard libertarian definition, is a sense not only that things could have gone otherwise but that the source of their going otherwise is us, not God. And even those who lack the libertarian intuition—which I reject as a feature of freedom but will bring back under the guise of self-creation—will want this account to say more about the possibility of sin. For if there are actions that count as theologically predetermined on this standard definition, they are those actions that God must create; this is the effect of rooting all indeterminism in God's freedom. And the only acts that God must create are those required by right reason, those whose omission, given the existing dispensation of creatures, is a sin. (The assumption here is that God is bound by his wisdom to produce only what is ordered, that she "who was beside him like a master workman" produces "nothing twisted nor crooked" [Prov 8:30, 8].) Which is to say that, on this account, the one thing that is predetermined to occur are those right actions that sometimes do not occur; and many things that must occur, like the acts of purely natural causes, are not predetermined to occur.

Which, in the end, is something like the inverse of what we want.

Negation without Premotion

The immediate solution is to jettison the strict definition of determinism in terms of sufficient antecedent conditions in

18. Cf. Suárez's discussion of a similar position he finds in Scotus (*DM* 19.3).

favor, at least for the moment, of a more amorphous sense of predetermination like the undefined way in which I have been working. But the amorphousness that saves us from the shortfalls of the standard definitions also undermines our ability to account for sin. This is true both of Lonergan's own account of the occurrence of sin, which is famously aporetic,[19] and of those traditional Banezian accounts that want to avoid the cruder conclusions of the Calvinists without the chimera of Maritain's negatable motions.[20] In neither

---

19. Lonergan's view is aporetic in principle: he thinks nothing conclusive can be said about the causation of the unintelligible that is sin, though he does take the unintelligibility to exculpate God. See Bernard Lonergan, *Insight: A Study of Human Understanding*, Philosophical Library (New York: Longmans, 1967), 667; Lonergan, *De Scientia atque Voluntate Dei*, in *Early Latin Theology*, vol. 19 of *Collected Works of Bernard Lonergan*, ed. Robert Doran, SJ, and H. Daniel Monsour, trans. Michael Shields (Toronto: University of Toronto Press, 2011), 349. But Lonergan says too little about how this unintelligibility allows us to be guilty while God remains innocent. Sin cannot be an entirely uncaused thing, since it has to be caused by the sinner. In *De Ente Supernaturali*, Lonergan holds that God's permission of sin is formally very different from our commission of sin (*Early Latin Theology*, 211), but he does not give an analysis of what that difference consists in—especially since "sin is not a positive entity" (203) and therefore seems to stand in relation to both us and God as an absence in the effect stands to the agent. More recent accounts that share his broadly Aristotelian view of causation run into the same problem, including Matthews Grant's, which argues for a kind of libertarian freedom for creatures while at the same time seeming to imply that God has the same sort of responsibility for our acts, and so our sins, that we have. See Grant, "Divine Universal Causality and Libertarian Freedom," in Timpe and Speak, *Free Will and Theism*, 214–33; cf. Matava, *Divine Causality*, ch. 7.

20. See, for instance, Garrigou-Lagrange's response to this objection (*Predestination*, 330). What we need is not an assertion of God's innocence but an explanation of it. Garrigou-Lagrange attempts both to hold that an efficacious grace is the cause of our not resisting God (330) and to deny that we resist God because we are deprived of efficacious grace (333), but this too relies more on assertion than explanation. At the very least, his "principle of predilection"—by which all differences in creation,

case is enough said about how God's causation of our sinful acts differs from our causation of our sinful acts in a way that makes the sin due to us and not to God.[21] Indeed, given ev-

---

including differences in the final state of rational creatures, are explained in terms of differences in how much God loves the thing (e.g., 221)—is not self-evident enough to support the obscurity in the account of sin that follows from it. Compare the slightly stronger, Báñez-Lemos-Alvarez account that Thomas Osborne presents in "How Sin Escapes Premotion: The Development of Thomas Aquinas's Thought by Spanish Thomists," in *Thomism and Predestination: Principles and Disputations*, ed. Steven A. Long, Roger W. Nutt, and Thomas Joseph White (Ave Maria, FL: Sapientia Press of Ave Maria University, 2017), 192–213, esp. 211. Osborne's reconstruction suggests that God causes the act but not the sin in something like the way that Jacob, when sleeping with someone he thinks to be his wife but is in fact her sister, is the cause of the act but not of its moral disorder. God is presumably not excused by an ignorance like Jacob's but by a higher knowledge, perhaps the knowledge of how this particular dissonance is to be used within the overall harmony of the cosmos. When God performs the act, unlike with the sinner, this higher harmony is the goal; and since God does not owe creatures anything, the act itself is not a violation of the rights either of the sinner or of the sinned against. Still, God's behavior here can be seen as wise only if the evil of, say, Ivan Karamazov's examples is necessary for or essentially ingredient in some larger good, if the good defeats and does not just outweigh the evil—for otherwise wisdom would require God to act for the good without the attendant evil. But as I said in the introduction, it is hard to see how this account of defeat could work when all good is an imitation of the One in whom there is no evil at all: evils are not necessary for or ingredient in the goods of the Godhead, so why should they be in our participations? Moreover, this account does not tell us enough about God's causation of the sinner's participation in the act (as opposed to God's causation of the act itself). For instance, why would God fail to inform the sinner of these higher harmonies, instead arranging it so that we perform justifiable acts for unjustifiable reasons and therefore incur damnation?

21. The worry here is threefold: First, God will be involved in sins in a way that threatens the divine innocence (see, e.g., Maritain, *God and the Permission of Evil*, 30–31) and the divine opposition to evil. Second, even if God's involvement is innocent, it will still predetermine us to sin in a way that prevents us from being guilty, because we could not but sin. See, e.g., Francis de Sales: "if [the will] cannot help willing evil, and thou

erything said so far, God is if anything more involved and more in control of our acts than we are, which tends rather to inculpate the divine and exculpate the human than the other way around.

What then is it to cause an act? On a broadly Aristotelian account, causation consists in a cause, an effect, and a relation of dependence in the effect that points to its cause, a real positive property that the effect has of being caused by this particular cause. In the case of our acts, we might think of the act having two such positive properties: a relation of dependence that points to us as cause and a relation of dependence that points to God. If we were to give a picture of how this works noncompetitively, the first relation would point along a kind of horizontal plane, and the second would point off the plane in a vertical direction toward the God who is sustaining the whole horizontal plane, including all its various causal relations, in existence.[22] There is also a corresponding nonreal

---

art the cause of its impossibility, what fault of mine can there be?" See *Harmony of Faith and Reason*, ch. 1, in Saint Francis de Sales, *The Catholic Controversy*, ed. Paul Böer Sr., trans. Henry Mackey, OSB (N.p.: Veritatis Splendor, 2012), 256. Third, even if God is innocent and we are guilty, still God cannot be said ever to have sincerely desired the salvation of all, as Scripture says in 1 Tim. 2:4 and 2 Pet. 3:9 (see, e.g., Most, *Salvific Will*, 142). Universal salvation would resolve the last of these, but in order to resolve the second, you would need universal salvation to be required just by the logic of creation and fall—and not by, say, God's free gift of self in Christ—which is much harder to reconcile with Scripture. And neither kind of universal salvation helps with God's responsibility for historical evils, which is the nub of the first worry.

22. Part of the reason for having these point in different planes is to suggest the ways in which God's causation is only analogously related to our own. There will be all sorts of important differences between our efficient causation and God's creation, for example, that God's causation is the source of all being and ours is downstream of it, that God's causation does not undermine our freedom whereas efficient causation by other creatures would, and so on.

relation or mere formality in the cause pointing to its effect: though the cause itself does not change in causation—"the fire does not change when it ceases to cook the potatoes and begins to cook the steak"[23]—there are new true descriptions we can give of it when it works effects in the world ("cause of the steak frying" and so on).

Now the trouble in the case of sin is that that aspect of the effect that we are interested in is precisely its defect, its relative lack of existence, and a nonexistent thing cannot ground a relation of causal dependence that points to its cause. An absence does not point in the way that a presence does, to God or us or both or neither; and since relations of dependence in the effect are what justify our ascriptions of activity to the cause—this fire is the cause of the steak cooking because there is a relation of dependence in the cooking steak on the fire—we seem to have no ground for making discriminations between the sinner as the cause of a defect and God as a cause of a defect.

But this problem is not particularly difficult. Sin involves an immanent act in which the person holds a volition they should not or fails to hold a volition they should.[24] The effect we are interested in, then, the thing that bears relations of dependence on its various causes, is not some abstracted act but the person herself as sinful. The sinner is what subtends those defects, and those omissions, in which sin consists.[25]

23. Lonergan, *Insight*, 663. The medieval dictum is *actio est in passo*: the action is in the patient, following Aristotle in *Physics* 3.3.

24. For Anscombian-Wittgensteinian reasons, I hesitate to say that this is all that sin is, as if we first formed a volition, sinful or not, that then itself produced a (morally indifferent) movement of the limbs or some such thing. My point is only that sin involves some form of volition, whatever else it may involve, and however the various involvements may relate to one another.

25. For those who have read to the end of this chapter: I later suggest that, on some views of foreknowledge, these sorts of relations may just

(If I continue to talk of the act as what is caused by the agent, or the act's relation of dependence on the agent, this is only to avoid confusing concatenations like sinner-as-agent and sinner-as-patient.)

If we have a ground for these relations of causal dependence, then, it is easy to distinguish between who is and is not the cause of sin. We simply identify different relations of dependence in the effect on its different causes. The sin points back toward the sinner as its deficient cause, as what makes it bad; it is therefore related to the creaturely agent in a way different from if the act had been good. The sin points to God as its nondeficient cause, as the cause that brought about the fullness of the act that the sin was in some sense trying to be, the act from which the sin is a defection. This means that the nondefective act and the defective act are related to God in the same way. "Because I have purged thee, and thou wast not purged" (Ezek. 24:13 KJV): we are related to Father, Son, and Spirit as those cleansed by them, even where we remain unclean. This is why we can ascribe the badness of the act to ourselves and the goodness of the act to God, because there are different real relations of dependence. This I take to be a metaphysically straightforward way of understanding what you might call the negationist accounts given by Bellarmine and Maritain and so on—accounts in which we are able to "produce" defects in our acts that are ascribable only to us and not to anything about God.[26]

---

be a way of talking about interrelations within the larger whole that is the cosmos; still, where here I am talking about changes in relation that ground these ascriptions, there I could talk about changes in the form of the world.

26. I am calling negation what Maritain calls nihilation. Nihilation suggests the existence of something that is then reduced to nothing, which for Maritain is the physical premotion. Negation is more neutral

The chief worry with this sort of account is that it, just as much as the Molinists, implies that we are the source of our acts' existence. Consider some good act that we do that was not predetermined by God. In this case, we have not negated the goodness of the act, even though we could have: we save the drowning man instead of watching passively as he dies, say. As Steven Long has argued, the negative of a negative is a positive, so the nonnegation of an act just is the act.[27] There is no separate choice not to watch passively: the choice not to watch passively just is the choice to save the man. If that choice is up to us and not from God, then we have taken God's place as the cause of being: we are the ones who initiate our diving into the water. If the choice is from God, on the other hand, then God is the one who decides whether negations occur, which is to say that God predetermines what happens.

What Long assumes in equating nonnegation with causation is that to negate is simply not to cause. Not to negate is not to not to cause, which is just to cause. The way out of Long's dilemma is to make a distinction between not-causing and negating. Consider first the innumerable other created agents who do not cause the defects of the act and are in no way responsible for the sin: the billions of people in the world who do not cause me to jump in the water to save the man (just as I do not cause myself to jump in the water) but who cannot in any way be said to negate my jumping in the water (unlike me, who does in some sense negate my jumping). Consider

as to what is being contradicted: not, for me, a created something like premotion that is then brought to nothing but simply God's will, or the uncreated Act as it bears on this feature of creation.

27. Steven A. Long, "Providence, Freedom, and Natural Law," *Nova et Vetera* 4 (2006): 585. See also O'Neill's response to Joshua Brotherton (*Grace*, 287).

second, in a more theological vein, God's relationship to the damned. Catholic teaching condemns the Calvinist view that both the saved and the damned are predestined to their final destination, and Long's Banezian view has traditionally held only a single predestination of the elect to beatitude, a view not explicitly condemned by the Church. But what is the difference? In both cases, God sustains the damned in whatever existence they maintain and fails to sustain the salvation they lack. Banezians argue that the Calvinist position involves some kind of positive reprobation in which God causes the damned not to be saved, whereas they affirm merely a negative reprobation in which God fails to cause the salvation of the damned. But notice that this argument assumes some real difference between causing something not to be (causing the damned not to be saved) and not causing something to be (not causing the damned to be saved). Absent that, it becomes a merely verbal question whether we say that God permits their damnation or causes it; the underlying reality is the same. And this underlying reality has been condemned by the Catholic Church. For the Banezian to remain Catholic, then, they need some real metaphysical difference between causing-not, which I will identify with negation, and not-causing.

Notice then where we are: Long's objection suggests that those who want some indeterminacy in creation are going to need a distinction between negation and not-causing. The pressures of magisterial teaching suggest that Catholics who want an entirely predetermined creation are going to need this distinction as well. How then do we draw the distinction? In particular, can we do it in terms of the relations of causal dependence we have already laid out?

My proposal is that, in the case of not-causing, there is no dependence relation to ground blame or praise; in the case of negation, there is. In particular, in negation, the act's relation of dependence attributes to the agent not just the existence of whatever is present but also the nonexistence of whatever is absent. If there is an act with metaphysical components X and Y that is negated to exist only as X, then the act's relation of dependence points to the negating actor as both the cause of X's existence and the cause of Y's nonexistence. This is what makes negations different from mere partial causations, in which X is attributed to the agent and Y is not. With negation, something about Y is attributed: its nonexistence.

But now Long forces us to ask another question: is this negation relation, ascribing Y's nonexistence to a cause, not itself some new and positive thing? After all, we are not now saying that the agent merely fails to cause Y but that the agent causes Y not to be, and this seems like a positive statement that should correspond to something positive in the relation of dependence, something that is not present when the agent causes X and Y together. And if that is the case, then the agent has brought about some new being—whatever being characterizes this negation relation—that is not brought about by God.

But this is too fast. For there is no reason to think that this negation relation is anything but a vitiation of the full causal relation, in which X and Y both are caused by the agent. The negation relation is of course more than a mere absence of relation, but that does not mean that it is a different being than the full relation. The negation relation stands to the full causal relation in something like the way that the negated act stands to the full act: it is a partial version of the thing. To vitiate the act is to vitiate the causal relation as well.[28]

Now negating Y, because it is more than merely not caus-

28. Note that classically this doesn't produce a further relation of

ing Y, is in some measure an act. It is therefore directed toward some end, an end that is a good and not merely a destruction.[29] And because it is not some act different from the X-Y to which God moves us but only a vitiation of it, the end to which it is directed will not be different from, but only a vitiation of, that end. It will not make much sense to say that it is directed toward Y, since the act is a causing of Y not to be. But it can still be directed toward X. God moves us to perform X-Y, and we act for X in a way that also negates Y: Adam and Eve in the garden are moved to become like God by obeying God's commands; they choose instead, out of a desire to be like God, to negate their obedience.

Why? Do they not know that they could become like God through obedience—that God would even give them the fruit eventually?[30] Why must they have it now, and in having it lose it? Why does X become a reason for negating Y when we could do X and Y both? There is no answer in terms of reasons here; it is due finally to the defectibility of the will. We choose to act as if these goods were in competition; we choose to act so as to have them now instead of in due time; we choose our languor as sufficient in the face of a fuller love; we make our friends a reason to reject the stranger. We take the limited good as a pretext to avoid the fuller good, not because we think it is the only way to get what we want but because we just choose to want it in that way. Everything that exists has a cause, including a final cause or reason, but what does not exist—the gap between doing X-Y and doing

---

causal dependence in the first causal relation upon the agent, since relations of relations are not taken to be real things but only formalities.

29. On this presupposition of a teleological character to action, see the beginning of chapter 2.

30. As Gregory Nazianzus says (*Oration* 45.8).

X while negating Y—does not. The will simply does not make up the difference.

There will be more to say about reasons and causes and the explicability of action in the next chapter, but the point here is that the vitiated act of negation still has a cause: its efficient cause is the agent, and its final cause is this accompanying good for which it acts. This is the sense in which evil is only ever pursued accidentally, as the Aristotelians say. Still, because negation is not a mere failure to cause but a kind of perverted causing-not, Long's argument does not go through. For our nonnegation of the good act is our not causing the good act not to be, and this is really different from our not not causing the good act to be. Billions of people do not cause me to leap into the water; only I cause myself not to. Long is right that an agent causing a not nonthing is just the same as it causing a thing, which is to say, just the same as it acting. But that is different from not causing a nonthing: the negatives are distributed to different subjects, the nothingness and the causing respectively. "A man talking sense to himself is no madder than a man talking nonsense not to himself," says Guildenstern, madly, and it is the same madness that, with these modifications, would characterize Long's argument.[31]

At this point, it is worth noting the shift that we have made. What the turn to a Lonerganian account has indicated is that the difference between God and sinners in the case of sins should not be located in some entity antecedent to the act, like a shatterable premotion, but in the act's relation to what is antecedent to it. This relation is what we look to in order to justify different ascriptions of causal involvement, so it is in these relations that we should expect the difference between

---

31. Tom Stoppard, *Rosencrantz and Guildenstern Are Dead*, 50th anniversary ed. (New York: Grove, 2017), 68.

our involvement in sin and God's to show up. And this is true regardless of one's position on predetermination; it is true for anyone who wants to maintain that God's innocence does not stem simply from a kind of tautological blamelessness—as if God could do anything at all without blame, because it is not wrong when God does it—but from the way in which God is creatively involved in sinful acts.

Still, if this does not assume a stance on predetermination, we have now seen how it might imply one. For if an act and its perversion can have the same dependence on God, this suggests that God's involvement is not always sufficient to guarantee the outcome of our choices. God can purge us, and we can fail to be purged. At the same time, nothing that I have said here rules out God choosing to be involved with our choices in such a way that their outcomes are guaranteed. In these cases, our acts and their relations to us would depend on God in such a way that they would reflect without fail God's will for them. The vertical-plane creation-relations—the acts' dependence on God—would be different in these predetermining cases, but there is nothing preventing such relations from inhering in an agent and an action in a way that guarantees the real connection between the two—that is, there is no evident impossibility in having God's predetermining activity subtend fully human acts.[32] God's causation

---

32. We could of course exclude by definition these acts from being free, but, as the first section of chapter 3 reiterates, the standard philosophical accounts of libertarian freedom are not sufficient for such exclusion, and, as that section goes on to suggest, the biblical account of freedom cuts against it. We have, for instance, good reason to think that Christ evinces perfect human freedom, though his humanity is subject to the divine will in such a way that it cannot depart from it; that the saints are more free now than when they could sin; that sinners are less free; and that the damned have lost their freedom not because they are determined to one outcome but because that outcome is evil.

sustains and runs orthogonal to our own, and if God would have us produce some act without fail, then, faultlessly, we will produce that act. Which means that it is finally up to God, not us, whether we can fail or not, and up to us, not God, whether we do.

Notice, finally, that we now have a more precise way of accounting for predetermination in terms of sufficient antecedents. For we can now say that, in cases of predetermination, the causal dependence of the act upon God (the act's property of having been created by God) is sufficient to fully characterize the subsequent causal dependence of the act upon the created agent (the act's property of having been caused by the agent). Should God cause the act in such a way that it bears this special predetermining relation to its uncreated Cause, then the act will be produced in such a way that it bears also an undefective relation to its created cause—which implies that it will therefore be undefective.[33] So there may not be a causally sufficient antecedent to the act itself, but there can be a causally sufficient antecedent to the act's having been produced by the creature—and this allows us to make some metaphysical sense of predetermination.

The Malignity of Sin

What I have said implies that every act of negation is ingredient within some larger act that provides its motive force; there is an X for every negated Y. Premotionist accounts like

---

33. Note that choosing the sufficient antecedents in this case is tricky because causal relations are posterior, not antecedent, to the effects in which they subsist (because they are accidents: see *ST* I.45.3ad3). This is also why I use the language of "having been caused by X" rather than "being caused by X."

Maritain's have tended to identify negation as a nonact rather than a vitiated act—hence Long's dissatisfaction—and so do not need this larger ingredient. Following Thomas, they identify this nonact with a nonconsideration of the rule of right reason.[34] When we act well, we consider the proper ordering of available goods—our will directs our intellect to the consideration of the rule—and then act in the way that that ordering indicates is most appropriate. When we act defectively, we do not consider the proper ordering of available goods—the will does not elicit that act, at least not at the moment of choice—and instead focus on some particular good. There is therefore a nonact at the heart of every sin: a (volitional) failure to keep in mind while choosing what right reason recommends for that choice.

Still, this account of nonconsideration is perfectly consistent with an emphasis on vitiation rather than straight negation. For the rule of right reason, if we are being precise about it, is not so much an object of consideration as it is the measure for considering the various objects of action. When we do not consider the rule but consider instead some partial or particular good, we are not failing to perform some distinct act of consideration of a thing called "the rule" so much as we are engaging in a partial act of consideration of the fullness of goods to which the rule would have us attend. This is a defective consideration, not an absolute nonconsideration.

And the same is true if we allow these nonacts a more diverse role in our sins, not just in our consideration of the rule but even in the very choice, keeping the rule in mind, to act for this particular good rather than in response to the larger set of goods that right reason recommends to it.[35] Here, too,

---

34. See, e.g., *De Malo* 1.3.
35. Thomists generally do not allow this possibility because of how

there might be relative nonacts, for our sinful choices consist less in an exaggerated love of a particular object than in a minimization of our love for other relevant goods. This is true not just of acts of sloth—classically, the vice of failing to love the good enough—but also of other acts of misdirected love: lusts that consist not in overvaluing sex or money or power but in failing to value the other real goods in play in a sufficiently serious way. Indeed, there is a sense in which all sin is like this, for making an idol out of a thing is not really to love it at all. The egoist does not suffer from a surfeit but a deficit of self-love; he does not love himself nearly so much as the saint. His little selfishnesses are half-acts, not quite so advantageous to himself because obstructing their advantage to others. We do not love ourselves too much but only God too little, and neighbors too little, and ultimately ourselves too little. There may be an excess to the phenomenal character of our disordered loves, since it seems to us that we have exalted these objects of our affection; but this seeming is born not from the exaltation of our idol but from the degradation of all else—which indeed, finally, is the degradation also of what we idolized. We do not, in so doing, go beyond or outside of what God moves us to but fail to attain to the fullness of God's will for us.

Part of my point here is practical, even existential. Sin is an odd mixture, a nothingness that is not inert but catching. We have to capture both its hollowness and its dangers. Maritain does not quite strike the right note on either point: not on the dangers, because he sees it as a not causing instead of a causing not; and not on the hollowness, because he leaves the good act, proceeding from the consideration of the rule,

---

they see the will and the intellect interacting in action, but I am leaving it open here.

too much in parallel with the bad act, proceeding from some more narrow consideration.[36] That is, too often his rhetoric has negation route us from one act to a different act; God sees our defective consideration and then moves us to the (entirely other) act to which it is directed. This emphasis on alternative options makes a certain everyday sense: if we are choosing between doing work due tomorrow and watching a movie, it is not clear how proceeding to watch the movie could be a vitiated version of doing the work. But what this obscures is the sense in which the *choice* to watch the movie is vitiated, is less responsive to the relevant goods of the situation, even if God responds to that defect by moving us to a different act. It is in that sense that our sins are not some different doing but a defective doing.

Since the defect here is catching, it is in effect a kind of sickness, both repulsive and fearsome. If experience forces us to recall its fearsomeness, we should not mistake it for good health. As Simone Weil says, "Nothing is so beautiful

36. Father Most faces the same problem in his attempt to accommodate the freedom of specification (the ability to choose A or B) with the negationist version of freedom of exercise (the ability to choose or not choose A): "Whenever a man makes a choice between several alternatives: God could send him, even in the first logical moment, several specified graces.... Man could then resist all, or all but one" (*Salvific Will*, 468–69). Notice how close this is to Suárez's view, that we determine the "mode" that God's concurrence takes (n. 4 above). As with Suárez, God's role as the source of all actuality is usurped here, since the rejection of alternative motions makes this one actual, or its full effects actual, which is necessarily a positive thing. For Most's rejections to be truly, purely negative, all of the acts associated with God's motions would have to be fully actual already, and then all but one rejected, but this is impossible (since the acts are contraries).

Below, I will speculate that it might even be more elegant to say that, *sub specie aeternitatis*, the freedom of specification is usually no more than a kind of freedom of exercise, that the Bs available in some morally significant act are in fact degrees of not A.

and wonderful, nothing is so continually fresh and surprising, so full of sweet and perpetual ecstasy, as the good. No desert is so dreary, monotonous, and boring as evil. This is the truth about authentic good and evil. With fictional good and evil it is the other way round. Fictional good is boring and flat, while fictional evil is varied and intriguing, attractive, profound, and full of charm."[37] Philosophy has its culpability here, if not in quite the way of the fabulist then as the fabulist's point of departure: it allows evil to stand as the sort of thing that could outcharm the good, should fiction so incline. With a more anemic ontology of evil, our Satans would be far sicklier, nearer Dante than Milton.

Maritain may evaluate the situation differently, but I feel Weil not just in the ether but in my bones; this is why the disease is existential and the exigence of the remedy so great. A negationary account has such remedial powers, but they must be powerfully administered. We do not do more in doing evil, nor even do differently, but somehow cease doing, in whole or part. The metaphysics of action is already quite obscure; the commitments of the Thomist need not be those of a Catholic, to say nothing of other Christians; and there is much to be worked out—I shall add some more light, and much more obscurity, at the end of this chapter. My one point here is that it is not sufficient to emphasize, with the great current of twentieth-century Thomism,[38] that we always act *for* the good; we must also emphasize how inescapably we act *in* the good (though sometimes poorly),

37. Simone Weil, *On Science, Necessity and the Love of God: Essays* (London: Oxford University Press, 1968), 160.
38. Exemplary here are Leo XIII's encyclical *Libertas praestantissimum* and Servais Pinckaers, *The Sources of Christian Ethics*, trans. Mary Thomas Noble, 3rd ed. (Washington, DC: Catholic University of America Press, 1995).

how our acts, like our substances, shade in degrees away from their proper selves. For our sins are finally not a death but a wounding, a good act twisted from its goodness in some crucial respect. We negate not in clean breaks from being but in bits and confusion; we rebel only as parasites; and every idolater is, in the end, an ill-formed iconophile.

FOREKNOWLEDGE: WHAT IT MEANS TO SAY GOD KNOWS SOMETHING

Perhaps this is implausible; I hope it is also attractive. But whether we push both its attraction and its implausibility a bit farther will depend on how we view divine foreknowledge. For how God responds to our defections, for instance in moving us to some different act, will depend on how God foreknows those defections.

The easiest account here is some form of Molinism: God's knowledge of our sins does not depend on our choices but is prior to our choices and indeed prior to any creation at all. God knows what undetermined creatures would do in any given circumstance and can choose to set up the circumstances accordingly; he knows when we will defect and so can have a different act prepared in response to our defection. I want to leave this more straightforward option open.[39] But there are also attractions to a kind of simple foreknowledge, in which God's knowledge is not prior to but depends on our choices. God does not know what we would choose

39. Because Molinism has more resources for God to respond to sin, I will tend to frame subsequent chapters in terms consistent with the more restrictive conditions of simple foreknowledge, allowing the proponents of middle knowledge to dissent, and invoke their additional flexibility, as appropriate.

in some as-yet-uncreated circumstance but knows what we do choose by seeing us choose it, not before but at the moment of our choice—in the Boethian formulation, by seeing all that happens in his eternal present. He knows what will happen in the future because the future is already present to him. Since the attractions of this view are beset by many complications, I want to say something about it in what remains of this chapter.

What is God's knowledge, on the classical view? God does not change with creation; there are no new intrinsic divine properties. Instead, knowledge must be predicated of God in something like the way that cause or volition is predicated: based on features of creation. Since all being comes from God, the most straightforward way to account for God's knowledge of beings is as their (analogous) cause. That is, it is the same relation of dependence in the creature that grounds our ascription of "cause" and of "knowledge" to God: God is the rational cause of the thing. This is the sort of practical knowledge that predeterministic accounts appeal to, where God is a craftsman who forms the world based on the prior plan he has for it in his head. God knows the world in the way the artisan knows her art, and the knowledge is the cause of the thing known.

All can agree that this sort of knowledge will work for the good things in creation, the things God causes. The trouble comes from defects, and in particular, defects of the negationist sort. Here the proponent of simple foreknowledge parts ways with a purely craftsmanlike account and appeals to God's timeless vision of things. God knows this sin by being present to it. The question is, given that God's knowledge is predicated based on a relation of dependence in the creature, and given that the relation of dependence upon God in the good act is the same as in a sin, what basis is there for distinguishing God's knowledge that sin occurs and God's knowledge that some undetermined good act occurs? God in both cases moves the agent to a good act; the act's dependence on God in both cases is the same. How then could the divine knowledge, which, as practical, tracks the divine causing, be different for the different acts?

But this mistakes how God's knowing tracks God's causing. It assumes that the term "cause" is predicated of God based on the same features of creation as the term "knowledge." If this were so, then knowledge would track causing in all the following cases: (1) if God causes X, then God knows that X; (2) if God causes not Y, then God knows that not Y; and (3) if God does not cause Z, then God does not know that Z. But we do not say that God does not know the Zs that God does not cause—unicorns, for instance. Rather, God knows that not Z. So we might deny the distinction between (2) and (3) and translate all cases of "God does not cause" into cases of "God causes not." This is roughly the Calvinist view: God not causing our salvation is equivalent to God causing us not to be saved. As I said, it is unavailable to the Catholic, who even when an absolute predeterminist must maintain a distinction between God's positive acts (e.g., predestining the blessed) and negative ones (e.g., reprobating the damned). God does not cause reprobation, or the sin which is its seed, and this not causing is really different from God causing it not to occur. But God knows of the reprobation, so God knows things that God does not cause.

Instead of saying that God knows insofar as God causes, then, we should say that God knows insofar as God is present in things as a cause is in its effects.[40] In the case of nonexistents, it is not so much that God is not present in them but that there is no thing for God to be present in. God is everywhere and does not fail to be present here. Instead, nonexistents fail to be a "here" at all, and God is present at their absence, as it were. So also God does not fail to know these things so much as they fail to be knowables, and God is present to this failure. But being present to this failure just is the knowledge that they do not exist. The corresponding implications here are (1) if God is causally present to X, then God knows that X; (2) if God is causally present to not Y, then God knows that not Y; and (3) if God is not causally present to Z, then God does not know that Z. On this view, since God is causally omnipresent and correspondingly omniscient, Z is an empty set. The difference from the earlier implications may be a subtle one, but it amounts to saying that "knowledge" is predicated of God not based on the mere relation of created dependence, as "cause" is, but based also on the thing itself, that in which the relation inheres. The formality of knowing is predicated on more than is the formality of causing; it extends beyond the relation to include its ground, the effect.

And this allows us to distinguish the cases we want to distinguish, between God knowing that a sin does and does not occur. For the act itself provides a basis for such a distinction. God is said to know that Mark sins not because Mark's vitiated act has a different relation on God but because God's knowledge reflects more than just these relations and extends also to the vitiation. God knows the sin because God's causal activity suffers it, not in that it has a different relation upon God but in that the created terminus of that relation is undermined. The immediate reason God knows that there are no unicorns is that God is present at the absence of unicorns, to which we can add that they are absent because God does not cause them. The immediate reason God knows that there is a sin is that God is present at the absence of the good act, to which we can add that the good act is absent because the sinner does not cause it.

We have to be careful in saying that knowledge of defects is itself a perfection, then. In us, this is grounded in the fact that the knowledge and the defect subsist in different entities, in the mind and the thing known, such that defect in the latter does not imply a defect in the former and might instead imply a perfection. But with God, knowledge of defects is a perfection because of a certain indistinctness between knowing and known, between God's knowledge of creatures and God's causal presence within them. God is more perfect for knowing defects in the sense that God's activity is what they defect from. This is why we can also speak, as the psalmist suggests, of God *not* knowing the way of the wicked (Ps. 1:6; cf. Matt. 7:23; 1 Cor. 8:3; 2 Tim. 2:19), because wickedness is a defection from God's causal activity. That is, we can sometimes speak of divine knowing in a way that does track the divine causing. But there is another sense, the sense in which God "will never forget the deeds" of those who "trample upon the needy" (Amos 8:7), in which Father, Son, and Holy Spirit know not just that which they cause but also the failure of that which they cause to live up to their causing. All of this is to say that the knowledge of defects, though analogous to a knowledge of vision in some ways, is still itself a part of God's practical knowledge, a knowledge that is bound up with God's making. The difference, in the case of defects, is that this practical knowing is strangely reflective and not effective, because the object is a negation introduced by the creature and not a being introduced by God.

Is this enough to satisfy a strong doctrine of providence? That depends. If we define providence in terms of control over events, then a strong doctrine of providence should put

God directly behind every event in our lives. "By identifying with this all-encompassing divine aim, we can be reconciled with the world's evils."[41] This has clear Stoic antecedents but muddier Christian ones. The attraction of Molinism is that it gives us some sense in which God is in control of what happens while still maintaining some sense in which the evil happenings are against his will (because God brings about only the world in which he knows these sins will happen, not the actual sins themselves). The feature of providence that the church fathers emphasize, by contrast, is not God's control over events but God as source and final guarantor of being and goodness; providence *provides*.[42] A strong doctrine of providence, then, is one in which God is the source of all that we have and are. Providence suffers no weakening for not being behind sin.

The trouble lies in accounting for how God responds to sin. While other versions of simple foreknowledge might appeal to a temporal God who can as it were change his mind,[43]

41. Derk Pereboom, "Libertarianism and Theological Determinism," in *Free Will and Theism: Connections, Contingencies, and Concerns*, ed. Kevin Timpe and Daniel Speak (Oxford: Oxford University Press, 2016), 115.

42. E.g., John of Damascus, *An Exposition of the Orthodox Faith* 2.29. Here the appropriate reaction is not reconciliation to the world's evils but resistance; "religion and secularism, by explaining death, give it a 'status,' a rationale, make it 'normal.' Only Christianity proclaims it to be *abnormal* and, therefore, truly horrible." See Alexander Schmemann, *For the Life of the World: Sacraments and Orthodoxy*, 2nd rev. and enl. ed. (Crestwood, NY: St. Vladimir's Seminary Press, 1973), 100. See the introduction, the section "In What Sense a Theodicy?"

43. See, e.g., William Hasker, "Why Simple Foreknowledge Is Still Useless (In Spite of David Hunt and Alex Pruss)," *Journal of the Evangelical Theological Society* 52 (2009): 537–44, and David Hunt's reply, "Contra Hasker: Why Simple Foreknowledge Is Still Useful," *Journal of the Evangelical Theological Society* 52 (2009): 545–50.

the problem is harder for a Boethian view that marries simple foreknowledge with strongly classical theism. For the classical God does not react to creation; as Maximus the Confessor says, "God's purpose cannot be contained within the boundaries of time, nor does it admit of change relative to the changes that take place among the things that are subject to it."[44] If God's plan does not change in response to the world, and if God is the source of all being, then are no new beings introduced in response to sin? Can God not respond to the fall, for example, with incarnation?

FOREKNOWLEDGE: THE STERILITY OF SIN

There must be a sense for every Christian in which God does respond to sin. For the proponent of simple foreknowledge, however, the response is somehow built into the very order of creation that precedes and encompasses the sin.[45] If pun-

44. *Ambiguum* 42, 1329b–c, translation in Maximus the Confessor, *On Difficulties in the Church Fathers: The Ambigua*, vol. 2, trans. Nicholas Constas (Cambridge: Harvard University Press, 2014). Cf. David Bentley Hart, "Providence and Causality: On Divine Innocence," in *Providence of God: Deus Habet Consilium*, ed. Francesca Aran Murphy and Philip Gordon Ziegler (London: T&T Clark, 2009), 47, who states: "And God . . . knows the good and evil acts of his creatures, and reacts to neither." This is a problem not sufficiently appreciated by those, like François Daguet (*Théologie du dessein divin chez Thomas d'Aquin: Finis omnium Ecclesia* [Paris: Librairie Philosophique Vrin, 2003]), who try to follow Maritain's line on God's involvement in sin and Thomas's line on the motive for the incarnation. Daguet acknowledges that Thomas himself is inconsistent on the question of whether God predetermines sin, but he does not acknowledge the extent of the inconsistency: that removing sin from the predetermination of God and upholding the unchangeability of God's will cast serious doubt on Thomas's infralapsarian christology.

45. This goes some way toward ruling out objections like David Lewis's, that God should at least prevent the consequences of evil free

ishment and redemption are the two archetypal responses to sin, then neither, on this view, can require new acts of God. Punishment must be nothing more than the sinner bearing the consequences of her choices. For "sin carries with it its own punishment";[46] "those who fly from the eternal light of God, which contains in itself all good things, are themselves the cause to themselves of their inhabiting eternal darkness, destitute of all good things."[47] What is brimstone but the "stones of fire" (Ezek. 28:14) for those who make themselves flammable, *theion* but the fatal flashing of God's glory upon a defected flesh?[48] Redemption, too, does not require some new initiative of the God who heals creation by elevating it: if the work of glorification on a sinful world is in part its healing, then the God who decrees our glorification from the beginning need not make some new decree when we grow ill. Incarnation anyway; only *this* way, this darkened but finally transfigured way, because of sin. So there are resources within Christianity for thinking that neither of the ways that God responds to our evil choices requires divine reaction.[49]

What I am after here is a sense of sin's futility, that it cannot

---

choices if not the choices themselves. See David Lewis, "Evil for Freedom's Sake?," *Philosophical Papers* 22 (1993): 154. For on this view God could not prevent the consequences once he knew the choice was evil: he committed to creating the world this way, with this whole history, then has to see where creatures will defect.

46. Bonaventure, *St. Bonaventure's Commentaries on the Four Books of Sentences of Master Peter Lombard* III d.20.q.6 ad 4.

47. Irenaeus, *Haer.* 3.39.4. For "it is a sinner's own works by which he is harmed" (Augustine, *Confessions* 2.6.13; cf. 1.12.19). See also Bernard of Clairvaux, *On Loving God* 13.36.

48. For a recent defense of this "divine presence" model of hell—hell as suffering the presence of God—see Zachary Manis, *Sinners in the Presence of a Loving God: An Essay on the Problem of Hell* (Oxford: Oxford University Press, 2019).

49. For more on punishment in this connection, see the next chapter;

get outside of God's order to force some further response but is defeated by the terms of that order itself. What I am after, if you like, is that other and much deeper problem of evil, the one that afflicts not God but the devil: not evil's existence but its inefficacy. "One's words are so crude, but I sometimes feel pity for that thing," says one of Graham Greene's characters of Satan. "It is so continually finding the right weapon to use against its Enemy and the weapon breaks in its own breast. It sometimes seems to me so powerless."[50] For all the efforts of hell, nothing finally comes out right. Indeed, in a sense, nothing comes out at all: sin is not fertile; it goes nowhere; it does not generate. We are not any of us in our essence the products of sin, conditional upon sin, brought forth from it. We owe our being to a decree of God that is not dependent upon the misdeeds that precede us. There is nothing else in creation but what God originally ordained. Mary Magdalene, seeing the risen Christ outside his garden tomb, mistakes him for the gardener. But is it a mistake, this God who walks in the garden in the cool of the day, made manifest now in all his glory? Has she not seen the Lord as he was meant to be, as he was described not just metaphorically but prophetically in the beginning? And what was the Christ before this great restoration, what is a carpenter, but a gardener of the fallen world? What is the creche but a bower *in regione dissimilitudinis*? What is the cross but a tree blighted by our disobedience? What has been added to this man, to his vocation, but "affliction and bitterness" (Lam. 3:19); what has been added that is not indeed a taking away? He was made no new thing,

---

for more on redemption, including a defense of supralapsarian Christology, see chapter 4.

50. From Graham Greene, "The Hint of an Explanation," *Commonweal*, February 11, 1949, https://www.commonwealmagazine.org/hint-explanation.

this gardener of our dissimilitude; he sums up no more, who "by summing up in himself the whole human race from the beginning to the end . . . has also summed up its death."[51] And if he is indeed our recapitulation, to whose life nothing was added by sin, then how much less is something added to the creation that "in him holds together" (Col. 1:17)?

Still—is it really plausible that there are no new things, just old things sullied and then made clean? Is all that is all that would always have been?[52] I have already suggested that the evil act is in some way the good act negated. But what sense does this make of those sins we commit when we should have done nothing at all, as Eve with her apple, and the long train of consequences that ensue?[53] Doesn't God need to move Eve to grasp the fruit, to bring it to her mouth, to bite it—all positive things? Even if her intention can be characterized as defective, its positive effects do not seem to be so much defective beings as different beings—the apple existing here rather than there, with this motion rather than that, and on and on.

I am not sure that a pellucid metaphysics can be given here. But notice that this is to characterize what occurs in such cases as concatenations of more basic metaphysical realities like the position, motion, and causal relations of objects (whether characterized in terms of substances/accidents or

51. *Haer.* 5.23.2.

52. Remember that we are talking only about beings conditional upon negation. There might be other defects, for example, the blight of the elm, that God permits in the old predeterminist way for the old predeterminist reasons, failing to supply the necessary assistance and bringing some other good out of it. These God would know in a straightforward way, as with the nonexistence of unicorns.

53. Including consequences that might precede the sins, as for instance Jesus foretelling Peter's denial—the denial being causally prior to the foretelling even if it is temporally posterior.

events/states of affairs). And one possibility for the Boethian is to take a more divine perspective on metaphysics generally and to deny that God sees concatenations in quite this way. For it may well be that God does not see the sweep of history as a conjunction of all these little beings but as a larger cosmic play of which these things are parts. Perhaps the apple does not have some different being when it is grasped rather than hanging, as if God has agreed to relinquish its branch-being and given it some new hand-being; perhaps instead these accidental descriptions of the apple are ways of breaking down a more cosmic reality, a reality into which these sorts of relations between parts are subsumed.

Consider for instance the following suggestion: on the Aristotelian account, a composite substance like a dog does not have distinctly existing relations between its parts; rather, these relations go to make up the dog's form. Disordering the relations between a dog's organs is not the introduction of new accidents in the organs but a diminishment of the dog's dogness; so also the color of the dog's liver is properly speaking a color of the dog. Now if we posit something like a form of the cosmos as a whole,[54] then we might see the relations between things in the world in something like the manner of relations between the parts of a dog, their disorder as only apparently a newness. Or—since the difference between an animal and the cosmos is that the parts of an animal are not themselves substances, whereas the parts of the cosmos are—we might picture the world not as a dog but as a kind of dance, where the dancers themselves are not subsumed into the dance but their actions and relations are. If, in this dance,

54. As Aquinas does; see esp. Oliva Blanchette, *The Perfection of the Universe according to Aquinas: A Teleological Cosmology* (University Park: Pennsylvania State University Press, 1992).

there are pauses called for that are not observed, these pre-
mature steps should be understood in terms of the dancing, as
a perversion of its order and indeed being, and not the dancing in terms of steps that have their own order and their own
being. The dance begun in the garden extends beyond just
this episode to the whole of Eve's life, the life that God sees
when beholding her "unformed substance" and decreeing the
"days that were formed for her when as yet there were none
of them" (Ps. 139:16), and her impatience does not yield some
new dance or some new days but merely disarranges the old
ones. Indeed, the dance extends out from Eve to the apple,
to Adam, to all the other dancers that share the stage both
now and then. Why not see God's single creative decree as
directed to these, and their dancing, as opposed to a myriad
of smaller realities out of which these are built? The appropriate metaphysics here, then, might be a kind of cosmic holism,
where the universe is a kind of social entity progressing toward its final perfection.[55] As a social entity, this cosmos does
not render its substantial components into mere parts—the
holism is not a monism, nor even, when paired with God, a
dualism—but it does render the dispositions and relations of
its parts into components of some one greater thing.[56] There

55. Blanchette, *Perfection of the Universe*, 148. See also chapter 4.
56. Though vaguely Thomistic, this is a stronger statement than
Thomism in general would accept. Thomas himself is committed to the
cosmos being a social entity and to social entities being more than mere
aggregates—having real forms and real activities and ends distinct from
the conjunction of the activities and ends of their parts (see, e.g., *In decem
libros Ethicorum Aristotelis ad Nicomachum expositio* 1.1.5)—but his actual
enumeration of what exists follows Aristotle's *Categories*, which has no
slot for social entities and no place for the cosmos as a whole. Are social
entities to be located in the category of relation, then, as an ordered set
of relations subsisting in individual substances? But then in what does
their order consist, and how does it yield the unity of form and of end
that Thomas wants? A bunch of relations do not a single form make. The

do not cease to be dancers in a dance, but there does in some deep sense cease to be distinct dips of the dancer—for the dips have been made part of the dancing.

Still, it is not clear the dance is adequate to apples and Eves and, in general, substances. For here the missteps produce new dancers; substances, not just accidents, are brought into existence by sin. Adultery has its children. Are the dancers, too, and not merely the steps, to be subsumed into components of the dance? I do not see why they have to be. It is not clear whether the offspring of adultery are essentially related to what produced them, that they could not exist just as much in that world where our tears never were (Rev. 21:4). Essences are obscure to us, certainly the essences of concrete individuals (if we can even make sense of individual essences), and perhaps the child of adultery is the same child, or even more the child it is, in the unadulterated creation.[57] And this may be true not just of substances, like

---

unity of *substantial* form is gained by displacing both the substantiality of its parts (the kidney and the liver do not have their own reality, on the Aristotelian account, but exist as parts) and the relations between its parts (the relation of kidney to liver is part of the substantial form, not an accident of the parts). What I am suggesting here is that a social entity might at least replace the second sort of reality for its own order and unity to be real (or at least, that if it is real, the second sort of realities need no longer be posited as distinct entities), though it need not replace the first.

57. One implication of this is that your biological relationship to these particular parents is not essential to you. Your DNA, for instance, is not essential. This last is not so far from Thomas, since DNA after all is detectable by the senses and so more like an appearance (*species*) than a substantial feature. Cf. *De esse et essentia*, ch. 6: "For their essential differences are unknown to us even in the case of sensible substances, whence we signify those through accidental differences that stem from the essential ones, as a cause is signified through its effect." The doctrine of transubstantiation commits all Catholics to some fairly strong distinction between appearances and substantial features, since the most careful observer will still find the DNA of wheat and not of a human being in the host.

actual children, but of certain dispositions that are important to our identity—things that might plausibly make us the sorts of dancers we have been called from the beginning to be. Adultery can be a deep and important love, even if defective; it is not just a causal relation. But who is to say that the adulterous do not love each other more in the world where they never adulter, of which this love is only a pale and perverted version? It is said of those who are married multiple times— as the bride of, successively, the seven brothers—that they do not lose the goods of each marriage but have them in some way taken up and perfected in the eschaton, where there is no marriage because there is something more than marriage. And could not the same be said, to what degree we do not know, of the creation that never fell, *down the passage we did not take*? Couldn't that woman have been related to those brothers in that lost world in something like the way she will be related to them in the coming world—a way that somehow contains within itself the faltering and successive relations we see now? There is much that is great that seems contingent on sin, indeed some of the greatest things of those born of women—but the least of the kingdom of God is greater still (Luke 7:28). And how much nearer is that world where sin did not occur, where death did not occur, to that life where it cannot occur?

If this puts a question mark against our more mundane metaphysics, it is in some sense also the mark of the beast; it is the mark that measures the precipitousness of our fall. The larger question here, after all, is one of divine foreknowledge, and the only sufficient answer therefore requires us to take a God's-eye view—a view distinctly unavailable to us after sin. But even the insufficient answer must make a start toward such a view.

There are questions about God which can persist in our mind for their enigmatic quality, like puzzles which remain still undeciphered. God's timeless knowledge or the predestination of the soul might be examples. They should perhaps be left aside after a time, not because we give up finding answers, but because our thought after a while has no love when we return to them. Other sacred mysteries of faith can be very different. They too overwhelm our intelligence, but not simply as enigmas that resist explanation. . . . It is a different kind of frustration they provoke. It is never simply intellectual, but one which stirs love. The difficulty they cause is the difficulty of unattained love.[58]

The obscurities of my subject are above all of the first kind of question. But the obscurity we approach here has the savor of the second sort: how do we see again the world as one united to God? How does the world itself in some deep and damaged way reflect its rupture from its lover? How do we see things through the eyes of our Beloved, things as they were meant to be, things as they at bottom are?[59]

All will grant that God does not see the world precisely as we see it, but running throughout these last suggestions has been a skepticism about the exactitude of our metaphysics that implies a very great difference indeed between our sight

---

58. Father Donald Haggerty, *Contemplative Provocations* (San Francisco: Ignatius, 2013), 42–43.

59. "Not content with knowing, through half a century, only of myself what was not truly me at all, I had carried the same ignorance into my dealing with others. . . . I had never once realized that the superficial appearance of others was something I must break through, a barrier that I must cross, if I was ever to make contact with the real man, the real woman beyond and behind it." See François Mauriac, *Viper's Tangle* (Tacoma, WA: Cluny Media, 2017), 249.

and God's. And this is especially so with regard to evil, which we fallen creatures are so quick to hypostasize, so eager to be charmed by. In a sense, then, this view of God's knowledge is not one that reflects our understanding of things, as if induced from empirical phenomena, but one that imposes itself on our understanding of things, ordering them in a new way. In that sense, it is a faint echo of foreknowledge itself, as effective and not reflective. I have already suggested a certain kind of reflective practical knowledge, and here we approach a complementary oddity: an almost effective speculative knowledge; a way of beholding that imposes itself on our beholdings, or a seeing that reshapes the eye. But it has this advantage, just in its unfamiliarity: if it is sometimes easy to forget, in reading Thomas's corpus, his final judgment that it was like straw, here the strawlikeness has been foregrounded. And the vanity of the endeavor comes also with a hope—the hope that we might be a little less surprised, when the morning comes, that it is so surprising.

REASONS, ACTION, AND BEATITUDE

Do not say, "Because of the Lord I left the right way";
for he will not do what he hates.
Do not say, "It was he who led me astray";
for he had no need of a sinful man.
Before a man are life and death,
and whichever he chooses will be given to him.

—SIRACH 15:11–12, 17

In the previous chapter, I argued that God as the efficient cause of creation moves us to our acts and that in some cases we can fail to move under this causation. We do not sin by producing our own effects independent of God but by rendering defective, not fully actual, the good to which God moves us. We are defectible only in some cases, however, since God as the source of both our capacities and our activities can also choose to move us to act without the possibility of failure. In this chapter, I want to suggest that something similar is true of God's final causality: that God draws us in a way that we can in some cases defect from, though in extraordinary cases we cannot. This parallel between efficient and final causality, and their respective defectibilities, is itself an argument from fittingness in favor of conceiving of our ability to sin in this way: an account that forbids us from initiating our own movements but allows us to fail under God's initiation can explain our ability to sin both as creatures coming from God and as creatures attracted to God. God's attraction here is mediated through the goods or reasons for which we act—we act for some good and so some godlikeness—so this will also double as a partial analysis of human action, an analysis that is broadly Thomistic.[1] But I will not give the sort of attention to emotions, habits, embodiment, and the like that a robust account of human action would require, for my interest here is situating the account in the larger metaphysics of God and creation, not in working out a moral phenomenology or an action theory. For that reason, I am committed more to the broad strokes of Christian Platonism that structure this work as a whole than to the scholastic psychology by which Thomas fills out his particulars. This preference should be evident already in the first section, which pursues the analogy between efficient and final causality. The scholastic psychological particulars will recede even further, and specifically theological considerations move into the foreground, in the second section, which considers how the beatific vision renders us unable to sin, and in the third, which asks why, if this is true, we were not created in beatitude from the beginning.

Acting for the Good

The metaphysical background of this project is immediately going to preclude a strongly voluntarist understanding of action. This strong voluntarism, sometimes associated with William of Ockham, thinks that we can will evil just as evil, *sub specie mali*. But three of the basic assumptions here—that evil is a privation, that all things have final causes, and

---

1. E.g., in conceiving the influence of reasons upon our acts purely in terms of final causality and not as partial efficient causes, as Scotus sometimes, and Ockham always, does. See Thomas M. Osborne Jr., *Human Action in Thomas Aquinas, John Duns Scotus, and William of Ockham* (Washington, DC: Catholic University of America Press, 2016), esp. ch. 1.

that something cannot be caused by nothing—together render this impossible. Evil is a nothing, motion comes from something, therefore motion does not come from evil. Put differently, strong voluntarism does for final causality something like what Molinism does for efficient causality. Where Molina sought some sliver of our efficient causation that was not moved by God, Ockham tries to make space for acts that are not drawn exclusively to the Good. Whatever causality God has, efficient or final, covers most of the case but not all of it. And this is to radically misconceive what it means to be a creature, and so also the character of the Creator.

Instead, final causation works in something like the way efficient causation works: we can remain unmoved by the good even if we cannot be moved by the bad. Just as nonthings do not need to be from or to be like God, so they do not need to be toward God. As I indicated already in the last chapter, this failure to be moved need not be for reasons; it is not a thing and does not need a (final) cause.[2] The partial act upon which this failure is parasitic will have a cause, but not the failure itself; there will be some reason for taking the fruit but not a reason for disregarding the command.[3]

2. "Since it is not a being, no cause can be assigned to it." See Bernard Lonergan, *De Scientia atque Voluntate Dei*, in *Early Latin Theology*, vol. 19 of *Collected Works of Bernard Lonergan*, ed. Robert Doran, SJ, and H. Daniel Monsour, trans. Michael Shields (Toronto: University of Toronto Press, 2011), 333.

3. Just because it is not an act does not mean it is innocent, of course, or even, Thomas thinks, involuntary (*ST* I-II.6.3). Moreover, unlike with efficient causation, there is no relation of dependence on final causes and so nothing like the negation relations that the last chapter argued for in the case of efficient causation. In cases of insufficiency, then, the reason or final cause is insufficient as that which does not bring about the effect, whereas the agent or efficient cause is insufficient as that which brings about the absence of the effect.

This analogy between efficient and final causality yields a kind of moderate voluntarism, then, in that it thinks explanation by reasons goes only so far. This sort of voluntarism, rooted in an ability not to will the good, is sometimes associated with Scotus, who entertains something like this position off and on in his corpus. The Scotistic sort of not willing involves an act by which the will suspends its own activity.[4] The will cannot refuse a wholly good object, but it can suspend itself so as to produce no act with respect to the object, producing instead this act of self-suspension.[5] Suárez is clearer in distinguishing this—what Alfred Freddoso calls an act of "reflexive specification"—from pure not willing.[6] The latter will be at the center of my account in a way that it is not for Scotus, since only the latter is truly a nonact and so nonrational. That is, even the will's suspension of itself is, as an act, directed toward some good; and as directed toward some good, it does not reveal the root of sin, which is the will's defection from the good. While this defection does consist in a partial and not total failure to act, the partial inaction is understood by clarifying what happens in the part that is not actual, not by appealing to some further partiality. Even so, the overall thrust of this Scotistic voluntarism—that the good cannot be hated nor evil loved but that both can fail to move—will also be my own.[7]

---

4. *Quodlibet* 16.17.

5. *Quodlibet* 16.20.

6. *DM* 19.4.9, translated in Francisco Suárez, SJ, *On Efficient Causality: Metaphysical Disputations 17, 18, and 19*, trans. Alfred J. Freddoso (New Haven: Yale University Press, 1994), 320.

7. "Hence, 'a nolition of the end' is a self-contradictory or meaningless expression, like 'seeing sound.'" Scotus, *Quodlibet* 16.21; cf. Thomas Aquinas, *ST* I-II.10.1–2.

Nor is this sort of voluntarism entirely foreign to the Thomists. Thomas himself thinks that reasons do not necessitate our acting; or, put differently, that the goods conceived by the intellect are final and formal causes of our act and the will alone is the efficient cause—an efficient cause that need not be exercised.[8] We still act for reasons, for any given act will be directed toward some good presented by the intellect that gives the act intelligibility as a rational activity. We even act, to use contemporary Anglo-American terminology, for contrastive reasons, reasons for why we did one act rather than another—for we will sometimes be able to account probabilistically for why we did X instead of Y. (One standard analogy is medical: the paralysis of some syphilitics is explained by their syphilis, even though there was some chance their syphilis would not have produced paralysis. So also here, the greater attraction of the reasons for X over the reasons for Y can explain why we did X rather than Y, though there is some chance we would have done Y instead.)[9] But these sorts of reasons do not determine, which is to say that the will's attraction to the good is not such that we must choose the greatest good present to our intellect. In other words, we can implicitly refrain from willing the good: here, in preferring a lesser good to a greater good; and in general, according to the sort of metaphysics of final causation that underpins my account, in not acting rather than acting. In

8. See *De Malo* 6.1; Osborne, *Human Action*, 14–17. Cf. Bernard Lonergan, *Insight: A Study of Human Understanding*, Philosophical Library (New York: Longmans, 1967), 619: "Critical reflection cannot execute the proposed action, for it is simply a knowing. Knowing cannot necessitate the decision, for consistency between knowing and willing becomes an actuality only through the willing."

9. The example is taken from Christopher Hitchcock, "Contrastive Explanations," in *Contrastivism in Philosophy*, ed. Martijn Blaauw (New York: Routledge, 2013), 11–34.

contemporary terms, we cannot give *exhaustive* contrastive explanations of why we did what we did, where an exhaustive contrastive explanation gives (a) a deterministic and not merely probabilistic account of X over Y, and (b) has Y range across all possible alternative acts. I will even suggest below that we cannot give perfect probabilistic explanations of our behavior: our ability not to act is finally immune even to probabilistic description. This will be the sense in which sin is unintelligible, even to God: there just is no reason that explains the thing.

Now if this sort of voluntarism, which is at the heart of modern libertarian accounts of freedom, is a consequence of our ability not to will the good presented to us, then it need not be read as a fundamental break with earlier Christian Platonist accounts, including even Thomas's. It has only to reflect at the level of final causality what the last chapter sketched at the level of efficient causality. God moves us, and we can fail to move; God draws us, and we can fail to be drawn.

A chief reason Thomas and Scotus and contemporary Christian libertarians all appeal to something like this voluntarism is to explain the origin of evil. For if the first sin is not to have necessitating causes, it must originate in the will rather than the intellect. As Tobias Hoffmann argues, Thomas himself is not finally clear on this point, but he can (should) be extended in this sort of mildly voluntarist direction. The angels' "attitudes with regard to the rule [of right reason] and their choice are not traceable to a previous cognitive state, but only to their *libertas voluntatis*."[10] The reasons we can give

10. Tobias Hoffmann, "Aquinas and Intellectual Determinism: The Test Case of Angelic Sin," *Archiv für Geschichte der Philosophie* 89 (2007): 151.

for their choice are not exhaustive contrastive ones: "Why did [the fallen angels] let themselves be motivated by an inadequate motive rather than by a good one? The preference for one reason over another is not traceable to a cause other than the person who makes the choice. Good and bad angels acted for a reason, but why only some acted for an adequate reason, while others acted for an inadequate one, escapes full intelligibility: there is no reason why some focused exaggeratedly on themselves instead of paying attention to the divine rule, other than that they were absorbed in themselves."[11]

If we do accept, more full-throatedly than Thomas, this sort of mild voluntarism, then we no longer need to worry so much about the intricate mechanisms by which he traces the origin of sin to a defect in the intellect—the nonconsideration of the rule of right reason—and that in turn to a nonaction of the will. As the last chapter suggested, some sins might have this sort of intricacy, but if choices can be traceable simply to the efficiency of the will in this way, then we could just as well allow other cases in which we consider the rule but then act for some more particular good than the rule recommends. We might see the goods available to us in proper relation to one another and still choose some partial good that the rule is telling us is (a) good in some respect but also (b) should not be acted upon. We simply elicit an act for the goods of (a) in such a way as to disregard the various other goods that make (b) the case.

Indeed, something like this needs to be the case for there to be sin, or at least for there to be initial sin—a sin not explicable in terms of some prior sin. "Whoever knows the right thing to do and fails to do it, for him it is sin" (James 4:17). It is not enough that we can act for lesser goods; we must

11. Hoffmann, "Aquinas and Intellectual Determinism," 153.

also at some level know them to be lesser in such a way that acting for them is wrong. That is, in our initial sins, we must have an awareness not just of the good we are acting for but also of the goods we should be acting for and are not. We do not choose the act under its description as a bad act—we choose it for its goodness—but in choosing just this goodness we have also some judgment in the intellect that it is wrong so to choose. It is those who knew God and did not honor him as God who are without excuse; it is the servant who knew his master's will but did not act according to it who is severely beaten (Rom. 1:19, 32; Luke 12:47). *That* is the heart of culpability.

Of course, there are extended forms of culpability, as when we are blind to the wrongness of our acts with a blindness that is itself the result of fault, or when we have only a confused or obscure sense of this wrongness.[12] And there are other ways in which an act can be bad that do not involve culpability, as when a great tragedy is produced by invincible ignorance. The intellectualist, who would tether the will more closely to the judgments of reason, is inevitably attracted to these extended cases; here the will still follows the intellect, even though evil results. Since these sorts of cases are endemic to our place in salvation history, after the fall and before the general resurrection, they also give intellectualism a certain empirical plausibility, or at least make its empirical liabilities less glaring. They can even make intellectualism seem real or concrete, and voluntarism, with its attention to remote, sometimes angelic cases, seem helplessly abstract. But it is precisely the suitability of intellectualism to

12. As seems to be the case with the servant who does not know the master's will and receives only a light beating (Luke 12:48); presumably this servant, a figure of the gentiles, is still held accountable to the law written upon his heart (Rom. 2:15).

our postlapsarian condition that disqualifies it as an account of how our choosing was created to work; it is precisely voluntarism's ability to account for first sins, when our faculties are not disordered, that gets closest to our natures. For the central question for those who believe that everything comes from God is not how sin spins itself off through the centuries but how it could emerge at all, either in the beginning or in subsequent ages.

This is to modify the standard Thomistic picture in a couple of respects, then. In the first place, it does away with the nonconsideration of the rule as an underlying feature of every sin.[13] Indeed, for those sins in which we do fail to direct the intellect toward the rule when we should, the source of culpability may well lie in this nondirection, not in the subsequent unruled act.[14] Second, Thomists in general talk of our coming to act as a single-minded process. The intellect and the will are held to interact in a complicated, eight-stepped way in this process, and this interaction occurs with a single object in view (even if it can be interrupted and redirected toward some other object).[15] Scotus I think is better here when he compares the intellection upon which we act to a kind of visual field that contains many objects, some more in focus than others, from which the will selects.[16] On this view, there is a clearer role for the rule of right reason in taking

13. For a recent account of similar concerns, see Michael Barnwell, "The Problem with Aquinas's Original Discovery," *American Catholic Philosophical Quarterly* 89 (2015): 277–91.

14. As seems to be Lonergan's view when he identifies this "contraction of consciousness" as the basic sin (*Insight*, 666).

15. Roughly *ST* I-II qq. 6–17.

16. *Ordinatio* II, dist. 42, qq. 1–4, nn. 10–11. For a dual-object view from a Thomist, see W. Matthews Grant, "Aquinas on How God Causes the Act of Sin without Causing Sin Itself," *Thomist* 73 (2009): 469; also Lonergan, *Insight*, 612, and Alasdair MacIntyre, *Ethics in the Conflicts of*

into account all the relevant goods: it governs how we view a landscape of objects, how we see their relationship to one another. When considering according to the rule, we know which we are to choose, though this does not guarantee that we choose it.

The analogy I have been working with is between efficient and final causality: between, at the level of efficiency, the primary cause and secondary causes and, at the level of finality, the universal good and particular goods. The attraction of the particular good is a kind of participation in the final causality of the universal good, just as secondary causality is a kind of participation in primary causality—participation in the sense that the superior cause acts in and through the inferior cause, neither replacing the causal force of the inferior nor having its own force displaced by the inferior in turn (i.e., these are not causal chains). And the pull of the universal good in normal (nonbeatific) cases is like God's general concurrence in normal cases, which is to say negatable. In brief, we are creatures and so have, in our willing, a kind of natural aptitude to be moved by God and to act for God; this aptitude is such that we can neither be determinately moved nor be determinately attracted by something other than God (the Good) without ceasing to be rational agents. Furthermore, neither God's motion nor God's attraction predetermines our agency in the ordinary course of things. As the next section will make clear, the parallel extends also to that extraordinary course of things in which God does predetermine us. For at both levels, this predetermination is not the destruction of freedom but the fulfillment of our natural aptitudes: our finality is consummated in the beatific vision, just as our source-

---

Modernity: An Essay on Desire, Practical Reasoning, and Narrative (New York: Cambridge University Press, 2016), 55.

hood, the sourcehood of one moved by God, is confirmed in beatific grace.

But this analogy is only rough. For the general concurrence by which God moves us is not exhausted by the activity of secondary causes, since secondary causes are not sufficient to bring the act into being; whereas the pull of the universal good may be exhausted by the pull of particular goods, since the universal good need merely attract, not bring into existence. We do not need also to desire God in order to want to eat, though we do need to desire the godlikeness of nourishment and life. But we do need also to be moved by God to perform the act of eating, since only God can sustain our acts in their existence. God pushes through but also alongside created agents; God need only pull through created goods. And this means that the pull of the universal good, because it is felt through its participants (or its participants as grasped by the intellect), can be selected between; whereas the push of the primary cause, because it provides the determinate being of every effect, cannot. God pushes to some one particular act; God pulls through many different goods. Put differently, what Suárez held for efficient causality is true of final causality, that we can select between the various options by which God might move (attract) us—though our selection will itself be the result of God's efficient causation.[17]

17. Like Suárez, Báñez also fails to observe this particular difference between God's efficient and final causality. In Báñez's case, he wants to make God's motions mediated in something like the way of God's attractions, positing a physical premotion like the moral premotion by which the good, grasped by the intellect, draws the will. In that sense, though Suárez does not share Báñez's view of physical premotion, something like Báñez's view is still the necessary condition of Suarezian selection: you need some space between God's causing and our doing such that we can

I have framed this account of human action within a larger metaphysics of final causality—that God is the end drawing all creatures on—without giving arguments in favor of this more general teleology. A widespread finality is more controversial than the view in which rational agents alone can be said to have a kind of goal-directedness, and much of the foregoing will hold true even if teleology is restricted to human beings. But let me say a little bit about how my broader view differs from contemporary anthropocentric ones in order to clarify the metaphysical background to these claims. I will use the philosopher Timothy O'Connor as a foil here, since he agrees with me and Thomas that our reasons are solely final causes and not partial efficient causes of our acts, but his final causality ends up taking a different form.

O'Connor basically concedes the early modern account of the break with Aristotelian metaphysics. That is, he basically concedes the separation of final causality from efficient causality and the rejection of the one in the name of the other by the sciences. Still, he thinks that human beings can act teleologically. To do justice to this, he posits a set of emergent features that constitute our agency—so far, so Aristotelian—and that act to produce end-regarding intentions. As emergent agents, we are the direct efficient cause of an intention that consists both in some act-type A and in some goal G for which A is chosen. The reasons we have in favor of G are then the reasons for which we act, and they explain our acts in a non(efficiently)causal, purely teleological way. Still, this does not tell us how our antecedent reasons make certain acts

---

select between various causings. My point here is that you get that sort of space with final causality but not with efficient causality—there is a moral but not a physical premotion—which is why the analogy between them, though helpful in some ways, is also misleading.

more or less likely, so O'Connor supplements these sorts of reasons *for which* we act with reasons *on which* we act.[18] The latter affect "the propensities of the agent-causal capacity"— the probabilistic disposition of the sole efficient cause, which is the agent, toward the act—without causing, even partially, the act itself.[19] The reason *for* which we act is then as it were endorsed from among these reasons *on* which we act, taken up into the intention as part of the agent's decision.

Notice, then, that final causality enters in only with the reasons *for* which we act, and these reasons do not explain the relative likelihood of certain acts over others so much as they explain the phenomenological datum that some (but not all) acts are chosen as goal-directed. But this is to make the final cause no cause at all, at least in Aristotelian terms. For Aristotle, final causes are ingredient in the operation of efficient causes; they tell us how efficient causes operate. This is why the early modern claim to reject final causes and keep only efficient causes is essentially incoherent (at least until Hume rejects efficient causes as well). Any account of causing, including both the various early modern ones and contemporary accounts of causal powers, will seem to Aristotle to include reference to both final and efficient causes. Masses accelerate toward one another because they "desire" proximity: Newton modifies, and quantifies, these desires but he does not banish them. At most he rolls them into efficient causality. This means that Aristotle's final causes are not just tacked on at the end for phenomenological purposes—as one

18. Among other problems, see Timothy O'Connor and John Ross Churchill, "Reasons Explanation and Agent Control: In Search of an Integrated Account," *Philosophical Topics* 32 (2004): 251.

19. Timothy O'Connor, "Agent-Causal Power," in *Dispositions and Causes*, ed. Toby Handfield (Oxford: Oxford University Press, 2009), 198.

begins to see already in Ockham[20]—but themselves govern the probability distribution of our dispositions. The earth accelerates toward the sun because the sun is more attractive than Jupiter; John stays home because time with his kids is more attractive than the party. There is no need, on this older view, for the distinction between reasons for which and reasons on which we act: we just have reasons, and these draw us with different force in different directions.

What is added with the human is not a new kind of causation but a shift in the normativity of the final cause, and this in three ways. First, because these are our ends, they govern our actions. They are normative for us as human in a way that gravity is not, or in a way that gravity is normative for us only as massive. Second, human beings are more valuable than nonrational creatures and as such their ends have more normative weight. The shift to the human is not a shift to the teleological from the nonteleological but a shift to a particularly valuable teleology, a particular actionable teleology. It is incumbent upon us in some strong way that all humans flourish; in some slight and defeasible way, that all roses flower; in little to no way, that all masses fall. These steps in importance are not just quantitative: it is a real violence that acts against human flourishing, an evil that cannot always be justified by its good consequences; it is in some extended sense violent to act against an amoeba, but hardly an evil in itself; it does a very diffuse sort of violence to prevent a rock from falling, a violence so diffuse that it is justified by any among the multitude of countervailing considerations (including even saving the energy it would take to make a decision about how we should behave toward the rock). This is not, as the early moderns take it, a sign that the inanimate

20. *Quodlibet* 4.1.

have no ends, or that their ends are essentially neutral; it is just a sign that their ends are always overridden. And human ends, by contrast, are so only in very particular ways, under very specific circumstances.

The third difference between human and other ends is that, unlike the rock, we can fail to act for our end. This has been the point of this section: we can not will the good, including the goods demanded by our nature. Our ends are norms in a prescriptive and not purely descriptive sense. This is why the indeterminism of our agency in the present chapter has not been modeled on the probabilistic interaction of subatomic particles, the way it is in much contemporary philosophical discussion.[21] It is not the case that our agency is probabilistically disposed by reasons in something like the way that the behavior of subatomic particles is probabilistically disposed by their various circumstances. For the behaviors of subatomic particles still follow the norms of their natures. It is good for the particle to behave according to whatever probability distribution it has, a good that we need not further in our own projects but still one by which the particle acts according to the designs of—the inborn tendencies given by—God. Whereas the whole point here has been to account for how we can act wrongly, not for our good, against our God-given natures.[22] If our finality were modeled on the

21. The most influential position here is Robert Kane's event-causal view (see, e.g., *The Significance of Free Will* [New York: Oxford University Press, 1998]), from which O'Connor's probabilistically disposing "reasons on" seem to be adapted.

22. Natures here means in particular the causal powers implanted in us by God. This leaves open two further questions: first, the degree to which these powers are shared across "natures" in the sense of species (e.g., human nature), and here classical Aristotelianism and contemporary evolutionary theory have much to work out; and second, the degree to which the observed propensities of creatures (especially living crea-

quantum, then we would have merely to behave according to the probability distribution given by our reasons; the less good and so less probable choice would not be wrong, so long as it occurs with the right infrequency. But what we need is some sense of how we choose against our natures, against our goods, and so against our (rightly ruled) reasons. It is not that these reasons dispose without determining us, but that they do in a sense determine us—and can be ignored. Adam had all the relevant reasons along with their unambiguous recommendation; he had neither disordered habits nor excessive emotions disposing him in favor of the worse; still he sinned.[23] He was less like the lepton than like the earth, bound in his courses; that his course was refused brings him no closer to the lepton, for the lepton cannot deviate from its probabilities any more than the earth from its orbit. The indeterminism of our sins, then, is not rooted in probabilities that we can calculate based on our attraction to various goods but in our ability not to act toward good at all—without reason, and so without odds.[24]

---

tures) are themselves already distorted by the fall, and here a theologization of empirical findings is called for. I note these primarily to point out that I have not taken sides in these disputes. Later in the chapter, I will use nature in a different sense again, as contrasted with grace or supernature.

23. The key premise here is that if God disposes you to a certain action 50 percent of the time, then it is not wrong to do it 50 percent of the time. Derk Pereboom has made a similar suggestion (*Free Will, Agency, and Meaning in Life* [Oxford University Press, 2014], 61–62), though for Pereboom the gravamen seems to be that we cannot be blamed if we are *constituted* in this way, whereas here I am emphasizing that these acts cannot be blameworthy if *God* constitutes us in this way.

24. This sort of chance incompatibilism is important if, as the next chapter argues, our ability to sin is the way in which we participate in our own creation. For what is the probability that God would create? And if we cannot assign an objective probability to it—if it is not only undetermined but also without determinate probability—and if self-creation is

DETERMINATION BY THE GOOD

What, then, of the beatific vision? Will we, in seeing God face-to-face, be able not to will the good? This is a problem that worries Scotus, and he points toward one possible solution: that God by grace maintains the will's enjoyment of beatitude such that it cannot cease willing. This is the solution by way of divine concurrence or efficient causation, though because Scotus at this point tends to conceive concurrence as God acting with rather than on us, making the activity of the primary cause external to our causing, our impeccability comes from something extrinsic and not intrinsic to us.[25] Here Scotus serves as a kind of premonition, both of Ock-

---

our way of having a hand in this act of creation as it touches us, then it makes sense that self-creation is without objective probability as well.

There is still a place for habit and passion and reason and all the other factors that probabilistically dispose our actions in various ways, whether as co-causes or in some noncausal fashion. The probabilities in question cannot be exact, however, because, first, there is always the undeterminable chance of grace turning us toward the good, and second, there is at least some of the time the undeterminable chance of rebelling against these dispositions. These inexact probabilities are quantifiable only to a band of uncertainty—for example, perhaps our dispositions are such that we will act in a certain way between a quarter and a third of the time—where the uncertainty here is not epistemic but ontic. God's probabilities might be absolutely unconditioned, but we should not expect ours to be quite so absolute. Still, inexactly specifiable probabilities can answer the major objection to this chance incompatibilism (the objection that our free actions seem to be rendered more and less probable by all sorts of things—see Timothy O'Connor, "Probability and Freedom: A Reply to Vicens," *Res Philosophica* 93 [2016]: 289–93, and Peter Furlong, "Libertarianism, the Rollback Argument, and the Objective Probability of Free Choices," *Pacific Philosophical Quarterly* 98 [2017]: 512–32) without entirely undermining its usefulness in dealing with so-called rollback arguments (as originally laid out in Lara Buchak, "Free Acts and Chance," *Philosophical Quarterly* 63 [2013]: 20–28).

25. *Ordinatio* bk. 4 d. 49 q. 6 n. 11 (ed. Wadding 10:455).

ham's more explicit treatment along these same lines and of those later figures who secure impeccability by having God interfere with our agency in some way.[26] Still, the Scotistic sort of solution can be readily translated into more Thomistic terms, and our goodness guaranteed by a grace that is more interior to us than we are to ourselves—a grace that therefore does not interfere with our agency but confirms it.

And this I think is part of beatitude. But it does not so much obviate an account of some kind of irresistible final causality as point in its direction: if it is a feature of God moving us efficiently that, in extraordinary and above all eschatological cases, we are made so good as to be impeccable, so also it may be a feature of God attracting us finally. But since I have also already suggested that efficient and final causality are disanalogous in ways that are relevant to this question, I need to say more about my account of beatitude to show how far this analogy goes.

My account is broadly Thomistic in the following three theses: first, that in the beatific vision, we see all things in God; second, that seeing all things in God means that in loving anything we love God above all; and third, that by nature we always love some things. From these follows a fourth and equally Thomistic

---

26. For the first, see the discussion in Simon Francis Gaine, *Will There Be Free Will in Heaven? Freedom, Impeccability and Beatitude* (London: Bloomsbury T&T Clark, 2003). Also Severin Valentinov Kitanov, *Beatific Enjoyment in Medieval Scholastic Debates: The Complex Legacy of Saint Augustine and Peter Lombard* (Lanham, MD: Lexington Books, 2017). For the second, I am thinking in particular of Jürgen Moltmann, *The Coming of God: Christian Eschatology* (Minneapolis: Fortress, 2004), 307, and, more generally, of a certain Barthian conception of the eschaton that undermines the sense of eternal life as *life* (e.g., the controversial statements in *Church Dogmatics* III/2 [Edinburgh: T. & T. Clark, 1960], 632–33). See Miroslav Volf, "Enter into Joy," in *The End of the World and the Ends of God: Science and Theology on Eschatology*, ed. John Polkinghorne and Michael Welker (Harrisburg, PA: Trinity Press International, 2000), 256–78.

conclusion: that "the will of the man who sees God in His essence of necessity adheres to God."[27] Let me take these in turn.

In this life, we see God in things. We move from a knowledge of creatures to a knowledge of the Creator; even in grace, we rise from our knowledge of the world to a knowledge of Christ to a knowledge of the Trinity. But this epistemic ascent undergoes a kind of beatific inversion. In the next life, we see all things in God and move from our knowledge of God to the knowledge of all creatures. In other words, though I will leave this vague, the order of knowing there follows more closely the order of being. Our present knowledge is analogical: we know the perfections that are in God only under a creaturely aspect (more on this in the next chapter). But our future knowledge will be katalogical: we will apprehend these perfections as properly divine, and we will see their instantiation in creatures as reflections of their divine source.[28] Of course, the specific actualities of creation cannot be derived from the divine essence, as if they followed logically given God's nature—God did not have to create. But as the grace of this life lifts up our eyes to the heavens (Isa. 46:20) through the one mediator Jesus Christ (1 Tim. 2:5), so the grace of the next shall trace for us the eternal Trinitarian love as it is in itself, to its manifestation in Christ, to the whole creation of which he is the head.[29]

Now the first way of knowing makes it possible for us to oppose God, since we can take particular goods in some

---

27. *ST* I.82.2c.

28. Thomas says that "he who sees God's essence, sees in Him that He exists infinitely" (*ST* I.12.7 ad3). Since infinity is the mode of God's existence, to know it is to know the divine being under its proper mode and not under a creaturely mode—that is, it is to know God in a more than analogical way. For an explication of analogy and modes, see chapter 3.

29. On the way in which we can see all creation in Christ, see chapter 4.

sense on their own, without grasping their intrinsic connection to the universal good, and so can choose them over
against God. In the field of vision that comprises our consideration of various goods, particular goods are viewed as
it were independently of one another and of their divine
source, exemplar, and end. They are a mirror of God, one
in which we need not see God nor, in seeing God, choose
him. Beatific knowledge changes this, for in beatific knowledge we know every particular good through its connection
to God. God is not merely one more item in the visual field,
which we might attend to or not; God saturates the visual
field. We cannot then single out some one particular good to
choose over against other goods, because our very access to
that particular good is always via a consideration of the Good
itself. The intellect, which gives the will its formal object—we
must be thinking of something in order to choose it—is filled
with God; we have always God in mind, not just as means but
as ultimate end to all other possible ends. When we act for
some good as conceived by us, and that good is conceived as
itself ordered to God, then God is always included as most
ultimate in what is willed as good—which is to say, in what is
loved. The goods that would motivate our negations already
involve an ordering of our selves to the higher Goodness.

It is not only, then, that God is loved as the producer of
this particular good that we love, as the artist is loved for
her art and the giver for her gift; nor only as the exemplar
of the thing, the Love that its loveliness bespeaks; nor only
as the end of the thing, a thing whose ends we as its lover
seek to make our own.[30] That is still to see God through the

30. The weight of the argument traditionally falls on the first and second of these—see, e.g., Bernard of Clairvaux, *On Loving God* 1–5, and
Augustine, *On the Trinity* 8.3.4, respectively. I have tried to indicate also
a role for God as final cause of the objects of our love, in part because,

thing. Rather, each thing is there loved as spoken by God, as bespeaking God, as speaking to God. To conceptualize the creature in the new creation is to conceptualize it as a thing-to-be-used, in Augustine's famous formulation; that is the thought of the thing even before any love has been elicited toward it; and the only love that can be had for such things is the love that refers beyond them.

It is precisely because all goods shall be seen in this way that there is no escaping it. Anselm suggests in one place that we can be determined by a knowledge more particular than the beatific vision—namely, a knowledge that our sins will be punished and our good works rewarded. For Anselm, this determines us because we act either for our own advantage or for justice, the good in itself; these are our only two motivations. If both affections are directed toward the same act, then we necessarily choose that act.[31] Putting aside the problem that punishment introduces—can God get us to love him in the right way merely by threatening retribution?—this view is still not adequate to our constitution. For postlapsarian reality suggests that our affections are more complicated than Anselm would have them: we overvalue any number of other created goods besides ourselves, putting them in the place of God.[32] Parents are constantly tempted to favor

---

as the next paragraph makes clear, I think the objects of sinful love are not just ourselves but any number of things. It is not enough to say, with Augustine, that our own goods are finally realized in God, for we might love other goods more than our own; just as it is not enough to say, with Kant, that we make the ends only of other rational creatures our own, when nonrational creatures too have ends, and have our love.

31. *On the Fall of the Devil* 23.

32. I owe this point to John Hare in particular. We even overvalue others to the point of undervaluing ourselves, in ways that an affection for advantage might accommodate only after much trouble, with many epicycles. See in this connection the influential early feminist critiques of Rein-

their children inordinately, for instance, in a way that is not straightforwardly advantageous to the parents, or not reducible to such advantage. Thus the sort of knowledge that would determine our acts would have to threaten retribution for our sin on all the things we might overvalue: obey God, or your children will suffer, and so on for the indefinitely many objects of our potential perversities. Such a threat is of course impossible for the God who said that "the son shall not suffer for the iniquity of the father" (Exod. 18:20); but even more, the universality of our affections favors something closer to Thomas's view, in which the will is structured by an affection for the good as such, not also by its own advantage.[33] The appearance of other affections distinct from our love of the good is a consequence of the fall, by which we come to have inordinate attachments to particular goods—often, but not always, the self.[34] That is, these other affections are distor-

---

hold Niebuhr: Valerie Saiving Goldstein, "The Human Situation: A Feminine Viewpoint," *Pastoral Psychology* 17 (1966): 29–42; and Susan Nelson Dunfee, "The Sin of Hiding: A Feminist Critique of Reinhold Niebuhr's Account of the Sin of Pride," *Soundings* 65 (1982): 316–27. If we take the biologists seriously as giving us some insight into our fallenness (as also our createdness), then evolutionary arguments about genetic preference, and not simply self-preference, are also in the background here.

33. As Thomas says, our end is not our own good but goodness itself: "Natura in se curva dicitur, quia semper diligit bonum suum. . . . Non tamen propter hoc amat quia suum est, sed quia bonum est: bonum enim est per se objectum voluntatis" (*Scriptum super Sententiis* II d. 3 q. 4 ad 2). See also Thomas M. Osborne Jr., *Love of Self and Love of God in Thirteenth-Century Ethics* (Notre Dame: University of Notre Dame Press, 2005), 94–112, 174–86, 198–200; Rudi te Velde, "Natura in se ipsa recurva est: Duns Scotus and Aquinas on the Relationship between Nature and Will," in *John Duns Scotus: Renewal of Philosophy; Acts of the Third Symposium Organized by the Dutch Society for Medieval Philosophy Medium Aevum (May 23 and 24, 1996)*, ed. Egbert P. Bos (Amsterdam: Rodopi, 1998), 155–69.

34. Cf. Augustine, *On Christian Doctrine* 3.10.16.

tions of the will's natural condition, not features of it. And this sort of will, one whose object is the good as such and that might have a distorted affection for any particular good, can be drawn from every disordered love only by seeing all of them as caused—efficiently, exemplarily, and finally—by the ordered love of the Trinity.

So much for my second Thomistic thesis, that seeing all things in God means that to love anything involves loving God above all. Still, this does not guarantee that we actually do love God, for we might not love anything at all. Thus the third thesis, that a total lack of love is impossible for our natures. This may seem obvious enough, but since there is a sense in which I will deny it below, it is first worth noting how far it is true. For it follows straightforwardly from the older teleological picture with which I am working that we only identify things by their desires, by the ordering of their capacities toward particular ends. What makes a lepton a lepton is that it is disposed to act (desires to act) in such and such a way. The will cannot, then, in Aristotelian terms, maintain itself entirely in potency and never actually decide on an act. For even potency of this kind is defined by reference to some background actuality: the potency of the will for various particular acts is based on a desire for the good in general that is intrinsic to the will and so is actual wherever there is a will. The will is the sort of potency that it is because it has an actual desire for goodness. A desire for the good in general is therefore in potency only where one is in potency for a will, that is, where the will itself is the *terminus ad quem* of the potency. Where the will is the *terminus a quo*, the will in potency to particular acts, some such general desire is already actual. This is what I mean by saying that some act—in this case, of a highly general kind—is necessary by nature for the will.

And our loves structure our other faculties as well. "For it is not only things pertaining to the will that the will desires, but also that which pertains to each power, and to the entire man. Wherefore man wills naturally not only the object of the will, but also other things that are appropriate to the other powers; such as the knowledge of truth, which befits the intellect; and to be and to live and other like things which regard the natural well-being; all of which are included in the object of the will, as so many particular goods."[35] This is particularly true of our intellect, as Wittgenstein and, in a different way, the phenomenologists make clear: the embodied, communal, linguistic character of our awareness structures it with certain commitments. The concepts by which we understand are constructed for particular uses; our understanding is not purely passive but already involves a reaching out toward certain things, an aversion from others, a discrimination within the intellectual field that is underlain with willings.[36] An understanding without these willings would not actually understand anything at all. It is not only that understanding requires a desire for the truth, then, but that understanding the truth requires loving things in a certain way; it requires finally, as the end of the last chapter suggested, that we see the world as God sees it, which is to say that we align ourselves and our purposes with God and God's. And this means that intellection in particular, but indeed all of our operations, rely on a kind of background activity of the will.

Now if in the beatific vision we derive all these other goods, like natural well-being, from God, and if in this deri-

---

35. *ST* I-II.10.1c.
36. See also Augustine, *On the Trinity* 8.2–3.

vation we love God without fail, then this means that the possession of the beatific vision elevates those natural activities of our will that we cannot avoid into a supernatural activity that we do not wish to avoid. God, considered merely as final cause, still does not force us to elicit an act. But the ordinary efficient concurrence by which God moves the will, paired with the extraordinary final cause of the beatific vision, is enough to secure impeccability, just as an extraordinary efficient concurrence paired with an ordinary final cause can also secure impeccability.[37] Once all things are seen in God, to love anything is to love the One who contains them. In that sense, the beatific vision determines us to the good.

I intimated in the last chapter that there might be a sense in which beatitude comes to all, and I am now suggesting that beatitude determines one to the good; is there then no space for damnation? How could the coming of beatitude be experienced by some as damnation—the suggestion of the last chapter—if it turns all to the good? The question here is what it means for the wicked to receive beatitude—or, since beatitude is our name for the glory of the Lord as received by the faithful, how it is that what is life for the righteous is damnation for the unrighteous.

Here my account diverges from Thomas somewhat. For the determination of beatitude as I have described it is a kind of *modus ponens*: if there is some natural willing, then there will be a supernatural willing. But that makes the enjoyment

37. The latter describing a case where, for example, God infallibly moves us to act rightly in some everyday act. That beatitude consists in both sorts of impeccability is not an unnecessary redundancy because impeccability is not the point of beatitude. Rather impeccability is a kind of mark or *proprium* of it: the thing that shows how extraordinary it is. It is only more glorious for having this surfeit of sinlessness.

of beatitude only as necessary as these sorts of natural loves—which is to say, necessary as long as we have natures.[38] Elsewhere I have suggested that that might not be true of the damned, that damnation might be a kind of inverted *epektasis* or progressive annihilation.[39] What I have here called the beatific inversion gives some hint of how this might work. For if in this life we can refuse the ascent to God from particular creaturely goods, so in the next life our refusal is inverted, and the lack of love for God works its effects downward into a lack of love for every good. One man's *modus ponens* is another man's *modus tollens*: the damned, too, see all things connected to God and reject them.

There may be a sense in which this is true on any account of damnation, but I mean it quite straightforwardly here: their refusal of all tends truly toward a refusal of all particular goods. God is all in all, and they prefer nothingness. This preference, this perversity, is never fully consummated because their negations are always themselves acts and so aimed at (ever more limited) goods—progressively vitiating their acts for the sake of progressively vanishing goods. But the tendency here is not toward a simple rejection of some goods, even of the universal good, in the name of some other, particular good—like the self. It rather pursues its partialities toward a complete negation, however impossible to attain; a nonexistence extended to all particular goods and so to all particular acts of the human person. The nonact of the will with respect to God becomes a nonact of the will with respect

---

38. Cf. Lonergan, *Insight*, 621.

39. An annihilation that has no after and so is strictly speaking never over, a kind of frozen final moment of death: Ross McCullough, "Darkling Lights of Lucifer: Annihilation, Tradition, and Hell," *Pro Ecclesia* 22 (2013): 55–68.

to ever more finite goods, and this in turn—because the will underlies all our faculties—slowly becomes a nonact of the person with respect to the various goods to which persons as such are oriented.

For this is what consummation involves: the unification of the whole person. Your attitude toward Christ shall rule your will, your will shall rule your soul, and your soul shall rule your self. The blessed see all creation in Christ and, open to the love of him, affirm both Christ and creatures. The damned see it, too, but they have habituated themselves not to choose the good; they have prepared themselves by their resolute rejection of the Savior to affirm neither Christ nor creatures. The demons are already some adumbration of this, for Lucifer fell not by some bare pride or even by some individual desire to earn his salvation but also and entwined with this by rejecting the incarnation of the Lord.[40] This is one fruit of a supralapsarian Christology, that Lucifer might reject not just grace but Christ, not just that help should come from God but that help should come from a man, the one mediator made not angelic but human. Adam's desire to be like God (Gen. 3:5) is a kind of shadow of the incarnation, by which God becomes like Adam—a shadow in its faintness and a shadow in its darkness. So, all the more, is Lucifer's desire to be like the Most High (Isa. 14:14). Adam at least was attempting to hasten what God would give in due time; Lucifer knew what was due and—proud because of his beauty, corrupt for the

---

40. "Nihilominus valde probabilis est sententia credens, Lucierfum de facto peccasse per superbiam, appetendo hypostaticam unionem, et a principio adversarium Christi fuisse" [It is nonetheless very likely that Lucifer in fact sinned through pride by desiring the hypostatic union, and from the beginning was the enemy of Christ] (Suárez, *De angelis* 7.13.13 [*Opera omnia* (Paris: Vivès, 1856–1878), 2:885].

sake of his splendor (Ezek. 28:17)—rejected it.[41] And this rejection is what will be given reign over his whole self, when all things are put under Christ's feet (Eph. 1:22) and the defeat of the devil becomes his debellation.

Even now, with Christ not fully regnant—even before the incarnation, with the humanity of Christ not yet existent—Lucifer already anticipates this unification of his self around rejection. So too the blessed and their affirmation; the course is set, if not yet traversed, at death. For the particular judgment already involves the beatific vision, and there is therefore a measure of unification of the self already here: we see that God underlies all things and we can will, not yet for all our other faculties, but for all our future willing. That is, we see God as the source and summit of every possible good—he is known there directly and not by analogy—and so as the necessary concomitant of every possible love; we know in that vision the stakes of every possible choice we could make; and we love, or not. Everything that we could deliberate over is made present to us and in some sense chosen at that moment. The blessed subordinate every good in every future choice to God in Christ; the wicked to their vanishing idol, which would finally destroy even their idolatry. But this decision does not end all future deciding—even the wicked will do more works before the end of time, or before sinking into that sempiternal time that characterizes their consummation—so much as it sets the horizon in which decision occurs, for or against God. We there commit ourselves, even if the effects of that commitment are not yet realized. The will is not yet entirely master of

41. Note also that if Lucifer rejects the incarnation for being human instead of angelic, then the first sin is not so much an individualistic pride as a communal one, a chauvinism or in-groupism rather than a self-reliance. (Again, there are both evolutionary and feminist insights in the background here.)

itself, for the wicked's choice against God is still counteracted in some measure by its love of the false gods, and the blessed still require the purgation of their dissident willings. Nor is it yet entirely master of the person, for the wicked's faculties still seek to some degree their ends, and the blessed's faculties in some measure await their actualization. This is true of the angels as much as us: Lucifer has still his loves, and still his acts, because Lucifer still awaits the final consummation; Michael has still his sifting to perform (Matt. 13:41), and though he is counted a saint because he long ago consented to perform it, he still awaits the grace actually to do the thing. But for both wicked and blessed, the particular judgment represents a kind of decision about all future decidings that ends not decision but the possibility of switching states.[42]

The glory of God, then, is purposed for all from the beginning of creation and is received by all when "God shall rule the man, and the soul shall rule the body."[43] But this glory—to make all things known in God as God is known now in them; and to make the whole of us subject to that knowledge—becomes for the wicked a consuming flame (Heb. 12:29;

---

42. To be clear, the vision of all things in God makes present at the particular judgment all future choices and allows us to choose them anticipatorily, as it were, but this is not strictly sufficient to ground our inability to switch states between judgments. God could give us this anticipatory choice and still allow us to change later. It does not so much imply our inability to switch as it demotivates an ability to switch: God has already given us a choice about these things, so there is no reason to give us a second shot at it (though of course God *could*). The Catholic Church teaches that God in fact does not: "Death puts an end to human life as the time open to either accepting or rejecting the divine grace manifested in Christ" (*Catechism of the Catholic Church*, 1021). I will leave it as an open question why it might be good to concentrate our future choices in this shorter horizon—those who have taken vows, including marriage vows, might have some insight.

43. Augustine, *The City of God* 19.27.

Deut. 4:24).[44] The potter does not mold forever; the clay is finally fired. There is a certain kind of resistibility to this highest grace, then, in that it is taken according to the mode of the receiver: the kiln perfects the well formed as much as it destroys the ill. But this is a different sort of resistibility than that of the lower graces that have so far occupied me. For the point of the lower graces is that they can be resisted by one who is not defective but merely defectible, which is indeed how they were negated by those first to fall. They are graces that enable but do not predetermine. Whereas these graces, whose mark is impeccability, must be immune from defectability because they come to do away with it—in one way or another. They do predetermine, in whichever way you would have them. These graces, in other words, as the summit of our life in the new creation, are more like that Eucharistic presence that forms the summit of our life in the old: life to the righteous, medicine to the sick—and death to the unworthy (1 Cor. 11:29).

BEATITUDE IN THE BEGINNING?

This all implies that if we had been given beatific graces at creation, we would never have sinned. The necessary loves of our created nature would have been elevated from the first into beatific loves, and Lucifer would have rejoiced in the inhabited world and delighted in the Son of Man (Prov. 8:31). Why then were we not? Of course, God did not owe it to our natures to elevate them in this way, since these things

---

44. Compare here Thomas on the exemplarity of the resurrection even for the damned (*ST* III.56ad3). The damned are not excluded from the paschal mystery; they are condemned by it.

are beyond nature. But—and here the traditional Thomists should take note—there are other ways the wisdom of the Creator might be besmirched besides an unfulfilled nature; there is in particular an unnecessary evil. And the question here is about the latter, about the wisdom of allowing our fallibility: not as a worry about what our natures deserve but as a worry about the long train of misery and oppression that our fallibility makes possible and, as it happens, actual.[45] It is a question not simply of divine hiddenness, of why God is not more manifest, but of the evils that hiddenness can engender.[46] Why then did we not begin in beatitude?

Thomas is sometimes read as saying that we could not have begun so.[47] "The corporeal creature instantly in the beginning of its creation could not have the perfection to which it is brought by its operation. . . . In the same way, the angelic creature in the beginning of its existence had the perfection of its nature; but it did not have the perfection to which it had to come by its oper-

45. That is, it is a question about whether Michael Murray's Necessity condition, as opposed to his Rights condition, is met. See Michael Murray, *Nature Red in Tooth and Claw: Theism and the Problem of Animal Suffering* (Oxford: Oxford University Press, 2008), 14.

46. If the question about beatitude were just about some lesser good and not about making possible great evil, then it would make more sense to think only in terms of what is owed. Divine hiddenness that does not involve evil is more easily solved by rights considerations alone—for instance, J. L. Schellenberg's work distinguishing hiddenness from evil makes the former into its own discrete problem by relying on Leibnizian intuitions about how a God of love must maximize his closeness to creatures. See J. L. Schellenberg, "The Hiddenness Problem and the Problem of Evil," *Faith and Philosophy* 27 (2010): 45–60. But these sorts of Leibnizian conditions are going to be rejected on the anti-emanationist line that I have taken here: presumably God does not have to maximize closeness for the same reason God does not have to create.

47. As in François Daguet, *Théologie du dessein divin chez Thomas d'Aquin: Finis omnium Ecclesia* (Paris: Librairie Philosophique Vrin, 2003), 129–30.

ation."[48] The question is how seriously we are to take this "could not have" for corporeal creatures. Thomas again:

> God could make a will having a right tendency to the end, and at the same time attaining the end; just as sometimes He disposes matter and at the same time introduces the form. But the order of Divine wisdom demands that it should not be thus; for as is stated in De Coel. ii, 12, "of those things that have a natural capacity for the perfect good, one has it without movement, some by one movement, some by several." Now to possess the perfect good without movement, belongs to that which has it naturally: and to have Happiness naturally belongs to God alone. Therefore it belongs to God alone not to be moved towards Happiness by any previous operation. Now since Happiness surpasses every created nature, no pure creature can becomingly gain Happiness, without the movement of operation, whereby it tends thereto.[49]

So perhaps it is not strictly true that corporeal creatures must start off without the perfections of their operations, since God could create them in the attainment of their end. This would contravene God's wisdom in some sense, however. Now does that contravention represent merely a less fitting but still possible world, or is it so unwise as to be uncreatable? Does making us work for our beatitude merely highlight the unnaturalness of our elevation, or is it essential to the thing? In his reply to the first objection, Thomas says that it is necessary "that the order in things be observed," but this is hardly more helpful.

48. *ST* I.62.1ad2.
49. *ST* I-II.5.7c.

One textual reason to think Thomas is not implying the metaphysical impossibility of original beatitude is that he explicitly contrasts it above with what "God could make." A second textual reason, and the first substantive reason, is that Thomas's reply to the next objection notes that Christ's soul is created immediately in beatitude. If this were impossible for God, then how is it actual in Christ? François Daguet appeals to the strangeness of Christ's personality, that he is not a human person but a divine person with a human nature, but it is not clear how this is relevant.[50] The worry here is at the level of natures, not persons: that beatitude so exceeds the nature of the creature that we must work our way up to it. But the creature here could just as easily be the human soul of Christ as it could be the angel Gabriel. A second substantive reason is that natures just cannot do that much work in limiting the state in which God creates us, since we are all in fact created with more than our natures. Adam and the angels both began in sanctifying grace.[51] And if it is possible for God to create us in a state exceeding our nature, then how is it that our natures prevent God from creating us in beatitude? This in turn points to a third and less definite substantive reason, which is that it seems entirely conceivable that a creature begin in beatitude. I can picture in my mind's eye an angel sprung immediately into God's presence; this angel is not, as I view her, any less a creature for her immediate felicity; the picture before me harbors no evident absurdity in its details. If it contains a metaphysical impossibility, then the impossibility is obscure. Absent some such impossibility, why not think that we could have been created blessed?[52]

50. *ST* I.62.1ad2.
51. *ST* I.62.3.
52. Note that even if this Thomistic line is right that we could not have been created in beatitude, it still has not explained our original pec-

Why then were we not? What is the order of things that the divine wisdom is choosing here to observe? In his discussion of the angels, Thomas appeals to merit: they were created without beatitude so that they could merit their beatitude. The premise here is that "no one merits to produce what he already enjoys."[53] But if merit at bottom names a relation between the goods God works in us and the rewards bestowed for those goods, is this really true? Can we not equally speak of meriting by a beatific love the *continuation* of our beatific enjoyment? The good and faithful servants did not own the talents that their master had given them in trust, nor the profits made from them; would it not still have been a reward if their master, upon returning, had allowed them to keep those talents in trust instead of setting them over even more? Was it not indeed part of their reward that they continued in stewardship of those talents, when the wicked and slothful servant was stripped even of the one talent he was given? Did they not merit the *continuation* of their stewardship? The intuition behind merit is that it would be not just unfitting but positively unwise for God to work sanctification in us without crowning it in glory. God's wisdom renders such a creation impossible, which is why (condign) merit falls under justice and not mercy, what God cannot fail to do.[54] But is it not equally unwise and so unjust for God to confirm the creature in beatitude and then subsequently take it away?[55]

---

cability. For God could have given Adam (Lucifer) an actual grace at the moment of his choice that predetermined it to the good.

53. *ST* I.62.4c.

54. *ST* I-II.114.6ad2.

55. This assumes some kind of temporal-like succession in beatitude, and this is a tricky question. There is perhaps a sense in which things are no longer successive after the final consummation. But even if this is true, and beatitude given in some quasi-eternal and so singular way at the general resurrection, there would still be a place for meriting the

And if so, then why can we not speak of merit in this case, in which the free actions of the creature in the first moment of beatitude make a claim on retaining beatitude in the next?[56] Thomas even concedes that his schema makes Christ less great than us in one respect, since Christ does not merit the beatitude of his soul, and he justifies this on the grounds that it is more great-making for Christ's person overall to begin in beatitude.[57] But why think we have to choose? Why not

---

continuation of beatitude prior to the end of time. Even the angels await the final judgment as their consummation; even they have to live out their beatitude until then as a mission that unfolds with the rest of that creation to which they minister. Which is to say, even they have to live it out as successive. This is why they continue to require grace and why Christ can become, with the incarnation, the instrument of that grace (cf. Thomas Aquinas, *De veritate*, q. 22 a. 7 ad5). Beatitude, then, must be compossible with succession, and this implies that we could have been created both sinless and successive in a way that makes merit possible. Alternatively, if one maintains not just a kind of succession but even a kind of *epektasis* in beatitude, then there is room for merit even on Thomas's schema—for in *epektasis*, we are constantly getting not just the same but ever higher graces.

56. The problem is only harder for congruous merit, where the reward is considered as God's recompense for the work we do (from him), as opposed to condign merit, where the reward is considered as God's continuation of the work he does in us. With congruous merit, not only can the same question be raised—why can't we merit the continuation of existing graces?—but we have also given up all pretensions to explaining why God *could not* begin us in beatitude. For congruous merit is rewarded only out of mercy, not justice; and how could it be the case that God had to give us an opportunity to merit congruously before beatitude if God is not bound by his justice actually to crown those merits in beatitude? If the connection between reward and merit is binding on God such that God has to provide the opportunity, then surely it is even more binding when, having taken advantage of the opportunity, we come to claim our recompense. Since the latter does not bind with congruous merit, neither should the former.

57. *ST* III.19.3c.

give Christ this greatness also, that he merits his graces going forward just as we do, though he begins in a better place?

I should note here that some of what is traditionally distinguished into merit and reward is made simultaneous on the present account. For it is not that God sees our souls and then decides whether to give us a fire that is infernal, purgative, or deifying; rather the whole world is fired with the Spirit, who consumes, cleanses, or consummates according to the mode of the receiver. The face of the earth is renewed by the breath of God (Ps. 104:30), though the wicked it chases like chaff upon the mountains (Isa. 17:13), and the lawless it destroys (2 Thess. 2:8; cf. Augustine, *The City of God* 20.12). The fit between eschatological merit and eschatological reward, then, is less a relation between what one does in one moment and the grace God decides to give in response than it is between the disposition of the receiver and the manner in which the Holy Spirit sets our hearts aflame. It is in this sense that our predestination to beatitude neither occurs before foreseen merits (*ante praevisa merita*) nor after (*post praevisa merita*). The first position is right to insist that we are predestined to glory before any consideration of our merits; the second is right that we experience that glory as beatitude conditional upon our state when we receive it. But, against the first, all are predestined to this glory, and against the second, merit and demerit do not determine God's choice of what to give us but only how we receive what God chose from the beginning. In that sense, our beatitude is as it were simultaneous with our merits (*simul ac praevisa merita*).[58] I will have more to say

---

58. I take the phrase from Jean-Pierre Torrell, in Thomas Aquinas, *Questions disputées sur la verité, Question V: La providence; Question VI: La predestination*, introduction and commentary by Jean-Pierre Torrell, trans. Jean-Pierre Torrell and Denis Chardonnens (Paris: Vrin, 2011), 353, though I do not use it to mean what he does.

about predestination in the fourth and final chapter. For present purposes, the upshot is this: to the degree that this sort of fit between the disposition of the subject and the experience of the object captures what we mean by rewarding merit, there is no reason the angels cannot begin in beatitude. For they, too, could be created with just such a fit. Indeed, what is meant by rewarding merits in this sense could exist not just in the continuation of their beatitude but at the first moment of their existence: they can be made righteous enjoying the rewards of righteousness.

So why not begin them in beatitude? It is useful to consider here a parallel question about parables—in some ways about the whole parabolic shape of Christ's first coming and indeed of our in-between times—for it is a question that Christ answers. Why not speak plainly, and reveal God's face? His teaching is a hard one: "for those outside everything is in parables; so that they may indeed see but not perceive, and may indeed hear but not understand; lest they should turn again, and be forgiven" (Mark 4:12).[59]

What are we to make of this? One answer points to what we have already said, that the truth unobscured would be condemnation to the defective;[60] it would be the vision of God that one cannot have and live (Exod. 33:20). "For God gives sight and understanding to men who seek for them, but the rest He blinds, lest it become a greater accusation against them, that though they understood, they did not choose to

---

59. I have chosen the Markan version of this passage for its difficulty; there is a Matthean version that is somewhat easier to explain away. See, e.g., Richard B. Hays, *Echoes of Scripture in the Gospels* (Waco, TX: Baylor University Press, 2017), 130–31. For a dismissal of the Markan passage that is rather too curt, see Hans Urs von Balthasar, *Truth of God*, vol. 2 of *Theo-Logic* (San Francisco: Ignatius, 2004), 73–81.

60. Cf. Bonaventure, *Itinerarium*, prologue, 4.

do what they ought."[61] This has a certain fittingness with the passage in Isaiah that Christ is quoting here, for the "lest they turn" is there preceded by the burning coal that purifies Isaiah's unclean lips and is followed by a destructive fire come upon idolatrous Israel (Isa. 6:6, 8, 13). The word of God in its plainness purifies the prophet but destroys the disobedient, and to veil it in parables at least palliates the destruction.[62] Still, this does not capture the sense in which Christ is claiming that parables actually forestall our conversion. Another answer points to a suggestion that will reappear in the fourth chapter when I consider Romans 9, that parables reinforce a temporary hardening of heart that God uses to spread salvation even farther afield. When this hardening has served its purpose—when the blindness of the audience has led them to crucify the Lord—even those previously hardened will have a chance to repent and be saved.[63] This explains the otherwise curious fact that anyone who reads about the parable now, disciple or no, reads also its interpretation: the blinding or hardening effect of the parable seems only meant for that one generation.

But there is also a third answer, true perhaps in a different way from the other two, or for different onlookers—an answer that will take us to the next chapter. This is that Christ is worried that plain discourse would necessitate the conversion of his audience, that Christ's "lest they should turn

61. Theophylact in the *Catena Aurea*, Mark 4, lecture 1.

62. If the last chapter's account of simple foreknowledge is true, then it may be not just Christ but the Scriptures that are dislocated by the fall, thrown out of joint and into a kind of obscurity. But God designs this dislocation to produce the kind of obscurity that is most helpful to our fallen condition, one that softens some of the danger of God's word.

63. Pope Benedict XVI, *Jesus of Nazareth: From the Baptism in the Jordan to the Transfiguration*, trans. Adrian J. Walker (San Francisco: Ignatius, 2008), 190–91.

again" is a worry about overwhelming with the nonparabolic. Anselm has something like this worry about the in-between times, that the effects of baptism not be too glorious: "For since people would see those converts to Christ instantly passing into incorruptibility, there would be no one who could even will to withdraw from the overwhelming happiness to be seen."[64] The chief advantage of this view as a reading of Mark is that it makes sense of a tension between this teaching, which is an interpretation of the parable of the sower, and the content of that parable itself. For if the sower is a parable about parables, as Christ intimates in verse 13, then it as much as its interpretation holds clues as to why Jesus spoke in parables. But where the interpretation suggests that different responses to the parable are due to the different manners of speaking—those who have been given the secret and those who have only the parable—the parable itself ties the difference to the condition of the receiver: the bad soil versus the good. These do not strictly contradict one another, but only because the manner of speaking is what makes the condition of the receiver relevant: it is because the parable seeds and does not transplant that it can fail to flower in some soils. It is because the disciples are particularly thickheaded (e.g., verse 41) that even plain language fails to overwhelm them. This takes up the first interpretation's emphasis on the disposition of the recipient, but in a new key, for here the point is that the veiling leaves open possibilities for the recipient that she would otherwise lack. "The possibility of refusal is very real, for the parable lacks the necessary proof."[65] Of course the soil analogy makes the audi-

---

64. *De concordia* 3.9, in Saint Anselm, *Anselm of Canterbury: The Major Works*, ed. Brian Davies and G. R. Evans (Oxford: Oxford University Press, 2008), 464.

65. Benedict, *Jesus of Nazareth*, 193.

ence's response seem predetermined by its condition, but soil is recognizably disanalogous in this respect; Christians have long recognized that its irrationality is not meant to imply our own. As Gregory Palamas says, "we are not inanimate, unfeeling earth which is cultivated and sown by others, but living, breathing, rational ground. For that reason we must make ourselves ready by means of repentance."[66] The parable also pushes against a straight predetermination: as Theophylact notes, Christ is seen not just in the sower and the seed but also in some way in the obstacles. "The stony persons are those who adhering a little to the rock, that is, to Christ, up to a short time, receive the word, and afterwards, falling back, cast it away." The question is not just the condition of one's soil but whether one finds Christ even in the soil's difficulties: holding fast to the path (Ps. 17:5), rooted in the rock (Ps. 18:2), wearing and not worn down by the thorns (Matt. 27:29). Christ has come in a veiled form that makes relevant our disposition to receive him, and he has come in a suffering form that makes even the difficulties of our dispositions a possible site of encountering his presence.

Why does Christ not speak plainly, then, or come immediately in his glory? Because he wants to make possible a certain kind of response on our part, one whose outcome is neither the same in all circumstances nor determined by the circumstances themselves but depends on us. Michael Murray has suggested that the kind of response in question is one that is free in a morally significant sense;[67] but since this

---

66. Gregory Palamas, "Homily 56: On the Holy and Dread Mysteries of Christ," in Saint Gregory Palamas, *Saint Gregory Palamas: The Homilies*, ed. Christopher Veniamin (Waymart, PA: Mount Thabor, 2016), 460.

67. Michael J. Murray, "Deus Absconditus," in *Divine Hiddenness: New Essays*, ed. Daniel Howard-Snyder and Paul K. Moser (Cambridge: Cambridge University Press, 2002), 62–82.

requires a libertarian account of freedom that contradicts my evident compatibilism, I should say more, first, about why an appeal to this sort of freedom is unsatisfactory, and second, about how to capture its goods under other guises. These will be the tasks of the next chapter.

EXEMPLARITY, ANALOGY, AND THE ABILITY TO DO EVIL

Who has had the power to transgress
and did not transgress,
and to do evil and did not do it?
We will call him blessed,
for he has done wonderful things among his people.

—SIRACH 31:10, 9

"If God can move the created will in an infallibly effi-cacious manner, and if God's antecedent will truly is the salvation of all, then why does God *not* ensure that all are saved by means of infallibly efficacious outpourings of grace?"[1] Put differently, why does God preserve our freedom in its fallibility? What good is fallibility if every good is an imitation of God, for whom evil is not possible?

One possibility is that the relevant good is not an imi-tation of God at all. It is not self-evident that all goods are godlikenesses, and though both we and God are free, per-haps there is some good to a particularly creaturely freedom

1. Matthew Levering, *Predestination: Biblical and Theological Paths* (Oxford: Oxford University Press, 2011), 162. Levering ultimately con-cludes that "every attempt to resolve the question [of how to balance God's superabundant love with his providence and permission of per-manent rebellion] in favour of one affirmation or the other exceeds the bounds proper to theological reflection" (197). Still, it is too much mys-terianism for my taste to stipulate that here we must live with the sort of seeming contradiction that theological reflection on other paradigmatic mysteries—like the Trinity and the incarnation—labored hard to resolve. The point of that early reflection was that resolving the seeming contra-diction does not resolve but in some ways only deepens the mystery, and the same I think is true here. But it takes more than mysterianism to reach those depths.

that is not itself like God in any way. Richard Swinburne has endorsed such a view,[2] and Thomas himself can seem to flirt with it: "Things that do not belong to the praise of higher beings can be praiseworthy in lower beings. For example, ferociousness is praiseworthy in dogs but not in human beings, as Dionysius says. And likewise, not transgressing when one could belong to the praise of human beings but is absent from the praise of God."[3] But this tack treats God rather too much as the best thing and rather too little as the bestness of things. And should we so quickly concede that ground?

I indicated in the introduction that Euthyphro-type dilemmas give us some reason not to concede it. But there is another classical Christian reason against it, a reason that is finally also Thomas's: that you cannot get something from nothing; and since all creation is from God, all the thingness or perfections of creation are contained in God. Further, since God is not from anything, including from parts, God is not composed out of the combination of these perfections but is identical to them. God is not just good but goodness. This, while much too quick to convince the skeptic, is notable for two of its implications. First, it implies that our language about God is at best analogous, since, as the third and fourth sections of this chapter will argue, we cannot univocally conceptualize the sort of "thing" that is identical with the perfections of all, and all possible, mutable things. This will be important scaffolding for the account of how our freedom and our peccability imitates God. Second, it implies that God

---

2. See, e.g., Richard Swinburne, *The Existence of God*, 2nd ed. (Oxford: Oxford University Press, 2004), 120. Cf. Seneca, *Epistle* 53.11. Recall also the implicit reliance on some such good by Adams-style defeat strategies that I noted in the introduction, p. 27 n. 37.

3. *De malo* 3.1ad10, trans. in Thomas Aquinas, *On Evil*, ed. Brian Davies, trans. Richard Regan (Oxford: Oxford University Press, 2003), 145.

is present in all creatures as that in which they participate. In particular, it implies the noncompetitive account with which I have been working throughout: that everything ontologically positive about our acts—both the acts themselves and our causing our acts, however those are conceptualized metaphysically—is from God. And this, too, will have important consequences for how we conceive of created freedom.

Let me therefore, in the first section, unpack the logic of participation by indicating some accounts of freedom that I find insufficient. In the second section, I will look to Irenaeus for a way to get the benefits of a freewill theodicy without the costs of these sorts of accounts. The third section will sketch Thomas's understanding of analogy in conversation with Scotus, and the fourth Scotus's understanding of univocity in conversation with Thomas, so as, in the fifth section, to fit the Irenaean suggestions into an account of God's exemplarity. Since this account both extends and reworks the Balthasarian project, the sixth and final chapter will compare Balthasar's own account of analogy and divine freedom.

Participated Freedom

The family of answers I would like to reject all imply that the ability to do evil—either at some time or at all times—is ingredient in our freedom. This is the most popular answer in contemporary Christian philosophy of religion and is defended in a certain form among the Thomists, so let me say something about the problems of participation in this connection.

Kevin Timpe provides a nice example of Anglo-American philosophy on these issues, in part because it represents the culmination of much analytic reflection, in part because of how close he is in some ways to the account I want to give.

Timpe thinks both humans and God are free because we are the ultimate sources of our acts, acts that are responsive to reasons.[4] Sourcehood, for him, implies incompatibilism, in the sense that our choices are not "causally determined by factors external to the agent; that is, . . . there exists [no] externally sufficient causal chain which brings about that action."[5]

As I noted in the first chapter, an account in terms of causally sufficient antecedents is going to have trouble accounting for theological determinism if God's causation of our acts is immediate and undetermined. God is not sufficient for particular created effects, since God could do otherwise; God's creative will is sufficient but not antecedent to such effects, since it is simultaneous with what it produces. Still, as I suggested there, there might be a way to account for divine predetermination in terms of the antecedent sufficiency of relations of dependence. On that account, the act's having been caused by God is antecedently sufficient for its having been caused by us. The question is whether this predetermination undermines our freedom. I think it does not, for two reasons. First, because Scripture tends to tie freedom to our ability to do good, not to our ability to do otherwise. The Father cannot do otherwise than freely love the Son; Father, Son, and Spirit are perfectly free in creating and cannot do evil. So also Christ as a human being; and the saints become more free when, beatified, they lose the ability to sin. Conversely, as Scripture everywhere affirms, the damned are less free. An account like

---

4. Kevin Timpe, *Free Will in Philosophical Theology* (New York: Bloomsbury Academic, 2013), 8. For earlier applications of this "source" view of freedom to God, see among others Edward Wierenga, "The Freedom of God," *Faith and Philosophy* 19 (2002): 434, and William Lane Craig, *Time and Eternity: Exploring God's Relationship to Time* (Wheaton, IL: Crossway, 2001), 261–62.

5. Craig, *Time and Eternity*, 109.

Timpe's leaves the freedom of the blessed and the freedom of the damned as rather too equivalent. Both are free in the sense of having stable dispositions based on undetermined choices in the past, dispositions that now determine them to good and bad respectively. This can tell us why the free acts of hell are worse than those of heaven, because they are constrained to evil, but it cannot say how they are worse *by lacking freedom.* Yet it is precisely the slavery of sin and the freedom of beatitude that the plain sense of Paul and the allegory of Exodus are at every opportunity emphasizing.[6]

Of course, we could just distinguish different senses of freedom and stipulate that the Bible prefers one and Anglo-American philosophy another. And since I am wanting to hold onto the idea behind the Anglo-American usage alongside the biblical idea, this could quickly become a semantic issue: why not distinguish F1 and F2 and continue in a quaintly, not to say vainly, mathematical precision?

Here there is a second reason to keep our usages more strictly biblical, for to tie an ability to do otherwise to free-

---

6. Compare also Timothy O'Connor's account, in which there are degrees of freedom but these do not correlate with one's goodness. See Timothy O'Connor, "Degrees of Freedom," *Philosophical Explorations* 12 (2009): 119–25. Though Jesse Couenhoven notes this distinction in Augustine's position, his desire to impute responsibility to the inheritors of original sin leads him to make rather little of it—the one determined by circumstances to sin is still seen as functioning properly. See Jesse Couenhoven, *Stricken by Sin, Cured by Christ: Agency, Necessity, and Culpability in Augustinian Theology* (Oxford: Oxford University Press, 2013), esp. ch. 5. Though I am agnostic here about Couenhaven's claim that we can be responsible for some evil acts that we are determined to do, in the next chapter, I suggest that we cannot be seen as functioning properly if we are entirely unable to do good (i.e., not just with respect to some specific acts but for any act whatsoever), as total depravity is sometimes taken to mean. For a comparison of the similar singlemindedness of the blessed and damned that does not lose sight of the differences, see Bernard of Clairvaux, *Steps of Humility and Pride* 21.51.

dom (or an ability to do otherwise than good to morally significant freedom) occludes the way in which our freedom imitates God's. It creates the ravel at the center of this chapter. Unraveling it will be easier if we do not identify this ability with freedom at all but with a different aspect of our agency. So I will hew to a rougher and more traditional definition of freedom as rational causality: this distinguishes it from coercion and involuntary action, both of which place unreasoning constraints upon our action. It also explains why the damned are less free, because they are not rational causes in the same way as the blessed: they are less rational because they act against the good, and they are weaker causes because they produce negations, or ontologically reduced effects. Their actions reflect stable dispositions, it is true, but this conceals the more fundamental truth that they are failing to execute themselves—or, if you like, that they are executing a failure of themselves. Finally, this rough definition should make clear the noncompetitive nature of freedom: we act as rational causes to the degree that we participate in, are upheld by, God's rational causality. When we produce an act, God has not stopped producing the act so that we can start—our starting is God's starting, too, for our causing is a positive feature and so of God.[7] Thus our being and our action is positively, not inversely, related to God's being and action.[8]

7. Timpe's divergence on this point leads also to his strange account of cooperative grace, in which he aims to show how "the agent is not a cause of her own salvation" (*Philosophical Theology*, 66). This yields the inversion of my conclusion in chapter 1: instead of the rejection of grace consisting in a relative nonact, as it does on my account, Timpe has the rejection of grace being a positive act (65) and our cooperation being an omission of this positive act. But why think that we should not be causes—secondary, but still real—of our salvation? Timpe is worried that this is Pelagian, because Timpe seems to presume that if we cause it, God does not. But that of course is exactly what we have to reject.

8. Karl Rahner, *Foundations of Christian Faith: An Introduction to the*

Still, we can keep Timpe's definition of freedom in terms of sufficient antecedent conditions of our acts, since God is not such a condition, and therefore God alone, along with what Timpe calls our agential structures, can determine our free decisions. Those whom God gives some share of his knowledge (causing our acts finally) or some share of his steadfastness in the good (causing efficiently) are in these very gifts given a freedom more like his, one that is therefore more perfect. They lose the ability to do otherwise, but their origination of their acts is in no way threatened—for God's origination does not threaten our own. The only thing we can originate in Timpe's sense, in the sense of initiating independently of God, is a negation.[9] This is why God's infallible origination perfects ours, since we are removed from the possibility of negating the acts to which God calls us and that are in some way most properly our own. Just as it would be a diminishment of divine freedom were God possibly to fail to act according to his nature, which is goodness, so it is an imperfection in us to possibly fail to act according to our own, which are goodnesses.

The problem is that this sort of participated freedom will not help us with the problem of evil in the way that Timpe rightly wants. It is (theologically) compatibilist. For theodicy, we need something else. But here, too, Timpe is useful. For he is quite right to point to a certain instrumental value to the ability to do evil that will be important for its justification—a point I will develop out of Irenaeus in the next section. The problem is that this ability is ours only by a kind

Idea of Christianity, trans. William V. Dych, rev. ed. (New York: Crossroad, 1982), 79.

9. David B. Burrell, *Freedom and Creation in Three Traditions* (Notre Dame: University of Notre Dame Press, 1993), 125.

of absence of God, a relative lack of grace, and the question is how that absence can be ingredient in some good. Since God's absence cannot be instrumentally valuable for those goods that consist in God's presence, for what goods can it be an instrument? Identifying these sorts of goods will be the task of the sections "Thomas (and Scotus) and Rupture" and "Scotus (and Thomas) and Rupture," so that the subsequent section, "Self-Creation," can fit our fallibility into them.

There is a Thomistic parallel to this Anglo-American tradition. Thomists sometimes make the ability to do evil part of our *defectible* freedom, which will eventually be elevated into an indefectible freedom that can do no wrong. Something like this distinction is going to be necessary on an account, like mine, that agrees so much with Thomas. Still, the relationship between defectible and indefectible freedom is rather too vague. Is freedom a genus of which these two are (higher and lower) species? Does defectible freedom have its own goods that distinguish it from the indefectible, goods that are lost in beatitude? Thomas even suggests that defectible freedom might be connected to the defectibility of our natures, as if a grace that worked infallibly in us would violate some essential fallibility. Thus Michael Torre:

> God gives the interior instinct of preparatory grace in accord with nature. Because his providence preserves, but does not destroy nature, he moves free creatures in accord with their defectability, and thus in a way that can fail: "evil cannot be kept from certain things without taking away their nature, which is such that it may or may not fail" (deficere vel non deficere). . . . Consequently, since God is most prudent, His providence does not prevent evil, but permits each thing to act as its nature requires that it act. For, as

Dionysius says, "the role of providence is to save, not to destroy, nature" (DV q. 5 a. 4 ad 4).[10]

This will have strange consequences if you think, as Torre and Thomas and I all do, that there are irresistible or infallible graces. For these graces will then be destructions of our nature. And the good of defectibility will be predicated upon the absence, not the presence, of grace—which is strange to say of any good, when grace is the presence of goodness itself.

The same problem besets those accounts that see our freedom as requiring a self-limitation of God.[11] What sort of good is this, which requires less of God rather than more? How could freedom be a perfection if it requires distancing oneself from the source of perfection? The whole logic of creation groans in travail here, as if our absolute analogical dependence upon God could be flipped inside out at its most concentrated point, in the freedom of the creature, in order to "make space" (a favorite image) for us by circumscribing God. But what is space from God but the void? And what is in the void to be valued? Whatever truth there is in these tropes

---

10. Michael D. Torre, *Do Not Resist the Spirit's Call: Francisco Marín-Sola on Sufficient Grace* (Washington, DC: Catholic University of America Press, 2013), 286. Thomas will sometimes also appeal to a diversity of goods: "Although a creature would be better if it adhered unchangeably to God, nevertheless that one also is good which can adhere to God or not adhere. And so a universe in which both sorts of creatures are found is better than if only one or the other were found" (*De veritate* q. 24 a. 1 ad16).

11. E.g., Hans Urs von Balthasar, *The Dramatis Personae: Man in God*, vol. 2 of *Theo-Drama: Theological Dramatic Theory*, trans. Graham Harrison (San Francisco: Ignatius, 1990), 271–73, which tries to hold a kind of *tsimtsum* or "making space" account in tension with a participatory account. My hesitations about Balthasar and especially his assumption that finite freedom always involves the "risk of drawing Lucifer's response" (272) will become clearer in the last section of this chapter.

requires great care in unpacking; this will in part be the task
of the final section.

IRENAEUS AND FREEWILL THEODICY

> But upon this supposition [that the first angels and human
> beings are prevented from transgressing], neither would
> what is good be grateful to them, nor communion with
> God be precious, nor would the good be very much to be
> sought after, which would present itself without their own
> proper endeavor, care, or study, but would be implanted of
> its own accord and without their concern. Thus it would
> come to pass, that their being good would be of no con-
> sequence, because they were so by nature rather than by
> will, and are possessors of good spontaneously, not by
> choice. . . . [T]he harder we strive, so much is it the more
> valuable; while so much the more valuable it is, so much
> the more should we esteem it.[12]

This is an example of Irenaeus's

> optimistic theological ground plan. . . . Whereas Augustine
> and Athanasius are full of plangent, almost gnostic lam-
> entation for the fact that, as changing creatures, they are
> removed from unchanging Being, Irenaeus sees in the very
> creatureliness of the creature, in the fact that its nature is
> to Become, that is, to change, the possibility of an unend-
> ing progression and development towards Being, towards
> God. . . . Instead of dwelling on the instability inherent in

12. *Haer.* 4.37.6–7. Cf. Damascene, *The Orthodox Faith* 2.30.

the condition of Becomingness, Irenaeus emphasizes the possibility of growth and development inherent in it.[13]

Notice two features of this Irenaean optimism. First, the value added by having to develop or strive for these goods is not exactly an additional good but a kind of mode of the original goods themselves. It is not just that we are wise but that we are wise through development, choice, will, and not originally, spontaneously, by nature.[14] This makes us not more wise but wise in an especially valuable way. Second, this way of being good is located precisely in what distinguishes us from God. It is bound up with becoming and indeed with our ability to do evil. We have these goods in a creaturely way, and even more in a voluntary and not just natural way. "The wheat and the chaff, being inanimate and irrational, have been made such by nature. But man, being endowed with reason, and in this respect like to God, having been made free in his will, and with power over himself, is himself the cause to himself, that sometimes he becomes wheat, and sometimes chaff."[15] This is to say that there is a scale of value that governs kinds of becoming, such that our way of becoming good is better than irrational ways of becoming good. Since these are both ways of becoming and so both modes of unlikeness to God, we might say that our way of becoming good is less unlike God than the irrational creature's. Let me say

13. Denis Minns, OP, *Irenaeus: An Introduction*, rev. ed. (London: T&T Clark, 2010), 84.

14. This is not to say we are wise by will instead of by grace, or that the striving Irenaeus speaks of is some kind of purely natural effort, for our willing is graced in any number of ways. See Roger Berthouzoz, *Liberté et grâce suivant la théologie d'Irénée de Lyon* (Fribourg: Beauchesne, 1980), esp. ch. 4, "La grâce de Dieu au fondement de la liberté."

15. *Haer.* 4.4.3.

something more about the first point before expanding upon the second in the next section.

Irenaeus is sometimes invoked as having a freewill theodicy, but we have to tread carefully here.[16] Standard contemporary freewill theodicies assume that freedom includes the ability to do evil and so think evil must be possible for us to be free. Unlike other theodicies, then, the freewill theodicy justifies the *possibility* of evil, and actual evil only through this possibility (because Adam so happened to choose wrong). Irenaeus suggests a further step: instead of justifying the possibility of evil by some actual good like libertarian freedom, he justifies the possibility of evil by the possibility of some good—in particular, by the possibility of having goods like wisdom in an especially valuable manner or mode, when they could be forfeited and are not.[17] That is, the emphasis here is not on the ability to do evil itself but on a particular value that emerges from the right use of that ability, the value of being wise when we could have chosen otherwise. In this it differs from Timpe's account, where the value attained is

16. E.g., by Minns, *Irenaeus*, 80–91. This use of Irenaeus may be in part a reaction to John Hick, who cleaves rather too cleanly Irenaeus's soul-making theodicy from Augustine's free-will theodicy.

17. Compare Dean Zimmerman: "Freedom is needed primarily as a necessary condition for other moral goods. The highest such good is the very possibility of creatures capable of displaying genuinely moral virtues—hard-won habits due, at least in part, to a lifetime of free choices" ("An Anti-Molinist Replies," in *Molinism: The Contemporary Debate*, ed. Ken Perszyk [Oxford: Oxford University Press, 2012], 176). Zimmerman is closer to Timpe than to Irenaeus on these points, however. Note also that the Molinists' God is going to know the outcomes of free choices before creation in such a way that the mere possibility of good outcomes is not enough to justify the creation of this world with its bad effects—because God would have seen the bad effects coming and known to avoid them. Whereas on a simple foreknowledge view, God would not know until creation whether he was getting the goods or the evils.

still a freedom in which the ability to do evil is ingredient, diachronically if not synchronically.

What this turn to modes of goodness allows is a way to preserve features of the freewill theodicy without relying on even this historicist notion of libertarian freedom (freedom that at some point must be able to work against God). For freedom need not contain essential reference to an ability to do evil either synchronically or diachronically for these modes to do work in a theodicy. Where freedom does ground such an ability, it does so as imperfect, a freedom not yet fully confirmed by grace nor yet firmly fixed on the good. That this ability requires freedom is clear: the sinful negations described in the first two chapters require certain characteristics of freedom, including the ability of the will not to be determined by created antecedents. Only the free can negate. But the possibility of negation occurs only when the will lacks a certain stability and a certain sight, when it is weak in the legs and dim in the eyes. Only the imperfectly free can negate. Thus while our freedom is itself a kind of perfection, like wisdom, and not a mode, it is a perfection whose use in certain imperfect circumstances can give a peculiar mode to the perfections that follow, either as preserved or as attained. God could have given us the perfections from the beginning, but how we hold them may depend in part on how we, as successive creatures, arrive at them. It is not itself good to begin imperfect, but it can be better to have begun so.[18]

None of this implies that we will always be so imperfect. Nor does it imply that any exercise of imperfect freedom exhibits or instantiates the relevant good, for misuses of this freedom will not preserve wisdom in us and so *a fortiori* will not produce a better mode of having wisdom. This is part of

18. Though, again, it does not make us more free to have begun so.

the force of identifying the ability to do evil with negation. Negation is not good for the overall order, because contrary to God's plan; nor, because negative, is it good in itself; nor, finally, can it ground the sort of added, Irenaean goodness of being produced in a particular way, because there is no real production here. The good of being won requires something won in the first place. Still, when this imperfect freedom is used rightly, greater perfection results than would without this initial imperfection—for there is, as Bernard suggests, a peculiar "glory of not sinning."[19]

THOMAS (AND SCOTUS) AND RUPTURE

Can this be made sense of on a participatory scheme, in which more God means more and not less of us? How could some value be dependent on the initial absence of the source of all value? To answer this, we need a more detailed account of how we resemble God, and this will be the object of the next two sections. My starting point is a distinction drawn by David Burrell between God's formal features and God's attributes. Attributes are things like wisdom, which are first divine and then communicated to us. Formal features describe how God holds his attributes; they "are not so much said of a subject, as they are reflected in a subject's very mode of existing, and govern the way in which anything whatsoever might be said of that subject."[20] Burrell lists as formal features of God things like simplicity, limitlessness, unchangeableness, and unity. Our wisdom is the same attribute as God's wisdom,

19. Bernard of Clairvaux, *On Grace and Free Choice* 7.22.

20. David B. Burrell, *Knowing the Unknowable God: Ibn Sina, Maimonides, Aquinas* (Notre Dame: University of Notre Dame Press, 1992), 47.

but God *is* this wisdom, "beyond measure" (Ps. 147:5) and without "shadow of turning" (James 1:17 KJV), whereas we merely *have* wisdom, limited and loseable.

For Burrell's Aquinas, these formal features or modes "are all to be understood negatively, whereas [Aquinas] will defend a practice of predicating positive attributes. Considerations of analogy, then, properly enter with such attributes; yet the demand for attention to analogous uses of language will be established as one establishes 'the distinction' through these formal features of divinity."[21] That is, the formal features delineate the difference present in any analogy between God and creatures; as such they are not themselves used analogously of God and creatures but negatively, as what God has that we lack.[22] This is why they are paradigmatically negative terms: without composition, without limit, without change, without number.

In other words, these formal features have a kind of apophatic logic upon which the logic of analogy is built. It is because God is simple that our ascription of wisdom to him can both signify the same thing as ascriptions of wisdom to creatures and elude our comprehension. It is the same wisdom as ours (same *res*) but also is identical with the same power as ours—which is to say, it exists in a radically different way (*modus*) from ours.[23] And because we cannot separate

---

21. Burrell, *Knowing the Unknowable God*, 47.

22. Cf. Thomas Aquinas, *Summa contra gentiles* (*SCG*) I.30.4. For Burrell's own account of these things, which is rather more skeptical of Thomas's use of *res* and *modus* than I am, see David B. Burrell, *Analogy and Philosophical Language* (Eugene, OR: Wipf & Stock, 2016).

23. "As regards what is signified by these names, they belong properly to God, and more properly than they belong to creatures, and are applied primarily to Him. But as regards their mode of signification, they do not properly and strictly apply to God; for their mode of signification applies to creatures" (*ST* I.13.3c).

out what exactly in our concept of wisdom belongs to the *res* and what belongs to the *modus*, our understanding of divine wisdom remains in this life analogical.[24] We cannot scrub the concept clean and apply it univocally to God; at most we can point to the way it gets ruptured by its reference beyond the world—for instance, by saying that it is identical to divine power.[25] It is not just that we cannot describe God; we can-

24. The view presented here is closer to Nicholas Wolterstorff's reading of Thomistic analogy than to William Alston's—to speak of Thomas's germination in those fields of analytic philosophy that stretch beyond Thomism—in that creatures and the Creator share the same perfections. But Wolterstorff's categories do not always match Thomas's own, and this creates unnecessary confusion. He contends that "in assertively uttering 'God is alive,' 'God is good,' 'God is powerful,' and the like, the predicate terms 'alive,' 'good,' and 'powerful' have exactly the same sense that they do when we assertively utter, about some human being, 'he is alive,' 'he is good,' 'he is powerful.'" Nicholas Wolterstorff, "Alston on Aquinas on Theological Predication," in *Inquiring about God*, vol. 1 of *Selected Essays*, ed. Terence Cuneo (New York: Cambridge University Press, 2010), 126. But Thomas is quite clear that "nomina [substantia divina] . . . habent rationes diversas" ("the names [of the divine substance] have diverse meanings" [*ST* I.13.4c])—the names themselves, not the predicating of them, as Wolterstorff holds. Thomas's view is rather more straightforward than Wolterstorff suggests. The meaning of "alive" is a combination of a signification of a perfection shared by God and creatures and the creaturely aspect under which we have experienced it. Meaning is not just the *res*, as Wolterstorff seems to think (along with Richard Cross, "Idolatry and Religious Language," *Faith and Philosophy* 25 [2008]: 194). This is why the names given to God are not synonymous, "because they signify [the one divine essence] under many and different aspects" (*ST* I.13.4c).

25. The rupture is unavoidable because analogy is itself an analogous term, above all when applied to the relation between God and creatures. The creature resembles God as the effect resembles its cause, but the term "cause" is not a univocal ground for analogous prediction but is itself analogous. That is, God causes us in *something like* the way that we cause our artistic productions, and just as our productions resemble us in a certain way, so God's productions resemble him—in a similar, but not identical, way. This is all to say that Thomistic analogy is irreducible to univocity, whether the univocity of "cause" or any other. Cf. Yves Simon, "On Order

not even describe the ways our descriptions fail God. "For the reality of God transcends our language not to any describable degree but 'infinitely'. And 'infinitely' [in my terms, a mode] is not itself the name of some measurement of the degree of difference between what we can say of God and what God is. It says, simply, that no such language of measurement is possible."[26]

This is where the Thomistic account differs from the Scotistic. Thomas and Scotus agree (a) that there is no reality shared in by God and creatures but a single reality in God in which the creaturely reality shares (i.e., not a generic wisdom or being of which divine and creaturely instances are species),[27] (b) that this sharing grounds an analogy between our concepts of God's wisdom and of our wisdom, and (c) that this analogy consists in the two concepts each being composed of parts, of which one part is the same across the two concepts and one part is different.

The two men differ in that Scotus thinks these parts can themselves be conceptualized, such that God's wisdom is a complex concept composed out of two simpler ones: wisdom and infinity. Thomas, on the other hand, thinks that God's wisdom is a concept composed out of a *res* and a *modus* and that these are not themselves susceptible of independent conceptualization. Rather, in this life, we know only the *res* of wisdom along with the *modus* under which we learn it, which is creaturely. The best we can do is to rupture the creatureliness of this concept in various ways—by denying things of

---

in Analogical Sets," *New Scholasticism* 34 (1960): 1–42. What I am calling rupture, Simon calls "abstraction *by way of confusion*" (12).

26. Denys Turner, *The Darkness of God: Negativity in Christian Mysticism* (Cambridge: Cambridge University Press, 1998), 42.

27. See Richard Cross, *Duns Scotus*, Great Medieval Thinkers (Oxford: Oxford University Press, 1999), 39.

it, by asserting its identity with properties differently defined, and so forth—which does not give us a new concept but just makes clear the brokenness of the old one.[28] That is, strictly speaking we have no concept associated with the denials and contradictions that point toward the divine *modus*: no concept of infinity, no concept of simplicity, no concept of uncreatedness. They are as it were operational terms whose role is a negative one, pointing to how we rupture the concepts we do have.

How then can we distinguish between terms that are literally true of God (God is wise) and those that are literally false (God is a rock)—that is, terms that are analogical and terms that are metaphorical? "Whatever names unqualifiedly designate a perfection without defect are predicated of God and of other things: for example, goodness, wisdom, being, and the like. But when any name expresses such perfections along with a mode that is proper to a creature, it can be said of God only according to likeness and metaphor."[29] So metaphorical terms include the creaturely mode as "part of the very signification of the name,"[30] whereas analogical terms signify the perfection without this mode. Is Thomas then committed to the idea that we can identify the *res* or perfection without the mode, so that we can know that what we are signifying is not essentially creaturely? Don't we have to peer inside

---

28. In this sense, my account is consistent with the "single *ratio*" account that Domenic D'Ettore traces from Capreolus through Cajetan—there is one concept that characterizes both divine and human wisdom. See Domenic D'Ettore, *Analogy after Aquinas: Logical Problems, Thomistic Answers* (Washington, DC: Catholic University of America Press, 2018), esp. chs. 3 and 5. But I am putting more emphasis on the changes that concept has to undergo when applied to God, even if those changes do not produce a new and different concept.

29. *SCG* I.30.2.

30. *ST* I.13.3ad1.

the analogical concept and conceptualize its parts to know whether the creaturely bit is just on the side of the *modus* or also on the side of the *res*?

Thomas and Scotus diverge on this point. Let us say that we want to deny that the ability to whinny is proper to horses, that all and only horses have it and that it therefore cannot be applied to nonhorses. There are three ways we could establish this. First, we could observe a nonhorse whinnying. Thomas and Scotus both deny that we have this sort of observational knowledge of God in this life. We cannot observe the non-creature in the way we can the nonhorse. Second, we could form a complete concept of whinnying and see no essential reference to horsiness in it. We would then know that there is nothing in the definition of whinnying that restricts it to horses. This, roughly, is Scotus's approach: we know being is indifferently finite or infinite, created or uncreated, because we can conceptualize it. Third, we might know a negative property about whinnying—that it is not essentially horsey—prior to, and not as a consequence of, knowing all its positive properties. This I take to be Thomas's approach.

How do we get the knowledge of this negative property? It is rooted in the fact that creaturely modes can themselves resemble God in a certain way. It will not be a resemblance by participation, because these modes are precisely what distinguish us from God. To participate in them would be to take some share in God's distinction from us, which would be a substantial and not merely accidental deification; it would in other words be our destruction. This is a sight of God that no one may have and live. Instead, the resemblance is apophatic, lying in the directionality of our denials. Of the things that are not God, some are more not God than others; and the apophatic theologian denies *toward* God.

Our modes resemble God's in this way, a kind of resemblance by approach. Simplicity, for instance, exhibits grades in created things: immaterial things are more simple than material things; the angels above all have their perfections in the simplest created mode. This simplest created mode is still not absolutely simple; it is still, in the dichotomy between simple and nonsimple things, inescapably on the nonsimple side; but it does have a kind of similarity to God's absolute simplicity that is not participatory but is a kind of approach toward the absolute. Or again, with Scotus's preferred mode: perfections can be more or less intense in creatures, as some are more powerful and more wise and so on than others, but only God has these perfections with *infinite* intensity. The more intensive modes of these perfections among creatures do in some sense approach the infinite intensity with which God has them; still, no creature has or could possibly have a perfection infinitely. Creatures don't participate in this infinity, since it is precisely the infinity that distinguishes God from them; they don't, in other words, have an analogical infinity, since "large" isn't properly speaking an analogue of "infinite"; rather they approach the infinity of God's perfections by various finite degrees.[31]

How do we distinguish between perfections and modes

---

31. Thomas for his part also acknowledges infinite intensity as a divine mode, and Scotus thinks infinity implies simplicity, though they do not mean exactly the same thing by the two terms. Thomas tends to move to the absolute by removal: simplicity is the removal of composition, infinity is the removal of limits, and so on. Scotus moves to the absolute by expansion: infinity is the expansion of finitude, simplicity is the expansion of something like integratedness, and so on. These are two ways of taking the Irenaean legacy, for Irenaeus too locates the divine difference in infinity and simplicity: "God's will differs from the human will, because in God thought and will are identical, and because God's will is infinitely more powerful than the human will." See E. P. Meijering, "Irenaeus' Relation to Philosophy in the Light of His Concept of Free Will," *Romanitas et Christianitas: Studia Iano Henrico Waszink A.D. VI*

then—between what is and what is not essentially creaturely? For Thomas, I think, we identify perfections as what endure across the various creaturely modes that point toward God. Being, life, wisdom all exist in this world in ways that exhibit a great deal of composition and in ways that exhibit very little composition.[32] This does not give us some complete concept

---

Kal. Nov. A. MCMLXXIII XIII Lustra Complenti Oblata, ed. Willem den Boer and Jan Hendrik Waszink (Amsterdam: North-Holland, 1973), 224.

32. Here it is worth raising a problem about perfection terms that the Denyses (Pseudo- and Turner) do not quite address. For there are really two kinds of perfections. The first are transcendental and apply to all things: goodness, being, beauty, and so forth. These have the sort of transcategorial character that makes them prime candidates for application to God: since they apply to all things, God can be identified with them without excluding anything from his exemplarity. See Denys Turner, *Faith, Reason and the Existence of God* (New York: Cambridge University Press, 2004), 189. Second, there are perfections that are neither transcendental nor essentially creaturely. Wisdom, for instance, is not a transcendental because rocks are not wise; still, God is wise. Unlike the transcendentals, these perfections do not describe all things, but unlike essentially creaturely terms, they need not exclude other perfections either. The key feature of these perfections—and they are relevant here because freedom is one of them—is that they contain no essential reference to limitation. They can be infinitized. This means that they do not serve as differentiae the way that, say, color does, by carving up the visible spectrum into different slices that are contrary to one another: if a thing is blue, then it is not red. Rather, they differentiate not over against a contrary but over against a contradictory: if a thing is rational, it is not irrational; if a thing is living, then it is not inanimate. They have something that the other species of their genus lack, not something that the other species of their genus have differently. This means that we can predicate life of God and still maintain that God is the source of every perfection in the nonliving. But we cannot say God is material without it implying that God lacks, and so is not the source of, spirituality. (I am taking spirituality and materiality as contraries here, not contradictories. We should be careful in saying God is spirit: we do not mean that God lacks the perfections of materiality; rather, we mean to deny of God the limitations of materiality. God is spirit not in an analogous sense—as if that intrinsically limited characteristic of angelic being could be made

of what they are, but it does suggest that there is something here that can exist without any sort of composition at all. We can derive from observation one negative property about these features, that they are not correlated with composition. And this implies another negative property: that they are not destroyed by the transition beyond composition altogether, that is, that they are not essentially creaturely. Of course, we do not know exactly how they will look on the other side of this transition, for the absolute removal of composition has consequences far stranger than its relative removal—one such consequence, for instance, is that goodness, life, and wisdom must themselves be really identical. But we can be confident that they survive the transition in some—ruptured—form.[33]

Scotus (and Thomas) and Rupture

This is not to say, as the Scotists sometimes accuse the Thomists of doing, that there is nothing positive in our conception of God, as if in approaching God through denials we were left with entirely empty concepts.[34] The denials are our way to a prebeatific conception of God, but the conception

infinite—but in an apophatic sense, as the intrinsic limits to animal being can be denied. Because we have less experience with spiritual than material things, we have a less distinct idea of what "spirit" means as a positive thing than what it means as a denial of its contrary, which is matter. Thus the word tends to get used for the second, the denial, as easily as it is used for the first, the affirmation.)

33. Cf. Burrell, *Analogy*, 162–63. And on 164: "any terms that we then go on to use of God must bear the mark of having been negated."

34. See, e.g., Claude Frassen, *Scotus academicus seu Universa Doctoris Subtilis theologica dogmata* (Rome: Ex Typographia Sallustiana, 1900), 1:146–47.

itself is formed not just of denials but of the substance of things denied. It is not just rupture but ruptured creaturely concepts. How far is this from Scotus's account then? In particular, if this implies a great deal of obscurity about our concepts of God, how much clarity does Scotus himself imply? For Scotus, God is conceptualized above all as infinite being, where we have a concept of being derived from creatures that is scrubbed of its imperfections and then raised to infinite intensity so as to fit the divine. But whence this concept of infinite intensity? It cannot itself come from creatures, since no creature is infinite. Scotus explicates it by analogy with quantitative (extensive) infinity: just as quantities come in grades called number and we can conceive of a numerical infinity, so also qualities or perfections like power come in grades that can have a similar sort of infinity.

But neither step in this conceptualization is obvious. First, it is not clear that we do have a concept of quantitative infinity, or at least a concept that operates in the univocal way that Scotus assumes. Scotus wants "being" to have all its same properties when infinitized, but it is not at all clear that mathematical infinities bear the same properties as that which they infinitize. I have in mind the suggestion in *kalam* debates that infinite sets may well break some of our basic assumptions about mathematical sets, either not being the same in number as sets to which they map one-to-one or not being greater than their proper subsets.[35] If that is true, then even mathematical infinities might look closer to Thomas's account, a kind of rupture of concepts derived from creaturely (and therefore finite) experience, than to Scotus's.

---

35. Paul Draper, "A Critique of the Kalam Cosmological Argument," in *Philosophy of Religion: An Anthology*, ed. Louis P. Pojman and Michael C. Rea, 6th ed. (Boston: Cengage Learning, 2012), 172–78.

Second, it is not clear how exactly the analogy between quantitative and qualitative (or in the case of being, entitative) infinity is supposed to work. It looks like what Thomistic commentators come to call the analogy of proportionality: A is to B as C is to D; numerical infinity is to number as omnipotence is to power. But if that is what our concept of qualitative infinity is at bottom, then it seems like Scotus has rooted his account of univocity in analogy. We know infinite being or power or suchlike on analogy with infinite numbers. This may be a more Cajetanian conception of analogy than Thomas's own view; but it is not univocity.[36] Alternatively, the analogy with quantity here might be merely indicative of the sort of thing meant by entitative infinity without defining the thing. But then the natural question is, how do we actually know its definition? If we do not get it from created things, because they are all finite, and we do not get it from Scotus's own account, because these are merely indications, then where does it come from? Allan Wolter appeals here to "a flash of insight,"[37] but it is not at all clear that this insight

---

36. We could of course note relevant disanalogies with quantitative infinity as well, as a way to specify what we mean by qualitative infinity, but this sort of specification is not the same as providing a clear concept of such infinity. It is significant that this positive feature (entitative infinity) seems always to be described in negative language (as with Richard Cross's explication in terms of logical *un*surpassability: *Duns Scotus on God* [Aldershot: Routledge, 2005], 98). This does not mean that the feature itself is negative, only that our conceptualization of it requires the sort of negating that points finite minds beyond the finite—in other words, that it requires rupture.

37. "But Scotus did not attribute this shift [to infinite being] to any special influence of divine ideas, as illuminationists do, nor did he regard it as something impressed upon our mind from above or as something innate or congenital. He indicated the psychological steps that one can take to lead up to the final state, but he regarded the flash of insight as an act of

gives us an actual positive conception of infinity rather than some kind of rupture of the finitude we see around us.

For entitative infinity has to do a lot of work for Scotus. In particular, it has to ground the sort of participatory metaphysics that he wants to pair with his doctrine of conceptual univocity. I have already noted that Scotus agrees with Aquinas in identifying perfections with God that creatures then resemble or participate in, not with something behind God that God and creatures both instantiate. Radical Orthodoxy has not been particularly fair to Scotus on this point, but they are right to be worried.[38] Their assumption seems to be that Scotus's logical doctrine—univocity—has to match his metaphysical doctrine, because that is how analogy operates in Aquinas. Scotus in fact uncouples these,[39] so that the analogy between God and creatures is rooted metaphysically in a God that creates (our being is metaphysically derived from God) but conceptually in a "being" that is differentiated into finite and infinite (our being is conceptually derived from some common concept).[40] Both

simple intelligence." See William Frank and Allan B. Wolter, *Duns Scotus, Metaphysician* (West Lafayette, IN: Purdue University Press, 1995), 151.

38. "Scotus asserted the metaphysical priority of Being over both the infinite and the finite alike." See Catherine Pickstock, *After Writing: On the Liturgical Cosummation of Philosophy* (Malden, MA: Wiley-Blackwell, 1997), 122.

39. Cf. E. Jennifer Ashworth, "Analogy and Metaphor from Thomas Aquinas to Duns Scotus and Walter Burley," in *Later Medieval Metaphysics: Ontology, Language, and Logic*, ed. Charles Bolyard and Rondo Keele (New York: Fordham University Press, 2013), 238: "Semantics and ontology are now independent, and the analogy of being is recognized as such." There is an alternative view that reads the places where Scotus endorses metaphysical analogy as margin notes about the position with which he is disagreeing. See D'Ettore, *Analogy*, 28–29.

40. For Scotus, this is not a generic concept because being is not a genus. It is contracted not, like a genus, by differentiae, but by intrinsic modes, like finitude and infinity. Cf. Daniel P. Horan, *Postmodernity and*

Thomas and Scotus do of course allow the same *words* to be used of God and creatures: God is wise, and we are wise. And one way to see the difference between them is that Thomas allows more slippage between these words and our concepts, such that our concepts can be broken open to track more closely their divine referent. "Wise" in "God is wise" refers to a ruptured version of "wise" in "Solomon is wise," and this ruptured concept itself refers to God in the least inadequate way possible. Scotus, by contrast, ties the concepts more closely to our language ("wise" refers to the same concept in both attributions) and introduces further concepts (finite and infinite) as a way to peg them to reality.

But the difficulty of "infinity" should be plain here, especially an infinity rooted in mathematical imaginings. For this sort of infinity has to be not just bigger than but actually the exemplar of finite things; it has to be not just a vanishingly large number but number itself. And that is just not how mathematical infinity works. Even the sort of strangeness you get when you infinitize quantity—the transformation of properties that seem essential to quantity itself, which was the first worry with Scotus's analogy—does not itself approach this sort of strangeness, which you get when you transfer quantitative to qualitative to entitative infinity. Whatever else infinite sets are, they are not setness. This is Radical Orthodoxy's worry; this is why they fault Scotus for the loss of a participatory metaphysics. Still, it is more charitable to Scotus—who is after all a real person, and beatified, which means he can hear us[41]—to say that he splits unsustainably the way

---

Univocity: A Critical Account of Radical Orthodoxy and John Duns Scotus (Minneapolis: Fortress, 2014), 182–83.

41. Even if Radical Orthodoxy does not accept his beatification, he at least *might* be able to hear us. This is a lingering worry with the Radically Orthodox, who occasionally evince a belief, or a desire for a belief, in

things are from the way we talk about them, and that others would reintegrate them by assimilating the metaphysical to the conceptual (univocity), even if Scotus himself, if pushed, would have done the reverse.

Indeed, Scotus the man seems to share the Radical worry. Notice the caution and the qualifications: "From the notion of the infinite in the *Physics*, then, applied imaginatively to something infinite in quantity, *were that possible* and applied further to something actually infinite in entity, *were it possible*, we can form *some sort of idea of how to* conceive a being intensively infinite in perfection and power."[42] Scotus does not even purport to give us a concept of infinite being, but only some sort of idea of how we might—maybe, possibly—go about conceiving it. This is the strangeness of Scotus's flash-of-insight epistemology, if such it is: it purports to clarify the concept but only at the cost of its communicability. He can at most prepare us; we have to have the flash ourselves. The weakness of such epistemologies is that the conditions of coruscation are so obscure. What if our consideration of the familiar infinities never catches fire? More worrisome, what if those we expect to be best conditioned to experience the flash report a different experience altogether—in particular, what if they report an inadequacy to conceptual thinking that points to something more like rupture than to an incommunicable univocal concept? For this indeed seems to be the ex-

---

fairies and wood nymphs and such things while treating (at least possible members of) the communion of the saints with the disregard due the no longer existent. Surely more respect is due the reality of the one before we even broach the reality of the other.

42. *Quodlibet* 5.8; translation in John Duns Scotus, *God and Creatures: The Quodlibetal Questions*, trans. Felix Alluntis and Allan B. Wolter (Washington, DC: Catholic University of America Press, 1981), 110. I owe this point to John Hare.

perience of the mystics: not a mere inadequacy of description but an inadequacy of description rooted in an inadequacy of conception. If such is true of those most familiar with the divine infinity, and if Scotus's own account of infinitizing is as hesitant and obscure as I have suggested, we might well wonder how clear we should take Scotus's own concept of infinite being to be. We might suspect, in other words, that this infinitizing is just a version of what I am calling rupture, and that Scotus's account, too, though in a different way from Thomas's, preserves the divine obscurity.

This sort of obscurity, however accounted, will work against Scotus's motives, which are to safeguard natural theology. The stated goal of the doctrine of univocity is to guarantee the validity of syllogisms about God by avoiding equivocation. Take the following syllogism:

1. All good agents optimize, where "optimize" means something like "allow the possibility of evil only where doing so makes possible goods that are at least as great (or incommensurably good)."
2. God is a good agent.
3. Therefore God optimizes.

Scotus wants to ensure that "good agent" means the same thing in (1) and (2) so that the deduction can go through. But has Scotus done any more to secure the soundness of this syllogism than Thomas did? Whatever he does for the validity of the argument comes at the expense of the premises. In this case, whatever we are to mean by "good agents" in the first premise, if it is to satisfy a universal quantifier whose domain includes God's agency, has to be defined in a way that survives infinitization. And if I am right that we just aren't very clear on what happens in infinitization, and that Scotus concedes that obscurity, then our concept of good agency will never, in this life, be very well formed. Instead of wondering, then, how much the fairly clear, creaturely concept of good agency cum optimization applies to God—that is, whether the syllogism is valid—we now have to wonder whether the rather obscure, "universal" concept of good agency includes optimization—that is, whether the first premise is true. Of course, we might still want to affirm that optimization applies to God in some way, but the point is that that "in some way" persists on any account. Reasoning about God is hard and not made easier by shifting the burden.[43]

Self-Creation

The upshot here is that if Scotus is as open to rupture as I have suggested, and if Thomas is as adequate in securing soundness, then perhaps there is less at stake in taking sides than either side has taken there to be.[44] And this suggests some

43. "'But is a blurred concept a concept at all?'—Is a photograph that is not sharp a picture of a person at all? Is it even always an advantage to replace a picture that is not sharp by one that is?" See Ludwig Wittgenstein, *Philosophical Investigations*, trans. G. E. M. Anscombe, P. M. S. Hacker, and Joachim Schulte, rev. 4th ed. (Chichester: Wiley-Blackwell, 2009), n. 71. "But it is, on the other hand, enormously difficult to discern these limitations, i.e. to depict them clearly. Or, as one might say, to invent a style of painting capable of depicting what is, in this way, fuzzy. For I want to keep telling myself: 'Make sure you really do paint only what you see!'" See Ludwig Wittgenstein, *Culture and Value*, trans. Peter Winch (Chicago: University of Chicago Press, 1984), 68. Burrell suggests that "there is no method for assuring proper analogous use" (*Analogy*, 242) but that analogy is a kind of tool in the craft of theology, and that only virtuous practice of this craft, and not something like rules of deduction, will guarantee the truth of our syllogisms (cf. 263).

44. It is worth noting, too, that what Thomas means by univocity, and

common resources—in particular, for my purposes here, it
suggests that on either account, exemplarity is going to involve at least three kinds of resemblance: univocal similarity,
when two things instantiate the same perfection; analogical
participation, when one thing instantiates the perfection of
a higher thing in a lower mode;[45] and apophatic *approach*,
when no shared perfections are instantiated but there is this
sort of approximation in the modes themselves of one to
the other (as large is closer to infinite, and less composed
is closer to absolutely simple). Both of the last two kinds
characterize our resemblance to God. Together, they give a
more precise way of describing the relationship between the
traditional *viae* of affirmation, negation, and eminence—the
via eminentiae itself encompassing the logic of affirmation
(the same perfection) and negation (infinitized and therefore ruptured). Thomas tends to think of this rupture in negative terms, because that makes clearer what happens to our
concepts: we absolutize by removing the creaturely defects
with which they are bound up. Scotus prefers a positive sort
of absolutization, because that makes clearer what happens
to our concepts' referents: they become more intense, more
real.[46] But I am less convinced than Scotus that the ways we

---

condemns under that name, is generic similarity, and Scotus expressly
denies that God and creatures fall under a common genus; likewise what
Scotus condemns by analogy is Henry of Ghent's doctrine, which is essentially equivocal, and not Thomas's, which stems from the natural theological arguments that Scotus wants to preserve. So we should be hesitant
about assuming an explicit contradiction between the two.

45. The higher thing in this case not instantiating the perfection at
all but being identical to it, which is what makes participation distinct
from univocal similarity. Again, Thomas and Scotus agree on this point.

46. See n. 31 above. Whatever the similarity, or at least noncontra-
diction, between their accounts, Scotus is still at bottom more ambitious
in wanting his concepts to track the underlying reality—even if it is an
ambition revealed as unfulfillable in the pursuit.

rupture can all be explained in positive, infinitizing terms, and Thomas's approach, though focused on simplicity, is less dogmatic about reducing all of our unlikenesses to a single master mode. So in what follows, I will tend to follow the Dominican. But on either account, the important point here is that, if we locate value in resembling God, both participation and approach represent value in a certain way. Which is to say that *approaching* God is a way for creatures to be good or valuable that is rooted in resemblance without being participatory.

This gives us a way to cash out the Irenaean intuition contrasting the goodness of our attributes with the goodness of how we bear them. Hard-won-ness is a mode of our perfections, a mode by which we can come to bear the perfections God originally implants in us. Irenaeus is not entirely explicit about how that mode represents an approach to God, but he does say that we are "making progress day by day, and ascending towards the perfect, that is, approximating to the uncreated One."[47] Irenaeus does not make much of it, but this line suggests one key unshareable feature of the divine that our hard-won-ness might approximate: uncreatedness.[48] Our approximation cannot of course be a participation, since God's uncreatedness is a prototypically divine formal feature: a negative description of the absolute difference between our way of being wise and God's way of being wise. God's wisdom is uncreated, and ours can only ever be created. Our approximation, then, can only be something like approach.

In what sense? I want to propose that we see the hard-won-ness of these goods as a kind of self-creation by which

47. *Haer.* 4.38.3.
48. Notice that it is not our creating that approximates God's creating but our self-creation that approximates God's uncreatedness. Why this is so will become clearer in the next chapter on Christ's self-creation.

"man . . . is himself the cause to himself."[49] This is not of course a creation *ex nihilo*—even the more restricted versions of that were ruled out in chapter 1—but at most a kind of *non in nihilum*. We create these goods in ourselves by not negating God's gift of them to us. The wise act that would make us wise—that would realize our habitual wisdom in an act, and contribute back to our habits in turn—might also be distorted in various ways to make us unwise. "We are in a sense our own parents," Gregory of Nyssa says, "and we give birth to ourselves by our own free choice of what is good. Such a choice becomes possible for us when we have received God into ourselves and have become children of God, children of the Most High. On the other hand, if what the Apostle calls the form of Christ has not been produced in us, we abort ourselves."[50]

Our self-creation, then, is so named not because it usurps God's role in creating but because it (a) shares "in the activity of the Creator and . . . in a sense continues to develop that activity" in such a way that (b) we control some of the contingent outcome of that creation.[51] We share or participate in God's creation as a rational secondary cause subordinate to the primary cause. But it is not qua participation that an act requires control over the contingent outcome of choice. Indeed, it is only as an imperfect participation that it includes this sort of control. Still, it is just this imperfection that makes possible a more complete *approach* toward God's uncreatedness, the approach of self-creation.[52]

---

49. *Haer.* 4.4.3.

50. *Homily 6 on Ecclesiastes.* Cf. *Life of Moses* 2.3.

51. John Paul II, *Laborem exercens*, 25.

52. Compare Katherin Rogers on Anselm: "the rational creature can, in however limited a way, mirror this divine aseity by contributing to its own being. It is a dim reflection of its Creator, but it is a true one in that,

The intuition is that rational agency is not sufficient for creation, that creation involves some kind of control over contingency in the sense of making a difference to the existence or nonexistence of the thing. This is where the Christian rejection of Neoplatonic necessity is important, not as a description of freedom as such but as a description of a particular (and less perfect) kind of freedom—but a kind that is essential to creation.[53] Because we are created, the real possibility of not existing is fundamental to our very being. This absolute contingency—contingent not just with respect to antecedent creatures but with respect to God—is the mode in which all creatures exist. Inanimate things are in no way the cause of themselves; living things are causes of themselves inasmuch as they are the source of behavior that affects not just things around them but also their own preservation and development; and rational things can operate as this source in a way that is contingent with respect to other creatures. They are not determined by created conditions to be the sorts of things they choose to be. But this is still farther from God's absolute lack of contingency than the self-created, who have some hand in the absoluteness of their own contingency— which is to say, a hand in their possibly not existing even when God calls them to exist. Rational creatures, then, exist on a kind of spectrum of self-creation, from those like the

---

through free choice, it participates in its own creation. This entails the mysterious position that the created free will is the originator of its morally significant choices." See Katherin Rogers, *Anselm on Freedom* (Oxford: Oxford University Press, 2008), 106. This is close to the present view provided that we only originate—in the sense of initiating without God— defects (cf. Anselm, *On the Fall of the Devil* 28). Of course, Rogers uses the language of "mirror" to gloss over the problems of relating our self-creation to God's uncreatedness, which is the central problematic here.

53. Notice that God's most perfect, and most free, acts are also the least contingent—above all the intra-Trinitarian "acts."

Holy Innocents who die before they could create themselves to those entirely unpredetermined to beatitude—one thinks perhaps of Mary here, whose choice undoes the undetermined Eve's[54]—and who therefore, if we take the progressive annihilation of the second chapter seriously, have a hand in the contingent existence of their whole selves.

The blessed, who see God face-to-face and so also participate in the highest degree in the intra-Trinitarian love, no longer have this ability. But they lack nothing for all that. For the blessed have already created themselves; it suffices for their imitation of God's uncreatedness that they have once done so, not that they are constantly doing so. Gold need not remain forever in the foundry to be well forged. This is why God might withhold the beatific vision for some time but not all time, to cultivate both the goods made possible by its absence and the goods made actual by its presence. At the end of the previous chapter, I noted that Thomas thought we began without beatitude in order to merit beatitude, because this gives a kind of self-generated character to the thing. "In a secondary manner anyone may be a cause, to himself, of having certain good things, inasmuch as he cooperates with God in the matter, and thus whoever has anything by his own merit has it, in a manner, of himself."[55] I suggested in that discussion the problems with this merit-based approach, but we can translate Thomas's point from the order of merits to the order of creative causality: by not negating when we could, we have these things, in a manner, of ourselves. And not just in any manner, not in a merely self-caused manner, but as self-created. Note then that the good gained by withholding

54. The *fiat mihi* echoing the language of creation, as I shall suggest in the next chapter, and applying the language to herself. The *fiat mihi* is a *fiat Jesus* but also a *fiat mater dei* and in that sense a partial *fiat Maria*.
55. *ST* III.19.3c.

beatitude is not "being able to self-create"—which is itself only a deficient, because defectible, form of true freedom—but "having self-created": it subsists in the perfections that are produced in this creation, as their mode. This is why it is different from naive libertarianism or Franciscan indifference, which is something more like a perfection that begins in us only to be eradicated, or at least rendered inoperative, by the grace of glorification—a grace that, in the end, destroys nature.

This fate befalls any attempt to locate the value of indeterminism in an ability or faculty instead of in the character of certain goods that come out of it. The same danger lies in distinguishing a defectible and indefectible freedom, as if the two were varieties of good. Defectible freedom is not some distinct natural condition that is destroyed by God's infallible action within us but an imperfect version of our indefectible freedom. That this indefectible freedom is realized only gradually is not to allow some space for our natural defectibility before its supersession but for the reasons Irenaeus saw from the very beginning: because progressive realization gives a certain character to what is finally realized. In that sense, talk of God's self-limitation stumbles toward a certain truth, for a progressive dissemination of glory requires beginning with less and building up. But this self-limitation, if we are going to call it that, is not for the sake of our freedom but for the sake of all those goods we will have said yes to in ourselves when God is all in all. And this all-in-all-ness occurs not as the dissolution of our freedom but when the whole creation is afire with God's glory, and nothing is consumed. It is not a withdrawal of God so that—somehow, perversely—we might be more godlike but God advening in such a way that our godlikenesses might be a little less unlike his.

ANALOGY AND BALTHASAR

Less unlike his. That self-creation is an approach toward uncreatedness is both confirmed by and explains the confusion of the great mass of contemporary theology that has gotten itself entangled in God as *causa sui.* It is confirmed by it because it shows how close the two modes are: self-creation is so close to uncreatedness that we have often confused the description of the one for a description of the other. It explains the confusion because self-creation is not a participation in uncreatedness and shares no features of it; in the very definition of the one is a denial of the other. To call God self-created, then, is not the same as calling God wise. To call him self-created is to call him not God.[56]

Note in this connection the ambiguity of the term "aseity." In some ways, aseity is a better description of our own mode of perfections than God's; God is not *a se* because God is not "from" anything at all. Barth is quite right here: "God as causa prima cannot be both causa and causatum, but only causa. Therefore 'aseity' cannot in any sense be interpreted as God's act of self-realization, His self-initiation, as though in a certain sense God arose out of Himself."[57] God is *non ex aliquo,* where we are *ex non aliquo* (*ex nihilo*). This confusion about aseity has dominated twentieth-century theology to such an extent that even its opponents get tarred with the

56. This is why Jean-Luc Marion makes the *causa sui* a condition of onto-theology. See Jean-Luc Marion, "Thomas Aquinas and Onto-Theology," in *Mystics: Presence and Aporia,* ed. Michael Kessler and Christian Sheppard (Chicago: University of Chicago Press, 2003), esp. 53.

57. *Church Dogmatics* II/1 (Edinburgh: T. & T. Clark, 1957), 305. Cf. Suárez, *De angelis* 1.2.15 (*Opera omnia* [Paris: Vivès, 1856–1878], 11:404: "Deus non est a se positive, sed negative tantum, quatenus non est ab alio" ("God is not *a se* positively but only negatively, insofar as he is not from another"). See also Frassen, *Scotus academicus,* 1:155.

brush. Thus Barth himself may be finally blackened in his doctrine of election, though the Barthians have been much exercised on this point.

And the same with Balthasar, whose ascriptions of passibility to God are tempered by the claim that God's *passio* is freely accepted.[58] Like other cases of the *causa sui*, this attempts to preserve God's transcendence by making his subjection to seemingly created conditions like suffering "up to him." God is created—but only by himself! As with Barth, however, it is not clear whether Balthasar is entirely guilty of this charge. If the idea of self-creation seems to baptize a certain kind of German idealism, let me consider Balthasar a bit more here as a way of showing how my own schema might ward off some of idealism's dangers.

Much hangs in interpreting Balthasar on how we understand talk of divine passibility. Perhaps it is not analogical at all, but only metaphorical.[59] That is, perhaps talk of suffering in God is like calling God a rock: not the ascription of some perfection term but signifying through a term that is essentially creaturely and so literally false when applied to God. The concept "rock" cannot be ruptured in the way the concept "being" can and still survive, which is why metaphorical terms operate with the same kind of apophatic logic that characterizes creaturely modes like complexity: they can strictly speaking only be denied, though denied directionally.[60] Still, in the case of metaphors, there are perfections

58. Thomas R. Krenski, *Passio Caritatis: Trinitarische Passiologie im Werk Hans Urs von Balthasars* (Einsiedeln: Johannes Verlag, 1990), 362–70. Cf. Barth, *Church Dogmatics* II/1, 303, and, among the liberationists, José Comblin, *Called for Freedom* (Maryknoll, NY: Orbis Books, 1998), 29.

59. For questions on this point, see Bernhard Blankenhorn, "Balthasar's Method of Divine Naming," *Nova et Vetera* 2 (2003): esp. 257–65.

60. Metaphor, indeed, comprises the bottom rungs of the Dionysian

associated with this essentially creaturely term, like steadfastness with rocks, that can signify the uncreated. God is
steadfast, is indeed the exemplar of the rock's steadfastness,
and in that indirect (read: metaphorical) way is rocklike.[61]

So if Balthasar talks of God's passibility as a metaphor,
perhaps all that is meant is to ensure the impassible God does
not lack the sort of dynamism that is associated with our passions. But this seems too weak. Balthasar wants a kind of suprapassibility in God that seems to function as the exemplar
of (certain features of) our own passibility, and this suggests
that the relationship is analogical: our passibility participates in God's suprapassibility. This goes beyond metaphor:
it would not make much sense to speak of God as a suprarock,
for instance, in which created rocks participate. The worry
with this is that our conception of passibility is essentially
creaturely, that "the imperfect way in which creatures receive
the divine perfection is part of the very signification of the
name itself."[62] And this is to destroy the very ground of analogical predication. For the foundation of analogy is that
God is the fullness of being, the sort of being that essentially
includes all perfections (as opposed to an *esse commune* that
excludes them, that admits of further specification).[63] And a
being that essentially includes all perfections cannot gain or
lose anything; it is therefore impassible. To deny this sort of
impassibility of God is not just to make a choice within the

---

ascent upon which the directionality of modes is modeled. See Turner,
Darkness of God, 35, 40–41.

61. Whether modes can themselves operate metaphorically, with their
own associated perfections, is hard to say. Part of the difficulty is that,
as any reader of poetry knows, metaphors can work without us having
clearly delineated the relevant concepts, or associated perfections, to
which they point. This can also make it difficult to know for every term
whether it is an analogy or a metaphor when applied to God.

62. *ST* I.13.3ad1.

63. Turner, *Faith, Reason*, 189.

analogical framework, as if one could choose to treat passibility as a perfection and therefore find an analogy for it in God, but is rather to destroy the framework at its foundation. It is not to make God the exemplar of more things but of less—in particular, it is to deny that God is the exemplar of whatever it is he gains or loses in his passibility (for if he can gain or lose it, it is not part of his essence, which means it has its existence apart from him, as something he can instantiate or not).

Balthasar wants to hold onto this foundation and accepts that this implies God is *actus purus*. But he claims that passibility need not contradict this, that there is a kind of active potency or receptivity that is compatible with, indeed contained within, pure actuality. Whence this conception of passibility? From a consideration of the grades of possibility or receptivity in creatures:

> It follows that the more perfectly an entity possesses itself, the freer it is, the less closed in on itself it is, and, therefore, the more receptive it is to everything around it. Entities without consciousness, such as stones, have no receptivity. Their essence is closed to itself, and so they are unreceptive to everything around them; because they are not subjects, there are no objects for them. Entities with less perfect interiority, such as plants, are capable of assimilating some little part of their environment, but they do so without becoming inwardly aware of the other as such. The same is true, albeit on a higher level, even of animals. . . . Nevertheless, because they lack self-consciousness, they are likewise incapable of setting the other over against themselves *as other*. The world is unlocked in its objectivity only to man.[64]

64. Hans Urs von Balthasar, *The Truth of the World*, vol. 1 of *Theo-Logic* (San Francisco: Ignatius, 2001), 45.

I take Balthasar's point to be not that these are grades of what is passible but grades of passibility itself. It is not just that perfections like vitality and rationality change *what* is passible but that they change the character of the passibility. There are grades of passibility, not just grades of vitality. And this is usually taken to mean that passibility, and not just vitality, can be a positive feature that exists eminently in God.

But the schema of this chapter suggests an alternative. That passibility or receptivity increases up the chain of being does not imply that it names a perfection, for it could name a mode of approach. God is properly speaking impassible, and this impassibility is a formal feature that distinguishes Creator from creature, which our grades of passibility approach. Our passibility is like our self-creation: it is the mode in which we have certain perfections. In the case of passibility, the perfection Balthasar seems to have in mind is something like communion. Unlike, say, ants, we act rationally, and this rationality gives a certain character—a greater passibility or receptivity—to our communion that makes it more nearly like God's impassible communion than is the ants'. In this it is like self-creation: our rational causality operating in certain conditions gives a certain character—a self-created character—to the perfections that result from it that makes it more nearly like God's uncreatedness.

Of course we know communion only under the guise of passibility, which is why the concept has to be ruptured in its application to God. But the point to fix and rivet is that it is "communion" we are rupturing by denying passibility, not "passibility" we are rupturing by infinitizing it. This is where talk of suprapassibility can be confusing, because it can suggest that "passibility" is the perfection term instead of "communion." Instead, the way I am suggesting we read Balthasar is to take this suprapassibility as indicating not an exemplar in which we participate but the direction of our denials. That is, we rupture "communion" by denying possibility, and the way we deny is up the chain of being. Since we are more receptive than the ants, we deny God's possibility by a certain kind of excess of receptivity. This "suprapassibility" does not indicate an operator with a value, the way analogous predication does—infinitized (operator) wisdom (value)—but the nature of the operation itself: to impassibilize a perfection is to make it transcend receptivity, just as to infinitize a perfection is to make it transcend number or amount. And something like this has been implicit in our other formal features as well. Uncreatedness, after all, is not just a denial of createdness—for the *nihil* lacks createdness too (and, for that matter, complexity and limit).[65] Uncreatedness is an *upward* denial of createdness; simplicity is an *upward* denial of complexity. This is why suprapassibility is different from suprarockness: not because the first is an analogical exemplum and the second isn't, but because there is no gradation to rockness that could give direction to the denial implicit in "supra-."

This explains Gerard O'Hanlon's suggestion that for Balthasar, "the term 'immutability' belongs to the more abstract, traditionally ontological level of speech about God ["the more properly analogical"], while the term 'supramutability' comes from the metaphorical level."[66] O'Hanlon, following Balthasar himself, does not give a worked-out version of what the metaphorical implies. It could just mean that God has eminently ("supra-") certain perfections as-

65. In this, Balthasar is doing for possibility what the Neoplatonists did for finitude: pointing to a way in which its denial gets us above creatures, not below them.

66. Gerard F. O'Hanlon, *The Immutability of God in the Theology of Hans Urs von Balthasar* (Cambridge: Cambridge University Press, 2007), 143–44.

sociated with mutability, like dynamic communion—while being himself immutable. But this is still too close to supra-rockness (God has eminently certain perfections associated with rocks, like steadfastness). Instead, I am suggesting that a metaphorical "supramutability" means not just that God has associated perfections, and not at all that God is infinitely mutable, but that God is immutable in a way less unlike our mutability than the rock's. He is unchangeable not as a non-entity but as a superentity.

Now the point of all of this is not to give a complete account of theological language: metaphor and analogy are ways of classifying our talk about God, but it is not easy to know how to classify every instance of theological speech, and we often do not need to know. But sometimes we do need to know, and sometimes, when we do, we need a more developed account of the classes than vague gestures toward "metaphor and analogy" or "images and concepts." Balthasar is a prime example of this need; worries about the darkness of his divine persist precisely because he is not always clear about where within the classifications his language should be located, nor even how we should go about deciding such questions. And this darkness has consequences, most notably the soteriological; for the God we become like must be without tears for our tears to be wiped away and free without the possibility of failure for our future to be secure. This is the point of identifying fallibility with the *imperfections* of creaturely freedom: to make the divine, and the divinized, the secure ground of our salvation.[67]

67. See here Karen Kilby, *Balthasar: A (Very) Critical Introduction* (Grand Rapids: Eerdmans, 2012), 119–22, following Alyssa Lyra Pitstick, *Light in Darkness: Hans Urs von Balthasar and the Catholic Doctrine of Christ's Descent into Hell* (Grand Rapids: Eerdmans, 2007); also Linn Marie Tonstad, *God and Difference: The Trinity, Sexuality, and the Trans-*

This is why to talk of passibility is also to talk about free-dom. For the worry with Balthasar is that the freedom of his God is shot through with passibility and its associates. (Nor was he unique; the influence of a kind of dialogical personalism on twentieth-century Trinitarian theology was in this respect widespread.) Thus you get "the possibility of predicating self-yielding surrender, omnipotent 'weakness,' dependence, expectancy, etc., as perfections of the Father's distinct mode of infinite freedom."[68] Thence you get talk of intra-Trinitarian risk, of surprise, of the mystery of one per-son to another based on their respective freedoms.[69]

There is a rhetorical and a substantive worry here. The rhetorical worry is that the "supra-"s drop out, and the im-plicit denials are obscured. That is, Balthasar's language starts to look more like *causa sui* language than *non causatum* lan-guage: identifying our approaching, but still absolutely un-like, modes with the divine. The substantive worry is that these associated terms may not be upwardly denied in the way that receptivity is. Is it true that our relationships get more risky and more mysterious the more perfect they are? It may be the case that our appreciation of the mystery of an-other person deepens as we get to know them, but our actual knowledge of them, absolutely speaking, grows; their mys-tery, absolutely speaking, shrinks. And in what sense does

---

formation of Finitude (New York: Routledge, 2017), ch. 1. It is significant that these objections come from women, though of course women are not the only objectors, since Balthasar associates receptivity and passibility with women in particular.

68. Margaret Turek, "'As the Father Has Loved Me' (Jn 15:9): Balthasar's Theo-dramatic Approach to a Theology of God the Father," *Communio* 26 (1999): 304.

69. E.g., Hans Urs von Balthasar, *The Last Act*, vol. 5 of *Theo-Drama: Theological Dramatic Theory* (San Francisco: Ignatius, 2003), 79. Cf. O'Hanlon, *Immutability*, 122n39.

risk increase? There is perhaps a sense in which human relationships are more risky than animal relationships—though
even here, animal relationships are in some ways more subject to the vicissitudes of circumstance and so more fragile
than ours; and the stones, who cannot react to opposition,
more than the animals; and the subatomic, which cannot
even act in a determinate way, more than the stones. But the
source of human risk is precisely the imperfections of our
freedom, its fallibility, and not freedom as such. The more
perfect our freedom, the less of this risk we see. Christ's love
for us is more perfect than our love for him, in part because it
is unwavering. We are more risky not because of our natures
but because of our ability to act against nature, an ability
that is not essential to us but is instead overcome. And this
suggests that, assuming Balthasar does want to deny, he is
denying in the wrong direction: toward an exaltation of risk
instead of toward its eradication.

In this, Balthasar courts making fallibility an essential
feature of freedom. He courts that spirit that Simone Weil
lamented in the first chapter, of thinking some admixture of
evil necessary to make the good more interesting: there is no
drama without risk; there is no life without some lingering
sense of loss. For Balthasar to consummate that courtship
would, as with a certain kind of philosopher and a certain
kind of Thomist, make freedom essentially linked to what
is itself essentially creaturely—fallibility, or a possibility that
is inextricably tied to fallibility—such that "freedom" is un-
avoidably metaphorical. This is at best confusing, since most
people think that calling God free is like calling God wise,
not like calling God a rock. At worst, it obscures any other
sort of freedom, in particular one that is suprapassible and
so impassible, which is to say one that is properly analogical. That is, at worst it suggests that God's freedom can *only*

be metaphorical, and in so doing, it prevents our freedom from being a participation in God's. The point of this chapter has been to specify in greater detail what we mean by things like analogy, metaphor, and apophasis, so that we can locate within that welter the proper logic for these claims about fallibility and freedom without preempting participation in the process. For in the end the worry is not just with the analytic philosophers who puzzle at the logic of participation, in particular participated freedom, but also with the imprecisions of the personalist theologians—and especially the liberties they take in the liberties they give to God.

FREEDOM AND SELF-CREATION IN CHRIST

As clay in the hand of the potter—
for all his ways are as he pleases—
so men are in the hand of him who made them,
to give them as he decides.
Some of them he blessed and exalted,
and some of them he made holy
    and brought near to himself;
but some of them he cursed and brought low,
and he turned them out of their place.

—SIRACH 33:13, 12

This chapter is an extension of the last, an application of exemplary causality to Christ's humanity and of self-creation to Christ. In the first section I consider the self-creation of the particular incarnate individual Jesus of Nazareth. The second and third sections set out the extent and constitution of the larger, mystical body of Christ—this is Christ's exemplarity as human—so that the fourth section can consider the self-creation of this mystical body. The final section takes stock of this in light of the apparent predeterminism of Romans 9, suggesting that the corporate understanding of election in these passages not only fails to undermine an account of self-creation but also points instead to the Christocentricity at the heart of this chapter.

Because much of this will connect with larger theological disputes that themselves require extended treatments—on Christ's temptations and sinlessness, on exemplarity and recapitulation, on merit and blame, on election and predestination—I can in many cases only lay out the connections as I construe them, not defend my particular construals. The point is to systematize some of the mix of Thomistic, Scotistic, and Suarezian theological implications that my account has generated, but this will necessarily leave some of these implications undermotivated, certainly to the skeptic. I can only recall what I said in the introduction, that my primary aim is to suggest the strengths and to expand upon the implications of one account, not to attack the implications or to expand upon the weaknesses of any other.

THE SELF-CREATION OF CHRIST

Freedom explains the emergence of moral evil; Christ is perfectly free; Christ cannot sin. It may already be clear how I want to respond to this dilemma: first, by identifying the source of moral evil not with freedom as such but with self-creation; second, by granting that Christ, as the perfect human, has both freedom and self-creation in the highest degree; third, by taking Christ's perfect freedom to rule out the possibility of sin; and fourth, by identifying Christ's self-creation with the divine act creating his humanity.

The fourth point is the only one that was not already suggested by the previous chapter. The assumption here is that the "self" that is the subject of self-creation is an agent or hypostatic term: it answers the question "who created you?" not "what created you?" The fact that my parents' humanity was in some way the cause of my humanity does not make my humanity self-created: *I* did not create myself. The "self" that is the subject of self-creation, in other words, is associated with persons, not natures. Natures do not act, as the christological councils suggest: persons act by means of natures. This means that when the divine Word creates his human nature *ex nihilo*, it is self-creation of the highest possible degree. Not only is the rational causality by which he makes his humanity more perfect than ours—acting in more complete understanding and control of what he is doing—but the humanity itself is more completely self-created, since it is made *ex nihilo* and not, as with us, fashioned from an existing self and under the pressures of circumstance. Of course, Christ does go on to act as a man to fashion himself further in this way (not, obviously, exclusive of his action as God), and this further human action, because it is necessarily sinless, does not have the character of self-creation. But the self-created character of his perfections is already entirely present; nothing is lost by an immediate impeccability on his part.

This is why Christ's self-creation need never involve an ability to do evil. The contingency involved in this self-creation is fundamentally different from ours—in particular, his contingency does not come from resisting the divine decision; his contingency just is the contingency of the divine decision. If all contingency is an "or not," the "not" of our contingency is an *in nihilum*, a negation of God's will for us and so an evil, whereas the "not" of Christ's contingency is a *non ex nihilo* and so indifferent. The first is the lack of a due good—even if not always one due our natures, one due in obedience to God—the second a lack of one not due. This is the difference that hypostatic union makes.

Is this sufficient to make Christ's perfections supremely hard-won, in the language of the last chapter? Or does Christ also have to struggle in some way for his perfections really to exceed in their manner of existence the fruits of our struggle? Put differently, is God's uncreatedness better approached by a struggling self-creation than one without struggle? Here we approach Weil's worries again, but with more resources in hand. Certainly struggle cannot be an essential feature of a perfection, for this would either require that there be struggle in the Trinity, as with a certain kind of Balthasarianism, or prevent God from possessing that perfection, as the premotionists and the defenders of defeat threaten to do (see p. 27 n. 37 and pp. 47–48 n. 20, above). But could it be incorporated into our approach to God, as self-created?

I think it can. Self-creation comes in degrees, and it will be greater the more aspects of ourselves it covers, including finally our relationship with God. This extensive greatness is complemented by an intensive greatness, in which we are more self-created because we confront our nothingness more deeply, staring more directly into the face of the abyss, as it were. To know more fully allows us to will more fully, and the more we appreciate the difference between the good to which God moves us and the evil that we could lapse into instead, the greater our role as rational causes in not succumbing to that nothingness. This is why Adam had to struggle in some minimal sense before the fall, if only against those temptations, or those tempters, which felled him: he did not need actual evil to have a deeper appreciation of his choice, but he did need to stare into the heart of the possible evil available to him in order for his rejection of that possible evil to be more complete. In this sense, at least some of the goods that defenders of defeat appeal to, goods associated with the struggle against evil, can be transposed into the struggle against possible or foreseen evil and incorporated into self-creation.[1] I suggested at the end of chapter 1 that sin might introduce no new goods,[2] and this implies that the goods we commonly

---

1. I am more skeptical about other examples—virtues like patience and rewards like gratitude—that require confronting actual evil and not just foreseen evil. The unfallen Adam might not be put in the circumstances to allow him to *display* patience to the same degree as the fallen Adam, but he can still have all that is virtuous in patience, and so be rewarded with the same level of gratitude. This presumably is the logic behind Thomas's view that Christ merits fully from his first moment of existence, not gaining additional merit by the struggle of the cross (*ST* III.34.3ad3).

2. This applies to both goods of participation and goods of approach. For

associate with our struggles are our instantiation in a fallen condition of goods that would have existed in a world preserved upright. But it is no stretch to allow some kinds of struggle to the unfallen world, especially if we include in it a fairly robust, Irenaean sense of growth into maturity. The world preserved upright is not the new Jerusalem but the road to it—the high road; the king's road; but still a road. The struggle of traveling that road may not involve suffering in quite the same way; we shall have to mind it, to keep to it, but not to toil along it (Gen. 2:15; 3:17). Still, we are created on the sixth day, not the seventh—let alone the eighth.[3]

It is less clear that Christ would have had to struggle without the fall, for the nature of his contingency is different. His self-creation, because it is rooted in his act as God, is not going to involve temptation in quite the way that Adam's did. Here we have to anticipate the rest of the chapter, however; for Christ is not just the best human being—not even, only, the perfect human being. He is the recapitulation of human beings, "the first-born from the dead, that in everything he might be pre-eminent" (Col. 1:18). Now this recapitulation implies not just that Christ is the best human being but that Christ is our sort of human being, a human being in the line of Adam; indeed Christ is the head of the line in a sense to be specified below. And it is an important feature of being united in one body—again, even without sin—that we share one another's struggles. That is, Christ does not need to struggle to be good in the relevant ways, but Adam needed it to be good,

---

goods of approach, too, are from God, in the sense that they are the mode in which God gives the participated perfections; and if sin is not the occasion of new giving, then it occasions no new approach.

3. My hesitancy here is driven in part by my skepticism about how much we can know in this life about the unfallen world, which is also, as the first chapter argued, the truth of this world.

and Christ needed it to be like Adam. Thus Christ in taking on fellowship with Adam joins himself to Adam's struggles as well. It is not shared struggle itself that represents some unique good then—this, again, is not found in the Trinity— but a kind of communion in which the struggles are shared, if struggles there are. And that gives us a sense in which even an unfallen incarnation might have included some kind of struggle, inasmuch as unfallen Adam did also.[4]

What is clear is that the actual incarnation did include struggle, and in precisely these recapitulatory ways. Paradigmatically, Christ fights the temptations of the desert and the temptations of the garden, the temptation to pleasures we would have and to pains we would avoid, as Maximus says.[5] And these match in some deep way the struggles of the line of Adam, which in this economy are shot through with the ravages of sin upon both desire and fear. Thus the threefold temptations of pleasure—"so when the woman saw that the tree was good for food (1), and that it was a delight to the eyes (2), and that the tree was to be desired to make one wise (3), she took of its fruit and ate"—Christ faces in his own encounter with the serpent. Good for food: "If you are the

4. This is not to take a position on whether, or when, Christ receives the beatific vision. For anyone who wants Christ to have the beatific vision before the resurrection is going to acknowledge its compatibility with struggle, given the actual life that Jesus led. But it does require that the beatific vision not spill over, as it were, to the whole humanity of Christ, that its effects remain initially confined to the rational faculties or some such thing. The Franciscan tradition, from which I have drawn my supralapsarian Christology, has tended to hold that Christ's body would have been impassible from the beginning in an unfallen world (e.g., Dominic Unger, "Franciscan Christology: Absolute and Universal Primacy of Christ," *Franciscan Studies* 2 [1942]: 436), but this seems rather too strong to me. (Again, given the obscurity of unfallen worlds, it is hard to be more definite than that.)

5. Maximus, *Ad Thalassium* 21.

Son of God, command this stone to become bread." Delight to the eyes: "And the devil took him up, and showed him all the kingdoms of the world in a moment of time, and said to him, 'To you I will give all this authority and their glory.'" Desired for wisdom: "'Throw yourself down from here. . . .' And Jesus answered him, 'You shall not tempt the Lord your God,'" "as you tempted him at Massah," seeking "the knowledge of the Holy One [that] is insight" by asking, "Is the Lord among us or not?" (Luke 4:12; Deut. 6:16; Prov. 9:10; Exod. 17:7).[6] And the temptation of fear—"I heard the sound of thee in the garden, and I was afraid, because I was naked; and I hid myself"—Christ faced too in a garden, only without hiding himself: "'Father, if thou art willing, remove this cup from me; nevertheless not my will, but thine, be done'" (Luke 22:42). Even if struggle is somehow ingredient in our intuitions about the value of self-creation qua hard-won-ness, then—for someone really to be self-created, he must have worked for it in some way—that intuition can be accommodated in Christ, both as he would have existed without sin and as he has existed with sin.

Still, there is a worry that however Christ struggles, it is not really like our struggles because it excludes the possibility of sin. It is not sufficient for hard-won-ness to sweat blood if one cannot also foreswear the good; it is not real temptation if indulging it is impossible. I have suggested that Christ's self-creation is the most perfect version of ours because it exhibits the greatest control over contingency and shares in our struggles, including, in this fallen world, in their agony. But the question piques because there is a deep intuition that we should not separate these quite so cleanly, even for Christ—that struggle and self-creation should not just be

6. Compare also the slightly different similarities of *ST* III.41.4.

present alongside one another but that the struggle should be ingredient in the self-creation in the way it is not, here, for Christ.

Yet even this can be accommodated. I do not mean, following some libertarian philosophers, to read into Christ some real possibility of succumbing to temptation; this is unworkable on classical theological premises.[7] I mean instead that we might connect the temptation to Christ's aboriginal contingency. Christ foresaw the garden in contemplating the incarnation. It is true that, keeping middle knowledge to one side still, Christ's decision to become incarnate is prior to the fall, and in that sense, he decided to become incarnate foreseeing only the *possibility* of sin. Even so, he knew what that possibility could occasion for him; even so, he accounted for it when he "sat down and counted the cost" (Luke 14:28).

In that sense, the deliberation in the garden is a kind of projection of the deliberation in the Godhead—not, as the more excessive Balthasarians might have it, as a kind of suprasuffering in the preincarnate God but as a measure of the suffering it could require of God in his flesh, and the gratuity with which he took both flesh and suffering upon himself. The suffering is only foreseen, in this case, and not yet actual;

---

7. This is true even with the attempt to make Christ's temptations range over the supererogatory, i.e., where Christ is tempted not to sin but to perform lesser, but still good, acts. See, e.g., David Werther, following Richard Swinburne, in "Freedom, Temptation, and Incarnation," in *Philosophy and the Christian Worldview: Analysis, Assessment and Development*, ed. David Werther and Mark D. Linville (London: Bloomsbury Academic, 2012), 252–64. The problem is what we do with Christ's divine will in these situations. Either Christ as God is reacting to his experience in the garden, which requires a passible God (God reacting to creation), or Christ as man is able to choose against what he as God wills, which is bad Christology. Neither option can be squared with patristic teaching as summed up in, for example, Maximus's mature thought.

but the garden is interestingly placed because its temptations do themselves spring from sufferings more foreseen than actual. Gethsemane is not Golgotha; there is no scourging there. It is true that Christ in the garden has *present* natural desires to avoid the foreseen evils, whereas in the Godhead these (human) natural desires are themselves only foreseen: he does not yet have the passions of self-preservation in the way he will. But I take these passions—at least in their innate aversion to evil, prescinding from whatever is essentially bodily in them—to be themselves analogous to aversions in the Godhead: not mere metaphors but some kind of participation in the one who is himself opposition to evil, or against whom evil is oppositionally defined. The preincarnate Logos is not repelled by evil in quite the way his flesh will be, no more than he deliberates in choosing in quite the way he will *ensarkos*; still there is something like deliberation and something like repulsion in the intellective and inveterately benevolent and in all ways unnecessitated choice to inhabit this intransigent world. And that suggests that there is something like Gethsemane in God, if only anticipatorily—but including now too the possibility of nonaction. He must reckon with the real evil he risks undergoing; he must choose whether to risk it or not; and, though not yet sensible, he is not insensible to its cost—*impassibilis, sed non incompassibilis.*[8]

These are the senses in which we can talk of Christ's perfections as hard-won. And this gives us enough to see why I have taken our mode of approach to be self-createdness, approaching uncreatedness, and not self-creating, approaching God's creative activity (in which the *non in nihilum* of our

---

8. Bernard of Clairvaux, *Sermons on the Song of Songs* (*SCC*) 26.5. This of course is only more acute if God does have middle knowledge, because then he foresees not just the possibility of the cross but the actuality.

actions would approach the *ex nihilo* of God's). For Christ's human will cannot do evil and so does not approach divine creative activity in this way. If such an approach were really valuable, then Christ's humanity would lack a value that ours had—indeed a very great value, since it is one that justifies the possibility of moral evil. Put the other way around, Christ "fully reveals man to man himself" and as such reveals what is good in us as what is supreme in him. This is why "in Him all the aforementioned truths find their root and attain their crown."[9] Because his humanity does not self-create in the relevant sense, I am suspicious of making this sort of self-creating central to a Christian anthropology. But because his humanity is self-created, drawn from nothing by the single subject that is him, self-createdness can bear such centrality.

This, too, is why I am hesitant to tie merit to self-creation, or to decisions that are only contingently good.[10] For if anyone merits, it is Christ; if anyone merits, indeed, it is in Christ. But Christ's decisions are only contingent for his divine will; his human will necessarily accepts them. If merit required an ability to disobey, then, Christ would not merit as a man. And this seems unfitting for two reasons. First, because it makes it hard to see how we, as members of Christ's body, can merit in him. If his humanity does not merit, then it is not clear why our humanity, remade in his image, should merit. Our access to God does not run parallel to Christ's humanity but through it, and the ability to merit, like the charity and freedom that

---

9. *Gaudium et spes* 22.

10. As Suárez for instance does (*DM* 19.8.11) and Irenaeus and Bernard might (*Haer.* 4.37.1–2 and *SCC* 81.6—it depends on whether meritorious choices are contingent with respect to created antecedents or also contingent with respect to grace). See also the early Augustine, *Against Fortunatus* 15, and compare with the later Augustine, for whom merits too are a gift of God (e.g., *Grace and Free Will* 6.15).

are its chief principles, is not derived *like* his but *from* his. This implies that merit requires freedom but not self-creation; like freedom, it is compatible with only being able to act well.[11] The second reason it is unfitting is for Anselmian reasons: because a human being should merit humanity's restoration, and the race of Adam merit for the race of Adam. If Christ merited only as God, there would still be a human being meriting—Christ is a single subject—but it would not be a human being meriting *as human*, which undermines some of the fittingness of the incarnation.

THE BODY OF CHRIST

All of this, including these last Anselmian reasons, relies on some kind of recapitulatory unity between Christ and us. What is this unity? This section will consider some preliminary characteristics before the more worked out account of the next section.

The first thing to note is that our communion is not primarily Adamic and secondarily Christic, for the unity in Adam is only an anticipation of our unity in Christ. Adam is "a type of the one who was to come" (Rom. 5:14), not as the model but as the modeled; he is a type in the way that circumcision is a type, as a "shadow of what is to come—but the substance belongs to Christ" (Col. 2:17).[12] The unity of the race of Adam is a shadow of the unity—which is to say the

---

11. Cf. *ST* I-II.114.4ad2.

12. This indeed is one of the supports for a supralapsarian Christology, that Adam is a type of Christ or is modeled on Christ in a way that is not exclusively due to his fall (because it characterizes, among other things, his headship, which is not so much the consequence of sin as what underlies and propagates the consequences of sin). See n. 28 below.

mystical body—of Christ: it is a unity taken up and fulfilled in the church.[13]

Second, this unity extends beyond the merely human. This is true already in some way of Adam the shadow, whose darkening dims the whole creation. But it is even more true of Christ the substance, by whom calf and lion and fatling together are led (Isa. 11:6), to whom all the trees of the wood sing for joy (Ps. 96:12), for whom sea and field and flood clap their hands (Ps. 98:7–8). As Thomas says of the angels:

> Now a multitude ordained to one end, with distinct acts and duties, may be metaphorically called one body. But it is manifest that both men and angels are ordained to one end, which is the glory of the Divine fruition. Hence the mystical body of the Church consists not only of men but of angels. Now of all this multitude Christ is the Head, since He is nearer God, and shares His gifts more fully, not only than man, but even than angels; and of His influence not only men but even angels partake, since it is written (Ephesians 1:20–22): that God the Father set "Him," namely Christ, "on His right hand in the heavenly places, above all Principality and Power and Virtue and Dominion and every name that is named not only in this world, but also in that which is to come. And He hath subjected all things under His feet."[14]

---

13. "The body of the Church, which enjoys the relation of the Son to the Father, *in which the entire world is embodied*, making it the body of Christ." See John D. Zizioulas, *Lectures in Christian Dogmatics*, ed. Douglas H. Knight, trans. Katerina Nikolopulu (London: T&T Clark, 2009), 13, my italics. Cf. *Haer.* 3.22.3, where Irenaeus uses Rom. 5:14 to explain why Luke's genealogy runs backward, from Christ to Adam instead of from Adam to Christ.

14. *ST* III.8.4c.

Both the logic (ordination to one end) and its scriptural support (subjected *all* things) point to Christ's headship over not
just rational creatures but all created reality—that is, that all
creation is finally the body of Christ,[15] even if some reject his
headship and so remain members only potentially.[16] "We are
members of each other. All of us. Everything. The difference
ain't in who is a member and who is not, but in who knows
it and who don't."[17]

Third, as I suggested in the first chapter, this unity in
Christ is not occasioned by sin. Though I cannot do justice
to the whole debate here, let me say briefly why, in addition
to my earlier reasons,[18] I reject the traditional Thomistic position, before noting how this affects an account of the larger
body of Christ. Thomas's argument is that, in matters of grace
like the incarnation, we can know only God's reasons for
acting from revelation and that "everywhere in the Sacred
Scripture the sin of the first man is assigned as the reason
of Incarnation."[19] But as Suárez notes, "If this word, 'every-

---

15. It is in this sense that the church "was created before the sun and
the moon" (2 Clem. 14.1), "before all things," because it is "for her sake
the world was framed" (Shepherd of Hermas, Vision 2.4.1).

16. *ST* III.8.3. Bernard is even harsher: "Him who will obviously not
return to the love of God you must regard not as almost nothing, but as
absolutely nothing, for he will be nothing forever" (*SCC* 50.7, translated
in Bernard of Clairvaux, *Bernard of Clairvaux: Selected Works*, trans. G. R.
Evans [New York: Paulist, 1987], 244–45).

17. Wendell Berry, "The Wild Birds," in *Wild Birds: Six Stories of the
Port William Membership* (San Francisco: North Point, 1986), 136–37.

18. These reasons were, at a general level, that a reading of the *felix
culpa* on which sin is not just the occasion but the condition of the incarnation makes good depend on evil in a way that I have throughout—with
Weil and much feminist theology—tried to resist; and, at a more particular level, that God could respond to sin in this way only on a Molinist view
of foreknowledge, which I do not want to commit to here.

19. *ST* III.1.3c.

where,' means frequently and most often, then the claim is obvious from an exploration of sacred Scripture. But if it is understood more exactly, as if no other cause or reason whatsoever were given, then it is difficult to credit."[20] Suárez cites Ephesians 1:12 and 1 Corinthians 2:7 as counterexamples, but we could expand this to any number of passages in which Christ is said to come for our salvation.[21] "For God so loved

20. "Si verbum illud, ubique, idem valeat quod frequentius et plurimum, res est obvia, et per se manifesta sacram Scripturam explorantibus; quod si ita exacte intelligatur, ut nunquam omnino alia causa vel ratio assignetur, difficilis creditu est." See *Summa*, 3a.4.12, q. 1, a. 3, comm. 4 (*Opera omnia* [Paris: Vivès, 1856–1878], 17:188). Cf. John Punch, *Commentarii theologici quibus Ioannis Duns Scoti quaestiones in libros Sententiarum, tom. III, dist. 7, qu. 3* (Paris: Sumptibus Simeonis Piget, 1661), 222: "Incarnatio non solum erat utilis ad redemptionem hominum a peccatis; sed ad multos alios fines: qui cum possent commode et congrue intendi, debet dici quod de facto intendebantur, et consequenter redemptio non erat sola causa. Probatur subsumptum, quia alia causa esset exaltatio naturae humanae, ostensio summe liberalitatis, sapientiae ac potentiae Dei; ostensio quidem liberalitatis, quia per incarnationem maximum donum possibile conferebat naturae humanae; ostensio etiam sapientiae; quia conferando istud donum naturae humanae, et non Angelicae, ostendit non fuisse debitum, nec connaturale ulli speciei creatae; quia nulli magis esset, quam Angelicae: ostensio denique potentiae, quia per incarnationem ostendebat facere se posse mysterium tam excellens, quod prorsus humanum captum superat, et mihi fere tam admirabile videtur, quam ipsum Trinitatis mysterium: sed haec motiva sufficere possent se solis, ut decerneretur incarnatio" (quoted in Trent Pomplun, "The Immaculate World: Predestination and Passibility in Contemporary Scotism," *Modern Theology* 30 [2014]: 538).

21. "The Scotist tradition also appeals to a large number of Scriptural passages to argue for Christ's absolute predestination and primacy (Prov. 8:22–9:6; Sir. 24:1–21; Wis. 7:22–8:1; Jn. 10:10, 18:37; Rom. 8:29–30; Col. 1:13–20; Eph. 1:3–10, etc.)" (Pomplun, "Immaculate World," 548). Note that the Scotists tend to emphasize that the end of the incarnation is the glory of the hypostatic union itself, and they tend to interpret those texts of Scripture and the fathers that speak of Christ as coming for our salvation in terms of Christ's coming as a possible and not impassible human being. I am instead taking the end of the incarnation to be our diviniza-

the world that he gave his only Son, that whoever believes in him should not perish but have eternal life" (John 3:16); "and this is eternal life, that they know thee the only true God, and Jesus Christ whom thou hast sent" (John 17:3) and, in knowing him, that "we shall be like him, for we shall see him as he is" (1 John 3:2). The eternal life for which Christ comes involves redemption from sin, but it is also more than redemption; as the Thomists themselves affirm, it is both a healing and an elevation. The only way to maintain that Christ comes just because of sin, then, is if the Scriptures told us that Christ's elevating mission, which the Scriptures also reveal, is not individually sufficient for the incarnation, or if they told us that this elevation, while individually sufficient, itself comes about only because of sin. But the Scriptures do not speak in those terms at all.[22] Instead, in the sort of cosmic Christologies of Ephesians and Colossians, we get closer to the opposite: a reason for the incarnation that precedes and makes no reference to sin.[23]

tion, a divinization that is included in what Scripture and the fathers mean by salvation; only the restoring (as opposed to the elevating) side of that salvation is conditional upon the fall.

22. Cf. Suárez, *Summa*, 3a.5.3, n. 9, and 3a.5.4, n. 22, in *Opera omnia* [Paris: Vivès, 1856–1878], 17:242–43 and 246–47. Suárez himself tries to save more of the Thomistic sentiment through a deft use of the doctrine of middle knowledge.

23. Even if these reasons could be incorporated in a *post hoc* way on the Thomistic view—for example, once Christ is set to come because of sin, he also takes up these other ends, as in Édouard Hugon, OP, "Le motif de l'Incarnation," *Revue Thomiste* 21 (1913): 276–96—that does not change the fact that Scripture itself does not give us this sort of *post hoc* account. Revelation gives us various reasons for the incarnation without any clear ordering between them. If Daguet is right that "Saint Thomas propose une analyse de notre divinization qui ne postule pas l'incarnation" (François Daguet, *Théologie du dessein divin chez Thomas d'Aquin: Finis omnium Ecclesia* [Paris: Librairie Philosophique Vrin, 2003], 225), that is a way of ordering the scriptural reasons that is not itself stated by

Of course, Christ does not fully head up the cosmos until incarnation, ascension, and finally judgment. While he may merit the graces that come to all creatures, including those that come at the beginning of creation, his humanity cannot be the efficient instrument of grace until, first, it exists, and second, it meets the conditions God has set for it: until it overflows with grace in the resurrection, until that overflow reaches from the depths to the heights in the ascension (Eph. 4:7-10), until it finally penetrates every spirit (Prov. 20:27; Heb. 4:12) at the end of time. Still, even the earlier communications of grace are done with an eye toward Christ, as the one from whom all grace will come. In that sense, all things are created for Christ: their ordination to eschatological consummation is from the beginning an ordination to membership in Christ's body.[24] The body of Christ is not just in-

---

Scripture and rather runs against much that is in the fathers. I defend a different ordering in my discussion below. For a nice summary of the Franciscan tradition, with its patristic and biblical support, see Unger, "Franciscan Christology," and Jean-François Bonnefoy, *Christ and the Cosmos*, trans. Michael D. Meilach (Paterson, NJ: St. Anthony Guild, 1965). For a Thomistic challenge, see Humbert Bouëssé, *La place du Christ dans le plan de Dieu*, vol. 1 of *Le Sauveur du monde* (Chambery: College Theologique Dominicain, 1951). A supralapsarian Christology closer to mine than Scotus's has gained a certain currency among Protestants, first with Schleiermacher and then especially with Barth: see Edwin van Driel, *Incarnation Anyway: Arguments for Supralapsarian Christology*, American Academy of Religion Academy Series (Oxford: Oxford University Press, 2008).

24. This is not to say, as the Franciscans tend to, that all other creatures are for Christ because of his greater dignity, except in that they are ordained to their fulfillment in the mystical body of Christ. The head of that body serves the whole just as the other members do, and in that sense the members are less ordained one to another than each is ordained to the whole of which they all are parts. There is a sense in which, say, the heart and lungs serve the brain; still, strictly speaking, all of these serve the whole that is the human being. It would be odd to say that the heart is

cepted at the annunciation, nor even at Abraham. On a supra-lapsarian account, its anticipation goes back in a strong way to Adam, indeed to the First Day; its physical appearance in Mary's *fiat mihi* is the fulfillment of its anticipated appearance in God's *fiat lux*. This I take to be the implication of the logic of Saint Thomas and the words of Saint Paul: all things are ordained to the glory of God from the very beginning, which is why we were "chosen in him before the foundation of the world, destined in love to be his sons through Jesus Christ" (Eph. 1:4–5)—for God's glory was always going to be through him who "was destined before the foundation of the world, made manifest at the end of times" (1 Pet. 1:20).

It is worth noting at this point the contrast between "before [*pro*] the foundation of the world" and "from [*apo*] the foundation of the world." The former is used in Ephesians 1:4 and 1 Peter 1:20 to speak of God's intention to become incarnate and join creation to himself, an intention that precedes creation and therefore also, on the simple foreknowledge account, precedes any refusal on the part of creatures (cf. the similar constructions of 2 Tim. 1:9 and Titus 1:2 and the ambiguously Trinitarian language of John 17:24). The second indicates not something before creation but something coeval with it, as the hiddenness of the teaching of the parables (Matt. 13:35), the persecution of the prophets (Luke 11:50), the slaying of the Lamb (Rev. 13:8, depending where you put the participle), and those excluded from the book of life (Rev. 17:8). These

---

made for the brain, not least because the brain also serves the heart: both are made for the person. So also here, both Christ and other creatures are for the divinization of the cosmos. See on this point, in a more Thomistic key, Bernard Lonergan, *Early Latin Theology*, vol. 19 of *Collected Works of Bernard Lonergan*, ed. Robert Doran, SJ, and H. Daniel Monsour, trans. Michael Shields (Toronto: University of Toronto Press, 2011), 525–26. As Daguet hints, it is precisely because the humanity of Christ is not the end of all things but is in service of others, of the larger whole, that he is so great (*Dessein divin*, 238).

need not be things, like the incarnation, that God intends before creation but are often things, like the crucifixion, that the world visits upon itself: in God's simple foreknowledge they would be seen from the beginning though not before the beginning, since they are part of God's plan only given sin.[25] What is true *before* the foundation is also of course true *from* the foundation, as with the preparation of the kingdom for the righteous in Matthew 25:34 (a preparation that is worked out in creation), but not always the other way around. And what is true *from* the foundation may be actively intended by God and not merely permitted, as the works of God "were finished from the foundation of the world" (Heb. 4:3), but it might also be the refusal of those intentions. This *pro/apo* distinction is surprisingly consistent across different New Testament writers: what is before the foundation of the world is intended by God and precedes all creatures; what is from the foundation is coeval with creation and therefore posterior to some creatures and to some creaturely choices. And this suggests that the glorification of Christ and his body, which is purposed *before* the foundation of the world, is a surety before and in spite of any refusal on the part of creatures—and that, while all particular individuals are initially written into the book of life that is that body, they can be blotted out going forward *from* the foundation of the world if they sin against God (Exod. 32:33; Ps. 69:28; Rev. 3:5; 22:19).

Put differently, what is foreknown before the foundation of the world (Christ: 1 Pet. 1:20) is also chosen by God (us in

25. I am departing at this point from the summary statement of evangelical Arminians, for whom Christ's *death* and not just incarnation is "purposed before creation"—a position in the Catholic debates associated with the Salmanticenses. See "A Concise Summary of the Corporate View of Election and Predestination," Society of Evangelical Arminians, February 13, 2013, http://evangelicalarminians.org/a-concise-summary -of-the-corporate-view-of-election-and-predestination/.

Christ: Eph. 1:4);[26] whereas what is known from the foundation of the world need not be. That is, before-knowledge is
the effective, practical knowing of the artist, whereas from-
knowledge includes the simple foreknowledge of vision.
I have already discussed these in the last section of chapter 1;
considering them now in a christological context will shed
more light on the ligature of Christ's body, and in particular
its differentiated relationship to its head.

RECAPITULATION

What does it mean for Christ to be our recapitulation? What
does his headship consist in? It depends on the type of thing
being related. Here three kinds of realities are usefully distinguished: first, those goods we have by nature; second, the
goods that come by grace; third, those negations that creation
visits upon itself. Christ as God is the exemplar in the full sense
of both of the first two of these—the *Logos* contains and communicates all perfections, whether natural or supernatural—
and the exemplar in no sense of the third. But what of Christ as
man? My contention in this section will be that he functions in a
differentiated way with regard to these first two categories and
in a real though inverted way with regard to the third. Together
this will yield seven different forms of relationship between the
members of the body and the humanity of their head; I will
italicize the term I am associating with each form.

26. This is part of why the proponent of simple foreknowledge should
think that God does not respond to sins in the sense of bringing new
goods into existence because of them—or at least, that God does not
bring new and different people into existence even, for example, in the
case of adultery. For the children of adultery, too, were chosen in Christ
before the foundation of the world and so before a consideration of sin.

Take the goods of nature first. There are certain paradigmatic perfections like spirit and matter that in general terms describe the character of creation and in specifically human ways are contained in Christ.[27] Christ's humanity is *paradigmatic* of all nature in this sense but is not exactly an exemplar of, say, specifically angelic intellection. For Christ's humanity strictly speaking lacks what is specific to an angel's intellect, and an angel is not intellectual by Christ communicating his human intellect to it or some such thing.

But there are also, second, the specifically human perfections, and these Christ does of course share. It is common in the Franciscan tradition to identify Christ as the exemplar of our humanity in the sense that God forms us after the *pattern* of Christ's human nature, a pattern that exists in God's mind even before it exists in history. This is the strongest sense in which Adam's headship could be a shadow of Christ's, since here even the human nature that Adam passes onto us is copied from Christ's human nature. The Franciscans then use this as an argument that the incarnation would occur without sin, since on this view the incarnation is a presupposition of, and so cannot be a response to, the propagation of sin.[28] I am less sure about this strongest sense, if only because the Scriptures seem rather more clearly to imply that Christ would come to

27. Cf. Maximus, *Difficulty* 41.
28. That is, it is because of our (coming) interconnectedness in Christ that we are interconnected in Adam, and it is because we are interconnected in Adam that sin is propagated, and it is because sin is propagated that we need redemption. Therefore our interconnectedness in Christ cannot be a consequence of redemption. Unger does not quite put it this way; I have tried to make his point slightly more acute. Note that to avoid this implication, Daguet separates Adam's headship more cleanly from Christ's (Daguet, *Dessein divin*, 90), in effect denying of Adam, as Thomas says in a somewhat different connection, that "others are called heads, as taking Christ's place" (*ST* III.8.6c).

elevate our natures even if there was no sin than to imply that our humanity was patterned upon Christ's. Still, the implicit urging of Saint Bonaventure has convinced me to include it here, both for its own fittingness and because, what gives that saint a certain pleasure, it brings my articulation of the aspects of Christ's headship to seven. Accepting this, then, gives us a second way in which Christ as human is the exemplar of our natural goods: not just paradigm but pattern.

As regards the goods of grace, Christ's relationship is even more intimate. Here, third, Christ is truly an exemplar, not just as a pattern in the mind of God but as a concrete *instrument* through whom grace is communicated. Christ is "our wisdom, our righteousness and sanctification and redemption" (1 Cor. 1:30); he contains in his humanity all those goods of divinization for which we are destined from the beginning, and he communicates them to us preeminently through the sacraments. Christ is exemplary here as human and not just divine: his humanity contains these graces as the iron contains the heat and enflames what it touches.[29]

Of course, some of these graces are communicated before the humanity of Christ exists. His divinized humanity might still be the exemplar of those earlier graces—Christ's face does not shine like Moses's but Moses's like Christ's—but it cannot be an instrument communicating these, even if it becomes one at some point in history.[30] Instead, fourth, for these graces—as of course for the ones he communicates instrumentally—Christ is not just the exemplary but also the *meritorious cause*, where a meritorious cause is that which

29. *ST* III.56.1.

30. For a Thomistic case that Christ takes over this role, see Jean-Hervé Nicolas, OP, "Le Christ et la création d'après Saint Thomas d'Aquin," in *Studia Medievalia et Mariologica*, ed. Carolus Balic (Rome: Antonianum, 1971), 87–93.

makes God's gift better befit the divine justice. This includes merit strictly speaking, in which the recipient establishes some sort of claim on the gift (see pp. 109–20 in chapter 2), but also things like satisfaction, in which obstacles to the fittingness of the gift are removed. Significantly, a meritorious cause can be temporally posterior to its effects: God can give Abraham grace at one time knowing that Christ will merit that grace at a later time. This is what allows Christ's meritorious work to underpin all grace, while his efficient work begins at the incarnation.

Now this is to speak of the goods of grace in a relatively undifferentiated way, as if Christ contained some single set of spiritual properties that were distributed to his members, which only in the distribution get differentiated into John's wisdom and righteousness, Paul's wisdom and righteousness, and so forth. And this by and large is the traditional way of talking. But I want to supplement this with a kind of Scotistic suggestion about Christ's representation of our individual perfections. For, fifth, Christ's humanity is not just exemplary of those created graces common to the saints but also has some seed in itself of the graces particular to individuals. The peculiar perfection of the beloved disciple is his particular love of Christ; but this love is preceded and produced by Christ's particular love of him. Christ loved him first (1 John 4:19; John 15:16); Christ's love summoned his response (Matt. 4:21). And this love Christ has for John is really different from the love he has for Peter. Written on Christ's humanity, then, are his many loves, one for each of us; these loves are what effect our own loving responses; and these responses are what constitute our individual supernatural perfection. So also with our other supernatural perfections: then we shall know fully not just *in the same way as* but *because* we are fully known (1 Cor. 13:12).

My contention, then, is that the inescapably individual character of sanctification is not produced by a general grace that is individuated in being received by those already constituted by nature as individuals. Rather, it comes individuated already in Christ. Of course, Christ's particular love of John differs from John's particular love of Christ in a way that Christ's general properties do not differ from John's. Christ communicates his wisdom and righteousness and general charity and so forth to John in a way that reproduces them in his disciple, whereas Christ's particular love of John elicits a reciprocal love that is not quite the same thing as what elicits it. This is especially clear when the object of Christ's love is not Saint John but Saint Michael, whose nature Christ does not share: Saint Michael's manner of loving Christ is presumably angelic, whereas Christ's manner of loving Saint Michael is presumably human, so Saint Michael's particular love of Christ cannot just be the reproduction in Saint Michael of Christ's specific love.[31] Instead, Christ is a kind of *inspiration* of these individual supernatural perfections but not an instrument of them; he has something corresponding to but not constitutive of their character. In that sense, Christ has registered in his humanity not just shared supernatural features but also individual ones. This is the third sense in which Christ as human is an exemplar of the goods of grace: as instrument, as meritorious cause, and as inspiration.

31. Saint Michael also precedes Christ's human nature in existence, though we might take Christ's human love of Saint Michael to sustain and so be logically prior to Saint Michael's love of Christ after the incarnation, or perhaps after the ascension—in something like the way that Christ's humanity becomes the efficient cause of Michael's general sanctification after the incarnation or perhaps ascension. Note that some of the proposals in n. 37 below might make Christ's humanity an efficient cause of Michael's sanctification even before the incarnation.

Moreover, these supernatural ordinations are particularly fitted to, though not required by, the natures of the creatures in which they are infused. Paradigmatically this is the fittingness of fellowship with God for the naturally friendly, the beatific vision for those with eyes to see. But it will equally well encompass whatever eschatological society the social animals shall enjoy; whatever turning is effected in the heliotropic by the One who outshines the sun; and, in brief, all that gilded glory in store for this silvered world. And again, it will encompass those more individual ends that make Christ the source of the particular and not just the specific or generic: Saint John is by nature a particularly intimate man, and with Christ is given a particular intimacy; he is a fisherman commissioned to cast subtler nets; he is a son of thunder sent thunderous visions. Saint Paul is a tentmaker who builds tabernacles across the known world; Saint Peter by nature a leader; Saint Simon by nature zealous; Saint Matthew by nature a collector of what is owed to Caesar. The particular character of creatures is not lost but elevated in their calling and, finally, their consummation; which is to say that their particular callings and the consummations of those calls indicate their characters. If inscribed in Christ is Saint Matthew's call to collect that coin owed to God, then indicated also is his character before calling as a coin collector. It is not that Matthew is owed this higher commission; it is that this higher commission fits what Matthew on any commission is, and is owed.

Besides Bonaventure's point about Matthew's generically human properties being patterned on Christ, then, and besides Maximus's point about Christ as the paradigm of other, even angelic, natures, we should add, as a third exemplarity of our natural goods and a sixth exemplarity overall, that even Matthew's individual natural perfections and even Michael's specific ones are written upon Christ's humanity in a more distant way, as *indicated* in the supernatural perfections that Christ does inspire.[32] This is the further sense in which Christ is a plan and not just a paradigm of the universe, and it deepens and in a way further Scoticizes (by emphasizing individuality) the intuition that inspired Scotus to make "the human nature of Christ the *motif* the Divine Architect was to carry out in the rest of creation. In Christ's soul God saw mirrored the choirs of angels; after his body the visible world was sculptured. The whole universe is full of Christ."[33] Christ's humanity no more has the specifically angelic perfections than a blueprint has the strength of a house or a key has the fastness of a lock. But his humanity is in some way the plan of those perfections; the music of the choirs can be read off his soul; for the whole of creation is written upon him as its consummation.

This is all to say that there is no natural destiny for the natural capacities. There is no aboriginal garden over which God watches but in which God does not walk, no final shining city lit by the merely celestial and not by the Son. The natural order need not find its fulfillment in the flesh of Christ, but in fact it does.[34] And so the natural order, too, can be read

---

32. And this goes beyond just perfections in the technical sense of the last chapter, for included in the individual perfections is also the self-created mode in which these might subsist.

33. Allan Wolter, "John Duns Scotus on the Primacy and Personality of Christ," in *Franciscan Christology: Selected Texts, Translations, and Introductory Essays*, ed. Damian McElrath (Saint Bonaventure, NY: Franciscan Institute, 1997), 141.

34. The fashion and the madness of twentieth-century theology has been to identify this ordination as natural, as if to be human is to be destined for Christ, or at least for consummation. This would make the present account simpler in some ways, but not more true. Much would have to be said to defend this view of nature and grace, but since the argument does not hang on it, the combative reader should refer to Lawrence Feingold, *The Natural Desire to See God according to St. Thomas and His Interpreters*, 2nd ed. (Ave Maria, FL: Sapientia Press of Ave Maria Univer-

off that flesh, for Christ would be different were our natures different. This is what I mean when I say that the rest of creation is written upon Christ as its consummation, as the gild of the lily tells the flower's form.

There are, then, three ways in which Christ contains the perfections of nature: as *paradigmatic* of generic features like spirit and matter, as the *pattern* of specifically human features, and as *indicating*, inasmuch as he is their consummation, particular perfections that he does not instantiate. There are also three ways in which he contains the perfections that are beyond nature: as an exemplar and then *instrument* communicating those graces that are common to all, as *meritorious cause* of every grace, and as *inspiration* of those graces specific to particular individuals.

This talk of how Christ contains the perfections of creation can sometimes seem to abstract from the narrative details of Christ's life, as if the gospels merely gave us some dispensable backstory to the perfect human you get at the end. So it is worth emphasizing here that the exemplarity of Christ is not just the exemplarity of some perfect humanity that Christ manages to achieve after a series of hardships but the exemplarity of a resurrected humanity into which that hardship has been written—written as overcome, but still, truly, written. That is, when Christ is communicated in the sacraments, it is his present, fully divinized life that is communicated, but it is this life as the culmination of his whole past: his virtues as habituated in the struggles and triumphs of his time on earth; his understanding reflecting the particular paths along which he grew in wisdom and stature (Luke 2:52); his loves conditioned by what he shared and

---

sity, 2004), and Steven A. Long, *Natura Pura: On the Recovery of Nature in the Doctrine of Grace* (New York: Fordham University Press, 2010).

suffered and pondered together with his mother, his family, his disciples.

Thus when Christ's wisdom is communicated to us, it is not just some abstract property representing ideal human wisdom: it is the wisdom formed by the concrete growth in stature of Jesus of Nazareth. When Christ's firmness in the face of temptation is given us, it is the firmness of one who resisted the pleasures in the desert and the pains in the garden. When Christ's perfection is given us, it is the perfection won through suffering (Heb. 2:10), the specific suffering of the cross. In that sense, what is exemplary in Christ and communicated to us by the Spirit is not just the result of his life but the events of his life: our wisdom is the wisdom of the boy posing questions in the temple; our victory over temptation is the victory of desert and garden; our perfection is the perfection of the empty tomb. This is why the saints are sometimes named by events in Christ's life: John has been given the long-suffering of the cross, Thérèse the littleness of the child Jesus, Anthony the firmness not first of the Egyptian but of the Palestinian desert.[35]

There will of course be something essentially individual in these perfections as they exist in Christ that is different from how they exist in us. But my point here is that these per-

---

35. "'Long before we were born—from a "human" point of view—Jesus met us somewhere, in Bethlehem, or perhaps Nazareth, or along the road to Galilee—anywhere. And one day among all the other days, His eyes happened to rest upon you and me and so we were called, each in his own particular way. . . .' My place for all time has been Mount Olivet, yes, in that instant—strangely in that very instant, when He set His hand on Peter's shoulder asking him the useless question, almost naïve yet so tender, so deeply courteous: Why sleep ye? . . . I am never to be torn from that eternal place chosen for me—that I remain the prisoner of His Agony in the Garden." From Georges Bernanos and Rémy Rougeau, *The Diary of a Country Priest: A Novel* (Cambridge: Da Capo, 2002), 202–3.

fections are shaped by the events that give rise to them in a way that makes those particular histories available to us. The histories are not exclusively on the side of what is individual about the perfections; they are in part what is communicated in them. And even as they are individual, even as they are incommunicable and so cannot have the exemplarity of an instrument, they can still serve as the sort of inspiration and indication of our individual perfections in the way that I have suggested already.

What this also means is that our suffering now is conformed to the image of his Son's (Rom. 8:29). The first six features of Christ's headship, taken together, describe how what is natural and supernatural both can be known by gazing on him—but finally, too, we gaze on him whom we have pierced. This is the third kind of reality—now not quite a thing—that God sees in Christ, and it yields the seventh sense of headship I have in mind. For Christ is not just an exemplary cause of the world's perfections but also a kind of exemplary effect of its vicissitudes. His headship is not just the source of the body's actions and perfections—"not I, but Christ in me" (Gal. 2:20)—but the central nerve in which the passions and distortions of creation are felt, "completing what is lacking in Christ's afflictions" (Col. 1:23).[36] In part, this is just what it means to be part of a social body: when a division of the army is defeated, the whole army suffers the defeat, the head especially, just as the general fights in some way wherever one of

---

36. Thomas does not mention this aspect in his discussion of headship in the *Summa*, but he does note it in his commentary on this verse of Colossians: "Or, we could say that Paul was completing the sufferings that were lacking in his own flesh, for what was lacking was that, just as Christ had suffered in his own body, so he should also suffer in Paul, his member, and in similar ways in others" (*Commentary on Colossians*, chapter 1, lecture 6, n. 61).

his soldiers is fighting. But it is more than this, for our general has already fought the battle before us, indeed already won the battle before us, and the soldiers fight with his strength. In some strange way, the general has anticipated his soldiers; he has seen and assumed in his time the struggles of his army across all time, that he might be their strength through the whole of history. There is a deep exchange here, in which the general's strength is what sustains the soldier, and the soldier's struggle is what assaults the general.[37] In that sense,

37. The metaphysics of this negative exemplarity, this sharing of defects between members and head, are more obscure than the metaphysics of positive exemplarity, the communication of perfections from head to members that follow something like the pattern of normal causation. The negation relations of the first chapter can help frame, but do not remove, the obscurity. If we stipulate that the suffering of Christ's passion is an effect of sin, then the causal relations in Christ that explain his wounds and his death will point back (either immediately or through intermediate causes) to sinners as those who "generated" the defects that were felt by him. We might speculate, given these stipulations, that his suffering bears a negation relation not just to the immediate agents of the crucifixion but to all sinners, to all of us who cry on Good Friday, "Crucify him!" The challenge here is that, on the Aristotelian understanding of causality, causes are temporally simultaneous with their effects: they have to be present in order to exert their influence, as it were. But sinners before the incarnation are not simultaneous with Christ's humanity at all, and sinners after the resurrection are simultaneous with an impassible humanity. There are several possible ways around this, however. First, you could say that this stricture on simultaneity is the normal condition of causation but not strictly necessary; God can miraculously make transtemporal causal relations, which he does in the case of the paschal mystery. Second, you could say that the paschal mystery is itself in some way outside of normal time, that it participates in God's eternity in some special way that makes it, as the supreme Trinitarian moment of history, in some sense present to and simultaneous with all of history. (Claims like this are sometimes made with respect to the Eucharist, which is not a second sacrifice in addition to Calvary but numerically identical with it.) Third, you could try to expand Christ's memories of past persecutions—"O Jerusalem, Jerusalem,

the cross is a kind of gathering up of all that the world does against itself and its spending upon Christ: in Calvary, Christ is, in some dark way, grumbled against with Moses, hunted with David, betrayed by Joseph's brothers, handed over to Daniel's authorities, scourged like a slave by the Egyptians: with Isaac, bound; with Job, mocked; with Abel, bled; with the Holy Innocents, struck down.

I suffer as a member of the body of Christ, then, and so Christ suffers in me. The death I have died in him in order that I may live in him is not just past, in baptism; it demands also now that "we suffer with him in order that we may also be glorified with him" (Rom. 8:17). "If we have died with him, we shall also live with him; if we endure, we shall also reign with him; if we deny him, he also will deny us; if we are faithless, he remains faithful—for he cannot deny himself" (2 Tim. 2:11–13). He cannot deny himself: how much more simply can one indicate the union of Christ with creation? Before the fall, this union is ordained for our consummation, but it is this same union that after the fall enables the suffering of the world to be borne by its model and its maker, and so be overcome. Even the afflictions of those members who are part of the body only potentially are borne by Christ as

---

who stoned the prophets!"—and anticipations of future ones—for example, in Gethsemane—to transmit these negation relations to him through a kind of causal chain: the sinner causes certain defects in himself or his neighbor, which Christ then sees, either recalling or foreknowing, and suffers. The less than pellucid thought here, the more luminous than lucid thought, is that if Christ experiences the communication of God's knowledge to his humanity, and God's knowledge, as I said in the first chapter, is a kind of practical knowing that both accomplishes and suffers creation, then the incarnation of this knowledge in Christ may extend beyond the reproduction of this knowledge in his mind and to an imprinting upon the whole of his humanity.

impeding the actualization of that potency. Their sins sever them as limbs from the head; their suffering is hindrance to that circulation of the Spirit by which the kingdom is realized. The suffering of all Christ's mystical members, then, is written upon his physical members, first as wounds and then, and forever, as scars.

I suggested in the first chapter that the object of God's knowledge is the cosmos as a whole, and this discussion has extended that point in two ways. First, it has established Christ as a kind of microcosms, "in whom are hid all the treasures of wisdom and knowledge" (Col. 2:3): in whose history all history can be read. "Since He is ontologically the summation of all reality, Christ cannot be without a knowledge of all that is contained within Him."[38] God can read off from his humanity both the creations and the destructions of the world. He knows the sanctification and the suffering of the saints as contained in him and the destruction of the damned as what has put itself outside his gates: he sees in his body both healed wounds and lost members. In that sense, he is summation as much as he is consummation, and the one because the other. If God knows all possible creatures in the divine Word, in whom all that could exist is contained exemplarily, then God knows all actual creatures in the Word made flesh, in whom all that does exist is contained by a variety of analogical exemplarities. And we, too, in that beatific inversion described in the second chapter, change from creatures who see in Christ the things of God to gods who see in Christ the things of creatures.

---

38. Zachary Hayes, *The Hidden Center: Spirituality and Speculative Christology in St. Bonaventure* (Saint Bonaventure, NY: Franciscan Institute, 1981), 206; cf. Bonaventure, *Hexaemeron* 1:10–20.

Second, this gives some sense of the unity of that cosmos, of the manner in which "all things hold together" (Col. 1:17). For these interrelations by which strength and suffering both are shared between members and head and members again are what constitute the cosmos as a kind of corporate whole, "imparting spiritual gifts to strengthen" one another, "mutually encouraged by each other's faith" (Rom. 1:11–12). "A body calls also for a multiplicity of members, which are linked together in such a way as to help one another. And as in the body when one member suffers, all the other members share its pain, and the healthy members come to the assistance of the ailing, so in the Church the individual members do not live for themselves alone, but also help their fellows, and all work in mutual collaboration for the common comfort and for the more perfect building up of the whole Body."[39] The end of the first chapter gestured at a kind of cosmic unity, and here we have its cause, indeed its causes: God moving all things (naturally by a general efficient providence and supernaturally by the special efficient work of the Holy Spirit) toward that full flourishing in the body of Christ (his mystical body being the formal cause, and his humanity the exemplary cause) that praises and "glorifies the God and Father of our Lord Jesus Christ" (Rom. 15:6) (the final cause).

The Self-Creation of the Body of Christ

The immediate upshot here is that we can speak of a self-creation of the mystical and not just the physical Christ, a

39. Pius XII, *Mystici corporis*, 14.

self-creation of "Christ, Head and whole Body, a sort of entire Man."[40] That is, the whole Christ forms a kind of corporate personality of which values can be predicated, and among these is that valuable mode of having perfections that is self-creation. This will first of all be the creation of all the members by the body's head, Christ; but it will also extend to the nonnegation of other members' perfections by those rational members capable of such negation. There is, in other words, a corporate subject to the reflexive act of self-creation—Christ along with those members of the body who are rational agents moved fallibly by God—just as there is a corporate object: the members in all their diversity. The sins of the church are not just the sins of private actors but in some way the sins of the corporate body. And when this subject could have sinned but does not, it gives a special value to our life together that it would otherwise lack, elevating our interconnectedness into a more fully self-created mode.

The value I am trying to get at here has to do with our interconnectedness, and one worry I am trying to address is that self-creation can at most explain why it is that we can harm ourselves, not why it is that we can harm one another. But it is the value of the one that makes possible those harms that worry the other. I can help or fail to help my fellow creatures, not just in my intentions but in fact. And were it not so in fact, were my failure at most merely intentional, creation would not hold together in the right way: the ligature of the body of Christ would be so loosened that it would cease to deserve the name body altogether. That is, our common life in Christ means, first, that many of our acts are directed toward other creatures and second, even if we think that the first effect of our actions is some kind of interior volition,

---

40. Augustine, *Expositions on the Psalms* 59.2.

that these acts must in general reach their external aims and wreak effects beyond the intentional if our sociality is to mean anything, and above all if we are to share some form of self-creation.

This social existence greatly magnifies the danger of our fallibility; and the more we are tied to one another, as with Adam's anticipations of Christ, the greater this danger grows.[41] Marilyn Adams is right that our freedom or self-creation alone does not explain how widely we can work our evil.[42] That involves other goods, including especially that interconnectedness by which we imitate the Trinity.[43] But my point here is not just that these two goods—self-creation and interconnectedness—have the sort of significance that starts to motivate the possibility of evil; nor is it that this interconnectedness implies a kind of other-creation alongside self-creation, as if our ability to harm one another somehow imitated the mutual constitution of the Trinitarian persons.[44] My point is that our interconnectedness constitutes a subject that itself evinces a kind of self-creation, and that this corpo-

41. Cf. John Paul II, *Reconciliatio et paenitentia*, 16: "by virtue of human solidarity which is as mysterious and intangible as it is real and concrete, each individual's sin in some way affects others. This is the other aspect of that solidarity which on the religious level is developed in the profound and magnificent mystery of the communion of saints, thanks to which it has been possible to say that 'every soul that rises above itself, raises up the world.' To this law of ascent there unfortunately corresponds the law of descent."

42. Marilyn McCord Adams, *Horrendous Evils and the Goodness of God* (Ithaca, NY: Cornell University Press, 2000), 38–39.

43. Cf. Robin Collins, "The Connection-Building Theodicy," in *Blackwell Companion to the Problem of Evil*, ed. Justin P. McBrayer and Daniel Howard-Snyder (Malden, MA: Wiley-Blackwell, 2013), 222–35, though Collins is still working in a greater-good-from-evil framework that is hard to square with God's exemplarity.

44. Not least among the problems with this suggestion is that the Trinitarian persons do not contingently constitute one another.

rate self-creation is an additional good beyond individual self-creation and corporate interconnectedness on its own.

Thus when, fallibly, I feed the hungry, there are three perfections that could fail to be: first, the satiety of the hungry person; second, my own virtuous act and its accompanying habits; and third, the connection between me and the hungry person that would be vitiated, and in a vicious way, by my failure to offer food. The last of these is, ultimately, a shadow of Trinitarian communion; but the point is not that the fallibility of my connections approaches some infallibility in the Trinity's but that the ultimately Trinitarian perfection is proximately available to us in the *totus Christus*, whose corporate subjectivity expands the scope of that valuable mode of having Trinitarian perfections that I have called self-creation. The whole Christ could fail to be: first and absolutely, because God could refuse to dwell among us, but second also, because the stones of that dwelling could chip away at one another, as also at the mortar between them. Were it just the first, were the self-creation of the body of Christ just the ability of the Logos not to become incarnate, then the individual members, with their individual self-creations, would have to be insulated from one another in a way that would ultimately, though perhaps not essentially, undermine the mystical body God wants to create.[45]

What this yields is a way of talking about our ability to affect the world and not just ourselves; or, rather, a way of talking about our ability to affect our larger self that is

---

45. Note that Christ's individual humanity is not just separate from and prior to this self-created corporate subject but also built up as part of it. It owes for instance much to his mother—even more if you think his original justice, not suffering the effects of original sin, is inherited from her as well (as is implied by the immaculate conception). Though since her humanity, too, is modeled on his, even her contribution has his as a prior (exemplary and meritorious) cause—*daughter of your son*, etc.

founded in Christ and encompasses the world. "How does your tongue cry out? 'It hurts me.' It doesn't say, 'It hurts my foot,' but it says, 'It hurts me.' O tongue, who touched you? Who struck you? Who disturbed you? Who troubled you? 'No one, but I am joined to those that are being trampled on. How is it that you don't want me to be pained when I'm not separate?'"[46]

Particular judgments about the value of this sort of corporate self-creation are going to be difficult: how to compare it to the value of having certain perfections, either individual or corporate, how to compare it to the value of the individual's self-creation, and so forth. In at least some of these cases, the kinds of value are going to be distinct enough that they are plausibly incommensurable: comparing modes with perfections, comparing individual with corporate subjects, and the like. And this means that Father, Son, and Holy Spirit will be left with a great deal of discretion, within their overall dedication to avoid those evils that outweigh any good they make possible, about which goods to prioritize and which evils to allow. For the purposes of theodicy, this means that God might allow the possibility of certain kinds of evils—like the loss of certain perfections—at least in part for the possibility of a very different kind of good, like the self-creation of the larger body of Christ. For the purposes of prayer, it means that God might forgo the possibility of some kinds of goods, like individual self-creation, for the sake of others, like the creation of one member by another who, for example, prays for her salvation.

The upshot is that this account is very flexible in its ability to track the faith as it is practiced. I adverted in the introduction to how strange it is on libertarian accounts that we should pray for the salvation of others. If God cannot actually effect

---

46. Augustine, *Tractates of the First Epistle of John* 10.8.

their salvation, then what are we praying for? Grades of probability? The pendant problem with a complete predeterminism, in which all events are up to God, is that our prayer does not seem to make the right sort of difference: the outcome might still be conditional upon our praying, but our praying is itself decided in advance, such that the real condition governing the outcome does not depend on us.[47] The point of the present account, in which God can work either fallibly or infallibly, is that prayer might incline God to work infallibly instead of fallibly, or vice versa. Which is to say that on the present account, the fallibility or infallibility with which God works the salvation of another can itself depend on a prayer that God works fallibly in us.[48] Part of the point of specifying the spread in the kinds of goods in play here is not to close down these options by appeal to the divine goodness, as if the triune God owed it to themself always to work fallibly because individual self-creation outweighed all other goods.[49]

47. Echoing here Peter van Inwagen's famous "consequence argument" in *An Essay on Free Will*, rev. ed. (Oxford: Oxford University Press, 1986).

48. He moves us fallibly to pray that our children will infallibly come to him; and our failure to pray can undermine the infallibility of their coming. This leaves them at most only fallibly Christian. Notice that for the Molinist, this could represent the possibility of a new good, the good of individual self-creation; for the Boethian, even this possibility would be a defection from the original possibilities: your individual self-creation is a less perfect form of the corporate self-creation God wanted, as the private good is a kind of narrowed form of the common good. (And this implies that here at least there would be some commensurability between individual and corporate self-creation.)

49. Notice also that self-creation is not essential to us. This is true not only in the contemporary sense of "essential" as identity-constituting, which after all only amounts to a triviality: we must first exist in order to self-create, so being self-created cannot be a condition for our existence (cf. Proclus, *Commentary on Plato's Timaeus* 260.10). Rather, self-creation is also not essential to us in the Aristotelian sense of something to which we are ineliminably ordered, as rationality is essential to human beings,

SCRIPTURE AND PREDESTINATION

The same flexibility allows the account to map more nearly the terrain of Scripture. God is fixed neither to fallible nor to infallible action. The Lord wishes to gather Jerusalem's children together, and they would not; the Lord hardens Pharaoh's heart. God wishes self-creation to Jerusalem, at least to those members in that epoch; God does not to Pharaoh, at least in those choices at that time. Jerusalem is given the chance to stand as a type of Mary instead of a type of Eve: one who chose to bring God into the world though she could have refused. Pharaoh is made to stand as a type of sin, which does not heed reason, which will not be persuaded, and whose bondage must therefore be fled. The goods at play here—self-creation, freedom, the fractaline form to history that the tradition calls typology, and so forth—are varied, and sometimes incommensurable. There is much more to be said both about these and about the many other passages arrayed for and against God's predetermination (is hardening a commission or a permission by God, does God's exhortation of us imply indeterminism about the subsequent choice,[50] and so forth), but it should already be clear that the present view will find it easier to account for this diversity than will a

---

even though human beings do not start out rational. Self-creation is unavailable to those who die as infants, for instance, including some who are baptized and receive beatitude—this follows from our general inability to switch states after death (*Catechism of the Catholic Church*, 1021) and their particular inability to make rational choices before it—and should we think that they lack something essentially human, in this Aristotelian sense? The Holy Innocents do not lack beatitude, do not lack full humanity, for lacking self-creation.

50. As in Irenaeus, *Haer.* 4.37: "If then it were not in our power to do or not to do these things, what reason had the apostle, and much more the Lord Himself, to give us counsel to do some things, and to abstain from others?"

more universally predeterminist or more uncompromisingly libertarian one.

That said, the thrust of this account has been against one way of reading certain passages: namely, as implying that God predetermines the damnation of at least some creatures. I noted above that merit is tied to freedom: it stems from those acts in which God most acts in us, which are our free acts. It is therefore compatible with predetermination to the good, as in the case of Christ's humanity. For just the same reason, demerit is incompatible with predetermination to evil. Here the analytic philosophers' habit of equating the two predeterminations, as if what matters most to freedom is whether we are predetermined and not what we are predetermined to, obscures the issue. As I indicated in the last chapter, to be predetermined to evil is not a different use of compatibilist freedom; it is not freedom at all. Sin is slavery, and the sin that results in *non posse non peccari* is slavery perfected. To be damned for what you were forced to do is not justice.

The analytic habit of decrying determination in whatever form as repugnant to freedom is merely the inversion of an older habit of identifying determination in its different forms as unavoidable—for example, because we are always in bondage, either to God or the devil.[51] The fruit of this earlier habit, when indulged as it is in Luther (for all his qualifications), is

---

51. A habit that reads Paul's talk of slavery to Christ (e.g., 1 Cor. 7:22; Eph. 6:6) in a more analogical than metaphorical way. The analogical way would have slavery to Christ be a real kind of slavery, perhaps the realest kind, in which our enslavements participate, rather than the slavery of the ancient world—Paul was addressing those who were actual slaves to "earthly masters"—being a kind of figure of service that can be associated with Christian service in at most a metaphorical way.

the Calvinist view that God has merely to arrange our doing of evil to make us deserve evil in return. As with the philosophers, this treats the good and the evil act rather too much alike, as if they were equally free and indeed equally acts. In fact, for God to arrange our doing of evil is to withhold grace from us, to attenuate our acting, to such a degree that we cannot possibly do right; and when this condition becomes total, such that we cannot perform any good actions whatsoever, this effectively undercuts the very grounds of merit and demerit, of praise and blame. It is to destroy our freedom, not redirect our slavery. Of course, we can bring this destruction upon ourselves by our earlier free choices and so deserve both this destruction and its fruit; but then, as with Augustine, the earlier choices must themselves be free and not attenuated in this way.[52] Here the Patristic contrast of the bestiality of the sinner with the beatitude of the righteous is more apt than competing bondages; here the fathers in general, including Augustine but especially the Greeks, are more reliable guides than those that come later.[53] The determinately good are praiseworthy because they are free; the determinately evil are not blameworthy because they are not free, though they may be blameworthy for their own determination if it is the result of some earlier freedom.

What of those passages that suggest the determinately evil

52. See the introduction, pp. 20–21 n. 28. Compare also Couenhoven's view mentioned in chapter 3, p. 126 n. 6.

53. I am thinking of those passages in which it is stated or implied that God condemns us only for those things we could have not done. E.g., Irenaeus, *Haer.* 4.4.3, in which the comparison with beasts is made (following Ps. 49:12), and 4.29.2; Origen, *Prin.* 3.1.20; Basil, *Homily Explaining That God Is Not the Cause of Evil*; Gregory of Nyssa, *Life of Moses* 2.74; Chrysostom, *Hom. Rom.* 16; Pseudo-Denys, *Divine Names* 4.35. As an example of post-Augustinian drift, see Thomas Aquinas, *ST* I.23.3.

are in fact to blame, as with the epigraph to this chapter from Sirach, and perhaps most famously with Romans 9:19–24?

> You will say to me then, "Why does he still find fault? For who can resist his will?" But who are you, a man, to answer back to God? Will what is molded say to its molder, "Why have you made me thus?" Has the potter no right over the clay, to make out of the same lump one vessel for beauty and another for menial use? What if God, desiring to show his wrath and to make known his power, has endured with much patience the vessels of wrath made for destruction, in order to make known the riches of his glory for the vessels of mercy, which he has prepared beforehand for glory, even us whom he has called, not from the Jews only but also from the Gentiles?

This would be a different book were it to attempt a reading of these and all other relevant passages on this point; and indeed, I do not think all readers of goodwill will converge on a single consistent account of these issues by a comprehensive consideration of the canon. That is why Christians continue to disagree; it is why in the last analysis this is a Catholic project that appeals to an authoritative tradition. But let me say something here not to convince the otherwise convicted but to clarify my own view, which is that this passage implies neither double predestination nor its Dominican simulacrum.[54]

54. In which God does not actively damn but simply refuses to supply with the required aid. "Lessius [an influential Molinist] rightly says that it would be indifferent to him whether he was numbered among those reprobated positively or negatively; for, in either case, his eternal damnation would be certain." See Joseph Pohle, "Predestination," *The Catholic*

Here I follow the "increasingly large number of [biblical] scholars who are convinced that Paul . . . is implying nothing about the salvation of individuals."[55] "Advocates of this general interpretation disagree over the extent to which Paul is focusing on individuals or peoples, but agree that no reference to the eternal destiny of individuals is present."[56] The heart of Paul's argument in these verses is about Israel; whatever else we, or he, would see in his words, Israel is a central referent of the "vessels made for destruction." And the chief problem with taking these words in a strongly predestinarian way is that the whole argument of this section of Romans is that Israel is not actually destined for eschatological destruction but for a temporary exclusion in which "a hardening has come upon part of Israel, until the full number of the Gentiles come in, *and so all Israel will be saved*" (11:25–6). Esau (9:13) and Pharaoh (9:17) are introduced not because they are fi-

---

Encyclopedia, vol. 12 (New York: Robert Appleton, 1911), http://www.newadvent.org/cathen/12378a.htm.

55. As Douglas Moo laments in *The Epistle to the Romans* (Grand Rapids: Eerdmans, 1996), 571. Moo's dissent on this point has not stemmed the increase—e.g., Leander E. Keck, *Romans*, Abingdon New Testament Commentaries (Nashville: Abingdon, 2005), 238, or Douglas Campbell's rather strong judgment that the historical, collective, and elective elements of these passages are "obvious and unavoidable." See Douglas A. Campbell and N. T. Wright, *The Deliverance of God: An Apocalyptic Rereading of Justification in Paul* (Grand Rapids: Eerdmans, 2013), 780 (cf. n. 34, where Campbell's apocalyptic reading ascribes double predestination language to Paul's opponent and seeks Paul's own account in the Christocentric election of Rom. 8). See also Brian Abasciano's more recent judgment that "in . . . Romans 9, which is a *locus classicus* for the doctrine of election, corporate election of one sort or another has become the most dominant type of election perceived by interpreters" ("Clearing Up Misconceptions about Corporate Election," *Ashland Theological Journal* 41 [2009]: 59).

56. Moo, *Epistle to the Romans*, 571, n. 9.

nally rejected—Esau is in fact reconciled, and nothing is said of Pharaoh's end—but because they have a certain typological significance for God's present treatment of Israel: "The antithetical role filled by Esau and Pharaoh in relation to Israel's election and redemption is now being filled by the bulk of Israel in relation to God's calling of the Gentile as well as Jew through the gospel."[57]

The passive construction "made [due, readied] for destruction," then, can be applied to eschatological destruction only in a Ninevehian way: as a prophecy about one's current course, not one's foreknown destination.[58] "The probably deliberate echo of the most famous of the scripture's potter passages (Jer. 18:1–11) would be an invitation to his Roman

57. James D. G. Dunn, *Romans 9–16*, Word Biblical Commentary, vol. 38B (Waco, TX: Word Books, 1988), 563.

58. As Thomas says, "*vasa apta in interitum*, id est, in se habentia aptitudinem ad aeternam damnationem" [*vessels ready for destruction*, that is, having in themselves an aptitude toward eternal damnation] (*Commentary on the Letter of Saint Paul to the Romans* [*Super Rom.*] 9.4 [793]). The classical Augustinian reading of Romans 9 takes it to describe the situation after the fall, in which God chooses to mold some of self-condemning humanity into vessels of honor and leave others as they are: "Deus liberam potestatem habet facere ex eadem corrupta materia humani generis, sicut ex quodam luto, nulli faciendo iniuriam, quosdam homines praeparatos in gloriam, quosdam autem in miseria derelictos. . . . Actus vero quem Deus erga eos exercet, non est quod disponat eos ad malum, quia ipsi de se habent dispositionem ad malum ex corruptione primi peccati" [God has the free ability to make from the corrupt matter of the human species, as from a kind of clay, and without wronging anyone, some prepared for glory while leaving the rest in their misery. . . . The act that God works on them is not to dispose them to evil, for they have of themselves a disposition to evil from the corruption of original sin] (*Super Rom.* 9.4 [793]). Cf. Augustine, *Grace and Free Will* 21.43: "He did not produce their evilness, but either it was originally drawn from Adam or it was increased by their own will" (in Peter King, trans., *Augustine: On the Free Choice of the Will, On Grace and Free Choice, and Other Writings* [New York: Cambridge University Press, 2010], 181; cf. *Admonition and Grace* 6.9).

readers to recognize that the divine purpose could be tempered and changed, that the pot made for a disreputable use could be remade into a work to be treasured."[59] As Origen remarks, this brings to mind 2 Timothy's use of vessel imagery: "In a great house there are not only vessels of gold and silver but also of wood and earthenware, and some for noble use, some for ignoble. If anyone purifies himself from what is ignoble, then he will be a vessel for noble use" (2 Tim. 2:20-21).[60] If we take "ignoble use" to mean final damnation, then, whether of individuals or groups, these sorts of passages do not suggest some initial infallible decree of God's. On the other hand, if we take the potter's sovereignty over the pot to indicate an infallible divine plan, then the menial use of some such pots does not lie in their destruction—"for in death there is no remembrance of thee; in Sheol who can give thee praise?" (Ps. 6:5; cf. 30:9; 88:10; 115:17)—but their status as those "parts of the body that seem to be weaker [but that] are indispensable" (1 Cor. 12:22). Either of those interpretations are consistent with Paul's claim that what is infallible about God's election is the *salvation* of Israel—if not for every Jew, at least as a corporate body. (As should be obvious from what I have said about hell, my reading of Paul is not just that some have more menial roles to play but that some are damned.) What is not consistent is the claim that God's infallible choice is for damnation, whether that infallibility comes through single or double predestination.

We can speak of a kind of infallible predestination from before the creation of the world, then, but its object is Christ, the corporate person, and its infallibility is rooted in the im-

---

59. Dunn, *Romans 9-16*, 565. Cf. his discussion of "made for destruction" on 559-60.

60. Origen, *Prin.* 3.1.20.

peccability of the head. The participation of individuals in this sure election is itself fallible to the degree that they are themselves peccable, which is to say, on my view, to a very great degree indeed.

Nor is this mix of fallibility and infallibility entirely at odds with an older Augustinian account.[61] There is a running problem of how to incorporate the predestination of Romans 8:29, which seems prior to creation both in Paul and in Augustine, with Augustine's account of Romans 9, in which God's election of some rather than others supposes the sinfulness of all[62]—a sinfulness that God did not work and that is therefore in some manner subsequent to creation.[63] My own reading of Augustine is that God wills from the beginning of creation that all are saved, and gives them, in Adam, a resistible grace to that end; but God also elects from the beginning some of creation to be saved no matter what, including Adam, and these ultimately all receive irresistible graces.

My own dissent from (this) Augustine lies not in denying God's discretion to give resistible or irresistible graces but in maintaining that those foreordained for merely resistible graces retain access to these graces after the fall. In other words, besides perhaps particular disagreements about the extent of irresistible grace or the number of those first to fall,[64] I am less convinced than Augustine that Adam's resistance is sufficient to block resistible grace from coming to the rest of

61. Here I am taking issue with William G. Most, *Grace, Predestination, and the Salvific Will of God: New Answers to Old Questions* (Front Royal, VA: Christendom, 2004), 23–27.

62. See n. 58 above. Also: "For God's foreknowledge and predestination has not singled them out from the mass of perdition" (*Admonition and Grace* 7.16, trans. King, *Augustine*, 198; cf. 12.37).

63. See the introduction, pp. 20–21 n. 28.

64. Taking Adam here to represent the first human beings, whether that is a couple like Adam and Eve or a tribe.

us. This accords better with the Greek fathers, whose exegesis of Romans 9 preserves more room even after the fall for free choice, which is to say for the continuation of that grace that makes us partakers in divine freedom (though not so completely as to be impeccable).[65] Still, on either account, there is a mix between the infallibility of the predestination of Christ and the fallibility of the predestination of at least some others. On Augustine's view, the Christ who is infallibly predestined includes in his body those specific individuals whose election is guaranteed from before the fall, and fallible predestination turns to sure condemnation for all other individuals after the fall. On the view defended here, the head and body that are predestined might include specific individuals but also includes the unspecified set of anyone who does not turn away, which is to say that it remains fallible across the span of our lives and not just the span of Adam's choice. What God infallibly decrees from before the foundation of the world, besides whatever particular acts within history are guaranteed against our refusal, is, first, the glorification of Christ and his body; second, the ordination of all things to membership in that body; and third, the fulfillment of that ordination for some nonrational creatures and at least some rational creatures (e.g., the Holy Innocents). God also decrees the fulfillment of that ordination for other rational (free) creatures, but in a way that can be refused and so experienced as destruction.

Now the point of all this, besides suggesting the flexibility of a compatibilist indeterminism in interpreting difficult passages, is that even those interpretations it does exclude

---

65. "And yet not even is it on the potter that the honor and the dishonor of the things made of the lump depends, but upon the use made by those that handle them, so here also it depends on the free choice," and so forth: Chrysostom, *Hom. Rom.* 16 (*Nicene and Post-Nicene Fathers*, First Series, 11:468).

point, in how they are excluded, to the larger project of this chapter. This is the upshot of opposing Calvinism with corporate election. For what I take, following contemporary biblical scholarship, to be the most plausible reading of passages dear to the double predestinationist not only fails to support double predestination but in fact points to the Christocentrism of creation that I have been limning all along. Election and predestination point to Christ, not Calvin—not even to Christ by way of Calvin. If one suggestion of the first chapter was that God knows creation in some way as a whole, a dance unfolding over time, the suggestion of this chapter is that God predestines creation in the same way, to reach its apex and apotheosis as one unified cosmos—a cosmos that is *from him and through him and to him. To him be glory forever. Amen.*

Works Cited

M ajor works, for example, premodern texts, are cited by the section numbers standard to the work. Unless otherwise noted, translations from Scripture are from the Revised Standard Version, translations from patristic works are taken from the *Ante-Nicene Fathers* and *Nicene and Post-Nicene Fathers* editions; translations from Aquinas are taken from the editions available at https://isidore.co/aquinas/; and translations from papal documents are taken from the Vatican website, vatican.va.

Abasciano, Brian. "Clearing Up Misconceptions about Corporate Election." *Ashland Theological Journal* 41 (2009): 59–90.

Adams, Marilyn McCord. *Christ and Horrors: The Coherence of Christology*. Cambridge: Cambridge University Press, 2008.

———. *Horrendous Evils and the Goodness of God*. Ithaca, NY: Cornell University Press, 2000.

Anselm, Saint. *Anselm of Canterbury: The Major Works*. Edited by Brian Davies and G. R. Evans. Oxford: Oxford University Press, 2008.

The Ante-Nicene Fathers. Edited by Alexander Roberts and James

Donaldson. 1885–1887. 10 vols. Repr., Peabody, MA: Hendrickson, 1994.

Arminius, James. *The Works of James Arminius: The London Edition.* Translated by James Nichols and William Nichols. Introduction by Carl Bangs. Grand Rapids: Baker, 1986.

Ashworth, E. Jennifer. "Analogy and Metaphor from Thomas Aquinas to Duns Scotus and Walter Burley." Pages 223–48 in *Later Medieval Metaphysics: Ontology, Language, and Logic.* Edited by Charles Bolyard and Rondo Keele. New York: Fordham University Press, 2013.

Augustine. *The Confessions of Saint Augustine.* Translated by John K. Ryan. New York: Doubleday Image, 1960.

Balthasar, Hans Urs von. *The Dramatis Personae: Man in God.* Vol. 2 of *Theo-Drama: Theological Dramatic Theory.* Translated by Graham Harrison. San Francisco: Ignatius, 1990.

———. *The Glory of the Lord: A Theological Aesthetics.* Vol. 2. Edited by John Kenneth Riches. San Francisco: Ignatius, 1984.

———. *The Last Act.* Vol. 5 of *Theo-Drama: Theological Dramatic Theory.* San Francisco: Ignatius, 2003.

———. *Truth of God.* Vol. 2 of *Theo-Logic.* San Francisco: Ignatius, 2004.

———. *The Truth of the World.* Vol. 1 of *Theo-Logic.* San Francisco: Ignatius, 2001.

Barnwell, Michael. "The Problem with Aquinas's Original Discovery." *American Catholic Philosophical Quarterly* 89 (2015): 277–91.

Barth, Karl. *Church Dogmatics* II/1. Edinburgh: T. & T. Clark, 1957.

———. *Church Dogmatics* III/2. Edinburgh: T. & T. Clark, 1960.

Benedict XVI. *Jesus of Nazareth: From the Baptism in the Jordan to the Transfiguration.* Translated by Adrian J. Walker. San Francisco: Ignatius, 2008.

Bernanos, Georges, and Rémy Rougeau. *The Diary of a Country Priest: A Novel.* Cambridge: Da Capo, 2002.

Bernard of Clairvaux. *Bernard of Clairvaux: Selected Works.* Translated by G. R. Evans. Preface by Ewert Cousins. Introduction by Jean LeClercq. New York: Paulist, 1987.

Works Cited

Berry, Wendell. *Wild Birds: Six Stories of the Port William Member-ship*. San Francisco: North Point, 1986.

Berthouzoz, Roger. *Liberté et grâce suivant la théologie d'Irénée de Lyon*. Fribourg: Beauchesne, 1980.

Blaauw, Martijn. *Contrastivism in Philosophy*. New York: Routledge, 2013.

Blanchette, Oliva. *The Perfection of the Universe according to Aquinas: A Teleological Cosmology*. University Park: Pennsylvania State University Press, 1992.

Blankenhorn, Bernhard. "Balthasar's Method of Divine Naming." *Nova et Vetera* 2 (2003): 245–68.

Boer, Willem den, and Jan Hendrik Waszink. *Romanitas et Chris-tianitas: Studia Iano Henrico Waszink A.D. VI Kal. Nov. A. MCMLXXIII XIII Lustra Complenti Oblata*. Amsterdam: North-Holland, 1973.

Bolyard, Charles, and Rondo Keele, eds. *Later Medieval Metaphysics: Ontology, Language, and Logic*. New York: Fordham Univer-sity Press, 2013.

Bonnefoy, Jean-François. *Christ and the Cosmos*. Translated by Mi-chael D. Meilach. Paterson, NJ: St. Anthony Guild, 1965.

Bos, Egbert P., and Medium Aevum (Association). *John Duns Scotus: Renewal of Philosophy; Acts of the Third Symposium Organized by the Dutch Society for Medieval Philosophy Medium Aevum (May 23 & 24 1996)*. Amsterdam: Rodopi, 1998.

Bouëssé, Humbert. *La place du Christ dans le plan de Dieu*. Vol. 1 of *Le Sauveur du monde*. Chambery: College Theologique Dominicain, 1951.

Buchak, Lara. "Free Acts and Chance: Why the Rollback Argument Fails." *Philosophical Quarterly* 63 (2013): 20–28.

Burns, J. Patout. *The Development of Augustine's Doctrine of Operative Grace*. Paris: Études Augustiniennes, 1980.

Burrell, David B. *Analogy and Philosophical Language*. Eugene, OR: Wipf & Stock, 2016.

———. *Deconstructing Theodicy: Why Job Has Nothing to Say to the Puzzle of Suffering*. Grand Rapids: Brazos, 2008.

———. *Freedom and Creation in Three Traditions.* Notre Dame: University of Notre Dame Press, 1993.

———. *Knowing the Unknowable God: Ibn Sina, Maimonides, Aquinas.* Notre Dame: University of Notre Dame Press, 1992.

Campbell, Douglas A., and N. T. Wright. *The Deliverance of God: An Apocalyptic Rereading of Justification in Paul.* Grand Rapids: Eerdmans, 2013.

Collins, Robin. "The Connection-Building Theodicy." Pages 222–35 in *Blackwell Companion to the Problem of Evil.* Edited by Justin P. McBrayer and Daniel Howard-Snyder. Malden, MA: Wiley-Blackwell, 2013.

Comblin, José. *Called for Freedom.* Maryknoll, NY: Orbis Books, 1998.

Couenhoven, Jesse. "Augustine's Rejection of the Free-Will Defence: An Overview of the Late Augustine's Theodicy." *Religious Studies* 43 (2007): 279–98.

———. *Stricken by Sin, Cured by Christ: Agency, Necessity, and Culpability in Augustinian Theology.* Oxford: Oxford University Press, 2013.

Craig, William Lane. *Time and Eternity: Exploring God's Relationship to Time.* Wheaton, IL: Crossway, 2001.

Cross, Richard. *Duns Scotus.* Great Medieval Thinkers. Oxford: Oxford University Press, 1999.

———. *Duns Scotus on God.* Aldershot: Routledge, 2005.

———. "Idolatry and Religious Language." *Faith and Philosophy* 25 (2008): 190–96.

Daguet, François. *Théologie du dessein divin chez Thomas d'Aquin: Finis omnium Ecclesia.* Paris: Librairie Philosophique Vrin, 2003.

D'Ettore, Domenic. *Analogy after Aquinas: Logical Problems, Thomistic Answers.* Washington, DC: Catholic University of America Press, 2018.

Draper, Paul. "A Critique of the Kalam Cosmological Argument." Pages 172–78 in *Philosophy of Religion: An Anthology.* Edited by Louis P. Pojman and Michael C. Rea. 6th ed. Boston: Cengage Learning, 2012.

Driel, Edwin van. *Incarnation Anyway: Arguments for Supralapsarian Christology*. American Academy of Religion Academy Series. Oxford: Oxford University Press, 2008.

Dunfee, Susan Nelson. "The Sin of Hiding: A Feminist Critique of Reinhold Niebuhr's Account of the Sin of Pride." *Soundings* 65 (1982): 316–27.

Dunn, James D. G. *Romans 9–16*. Word Biblical Commentary. Vol. 38B. Waco, TX: Word, 1988.

Feingold, Lawrence. *The Natural Desire to See God according to St. Thomas and His Interpreters*. 2nd ed. Ave Maria, FL: Sapientia Press of Ave Maria University, 2004.

Francis de Sales, Saint. *The Catholic Controversy*. Edited by Paul Böer Sr. Translated by Henry Mackey, OSB. N.p.: Veritatis Splendor, 2012.

———. *Oeuvres de Saint François de Sales*. Edited by Jean Joseph Navatel, Peter Paul Mackey, and Benedict Mackey. Annecy: J. Niérat, 1892.

Frank, William, and Allan B. Wolter. *Duns Scotus, Metaphysician*. West Lafayette, IN: Purdue University Press, 1995.

Frassen, Claude. *Scotus academicus seu Universa Doctoris Subtilis theologica dogmata*. 12 vols. Rome: Ex Typographia Sallustiana, 1900–1902.

Frost, Gloria. "John Duns Scotus on God's Knowledge of Sins: A Test-Case for God's Knowledge of Contingents." *Journal of the History of Philosophy* 48 (2010): 15–34.

Furlong, Peter. "Libertarianism, the Rollback Argument, and the Objective Probability of Free Choices." *Pacific Philosophical Quarterly* 98 (2017): 512–32.

Gaine, Simon Francis. *Will There Be Free Will in Heaven? Freedom, Impeccability and Beatitude*. London: Bloomsbury T&T Clark, 2003.

Garrigou-Lagrange, Reginald. *Predestination: The Meaning of Predes-*

tination in Scripture and the Church. Repr., Rockford, IL: TAN Books, 1998.

———. "Prémotion Physique." Columns 31–77 in vol. 13 of *Dictionnaire de théologie catholique*. Edited by A. Vacant et al. Paris: Letouzey & Ané, 1923–1950.

Goldstein, Valerie Saiving. "The Human Situation: A Feminine Viewpoint." *Pastoral Psychology* 17 (1966): 29–42.

Grant, W. Matthews. "Aquinas on How God Causes the Act of Sin without Causing Sin Itself." *Thomist* 73 (2009): 455–96.

———. "Divine Universal Causality and Libertarian Freedom." Pages 214–33 in *Free Will and Theism: Connections, Contingencies, and Concerns*. Edited by Kevin Timpe and Daniel Speak. Oxford: Oxford University Press, 2016.

Greene, Graham. "The Hint of an Explanation." *Commonweal*, February 11, 1949, https://www.commonwealmagazine.org/hint-explanation.

Gregory Palamas, Saint. *Saint Gregory Palamas: The Homilies*. Edited by Christopher Veniamin. Waymart, PA: Mount Thabor, 2016.

Gutiérrez, Gustavo. *On Job*. Translated by Matthew O'Connell. Maryknoll, NY: Orbis Books, 1987.

Haggerty, Father Donald. *Contemplative Provocations*. San Francisco: Ignatius, 2013.

Hart, David Bentley. "Providence and Causality: On Divine Innocence." Pages 34–56 in *Providence of God: Deus Habet Consilium*. Edited by Francesca Aran Murphy and Philip Gordon Ziegler. London: T&T Clark, 2009.

Hasker, William. "Why Simple Foreknowledge Is Still Useless (In Spite of David Hunt and Alex Pruss)." *Journal of the Evangelical Theological Society* 52 (2009): 537–44.

Hayes, Zachary. *The Hidden Center: Spirituality and Speculative Christology in St. Bonaventure*. Saint Bonaventure, NY: Franciscan Institute, 1981.

Hays, Richard B. *Echoes of Scripture in the Gospels*. Waco, TX: Baylor University Press, 2017.

Hitchcock, Christopher. "Contrastive Explanations." Pages 11–34 in

Works Cited

Contrastivism in Philosophy. Edited by Martijn Blaauw. New York: Routledge, 2013.

Hoffmann, Tobias. "Aquinas and Intellectual Determinism: The Test Case of Angelic Sin." *Archiv für Geschichte der Philosophie* 89 (2007): 122–56.

Horan, Daniel P. *Postmodernity and Univocity: A Critical Account of Radical Orthodoxy and John Duns Scotus*. Minneapolis: Fortress, 2014.

Hugon, Édouard, OP. "Le motif de l'Incarnation." *Revue Thomiste* 21 (1913): 276–96.

Hunt, David P. "Contra Hasker: Why Simple Foreknowledge Is Still Useful." *Journal of the Evangelical Theological Society* 52 (2009): 545–50.

Inwagen, Peter van. *An Essay on Free Will*. Rev. ed. Oxford: Oxford University Press, 1986.

Jackson, Sherman A. *Islam and the Problem of Black Suffering*. Oxford: Oxford University Press, 2014.

John of Saint Thomas. *Introduction to the Summa Theologiae of Thomas Aquinas*. Translated by Ralph McInerny. South Bend, IN: St. Augustine's, 2003.

Jones, William R. *Is God a White Racist? A Preamble to Black Theology*. Boston: Beacon, 1997.

Kane, Robert. *The Significance of Free Will*. New York: Oxford University Press, 1998.

Keck, Leander E. *Romans*. Abingdon New Testament Commentaries. Nashville: Abingdon, 2005.

Kelsey, David H. *Eccentric Existence: A Theological Anthropology*. Louisville: Westminster John Knox, 2009.

Kilby, Karen. *Balthasar: A (Very) Critical Introduction*. Grand Rapids: Eerdmans, 2012.

———. "Evil and the Limits of Theology." *New Blackfriars* 84 (2003): 13–29.

King, Peter. "Augustine and Anselm on Angelic Sin." Pages 261–81 in *A Companion to Angels in Medieval Philosophy*. Edited by Tobias Hoffmann. Leiden: Brill, 2012.

———, trans. *Augustine: On the Free Choice of the Will, On Grace and Free Choice, and Other Writings*. New York: Cambridge University Press, 2010.

Kitanov, Severin Valentinov. *Beatific Enjoyment in Medieval Scholastic Debates: The Complex Legacy of Saint Augustine and Peter Lombard*. Lanham, MD: Lexington Books, 2017.

Krenski, Thomas R. *Passio Caritatis: Trinitarische Passiologie im Werk Hans Urs von Balthasars*. Einsiedeln: Johannes Verlag, 1990.

Lamb, Matthew. "The Mystery of Divine Predestination." Pages 214–25 in *Thomism and Predestination: Principles and Disputations*. Edited by Steven A. Long, Roger W. Nutt, and Thomas Joseph White. Ave Maria, FL: Sapientia Press of Ave Maria University, 2017.

Levering, Matthew. *Predestination: Biblical and Theological Paths*. Oxford: Oxford University Press, 2011.

Lewis, David. "Evil for Freedom's Sake?" *Philosophical Papers* 22 (1993): 149–72.

Lonergan, Bernard. *Early Latin Theology*. Vol. 19 of *Collected Works of Bernard Lonergan*. Edited by Robert Doran, SJ, and H. Daniel Monsour. Translated by Michael Shields. Toronto: University of Toronto Press, 2011.

———. *Grace and Freedom: Operative Grace in the Thought of St. Thomas Aquinas*. Vol. 1. Edited by Frederick Crowe, SJ, and Robert Doran, SJ. Toronto: University of Toronto Press, 2000.

———. *Insight: A Study of Human Understanding*. Philosophical Library. New York: Longmans, 1967.

———. *Method in Theology*. 2nd ed. Toronto: University of Toronto Press, 1990.

Long, Steven A. *Natura Pura: On the Recovery of Nature in the Doctrine of Grace*. New York: Fordham University Press, 2010.

———. "Providence, Freedom, and Natural Law." *Nova et Vetera* 4 (2006): 557–605.

Long, Steven A., Roger W. Nutt, and Thomas Joseph White, eds. *Thomism and Predestination: Principles and Disputations*. Ave Maria, FL: Sapientia Press of Ave Maria University, 2017.

Works Cited

MacIntyre, Alasdair. *Ethics in the Conflicts of Modernity: An Essay on Desire, Practical Reasoning, and Narrative*. New York: Cambridge University Press, 2016.

———. *Three Rival Versions of Moral Inquiry*. Notre Dame: University of Notre Dame Press, 1990.

Manis, Zachary. *Sinners in the Presence of a Loving God: An Essay on the Problem of Hell*. Oxford: Oxford University Press, 2019.

Marion, Jean-Luc. "Thomas Aquinas and Onto-Theology." Pages 38–74 in *Mystics: Presence and Aporia*. Edited by Michael Kessler and Christian Sheppard. Chicago: University of Chicago Press, 2003.

Maritain, Jacques. *Existence and the Existent*. New York: Pantheon Books, 1949.

———. *God and the Permission of Evil*. Milwaukee: Bruce, 1966.

———. *The Sin of the Angel*. Westminster, MD: Newman, 1959.

Matava, Robert Joseph. *Divine Causality and Human Free Choice: Domingo Báñez, Physical Premotion and the Controversy* de Auxiliis *Revisited*. Boston: Brill, 2016.

Mauriac, François. *Viper's Tangle*. Tacoma, WA: Cluny Media, 2017.

Maximus the Confessor. *On Difficulties in the Church Fathers: The Ambigua*. Vol. 2. Translated by Nicholas Constas. Cambridge: Harvard University Press, 2014.

McCabe, Herbert. *God and Evil: In the Theology of St Thomas Aquinas*. New York: Bloomsbury Academic, 2010.

McCann, Hugh. *Creation and the Sovereignty of God*. Bloomington: Indiana University Press, 2012.

McCullough, Ross. "Darkling Lights of Lucifer: Annihilation, Tradition, and Hell." *Pro Ecclesia* 22 (2013): 55–68.

McDonnell, Eunan. *The Concept of Freedom in the Writings of St Francis de Sales*. New York: Lang, 2009.

McElrath, Damian. *Franciscan Christology: Selected Texts, Translations, and Introductory Essays*. Saint Bonaventure, NY: Franciscan Institute, 1997.

Meijering, E. P. "Irenaeus' Relation to Philosophy in the Light of His Concept of Free Will." Pages 221–32 in *Romanitas et Chris-*

tianitas: Studia Iano Henrico Waszink A.D. VI Kal. Nov. A. MCMLXXIII XIII Lustra Complenti Oblata. Edited by Willem den Boer and Jan Hendrik Waszink. Amsterdam: North-Holland, 1973.

Melanchthon, Philip. *Melanchthon and Bucer.* Edited by Wilhelm Pauck. Philadelphia: Westminster John Knox, 2006.

Minns, Denis. *Irenaeus: An Introduction.* Rev. ed. London: T&T Clark, 2010.

Moltmann, Jürgen. *The Coming of God: Christian Eschatology.* Minneapolis: Fortress, 2004.

Moo, Douglas J. *The Epistle to the Romans.* Grand Rapids: Eerdmans, 1996.

Most, William G. *Grace, Predestination, and the Salvific Will of God: New Answers to Old Questions.* Front Royal, VA: Christendom, 2004.

Muller, Richard Alfred. *God, Creation, and Providence in the Thought of Jacob Arminius: Sources and Directions of Scholastic Protestantism in the Era of Early Orthodoxy.* Grand Rapids: Baker, 1991.

Murphy, Francesca Aran, and Philip Gordon Ziegler, eds. *Providence of God: Deus Habet Consilium.* London: T&T Clark, 2009.

Murray, Michael J. "Deus Absconditus." Pages 62–82 in *Divine Hiddenness: New Essays.* Edited by Daniel Howard-Snyder and Paul K. Moser. Cambridge: Cambridge University Press, 2002.

———. *Nature Red in Tooth and Claw: Theism and the Problem of Animal Suffering.* Oxford: Oxford University Press, 2008.

Nicolas, Jean-Hervé. "La volonté salvifique de Dieu contrariée par le péché." *Revue Thomiste* 92 (1992): 177–96.

———. "Le Christ et la création d'après Saint Thomas d'Aquin." Pages 79–100 in *Studia Medievalia et Mariologica.* Edited by Carolus Balic. Rome: Antonianum, 1971.

O'Connor, Timothy. "Agent-Causal Power." Pages 189–214 in *Dispositions and Causes.* Edited by Toby Handfield. Oxford: Oxford University Press, 2009.

Works Cited

———. "Degrees of Freedom." *Philosophical Explorations* 12 (2009): 119–25.

———. *Persons and Causes: The Metaphysics of Free Will.* New York: Oxford University Press, 2000.

———. "Probability and Freedom: A Reply to Vicens." *Res Philosophica* 93 (2016): 289–93.

O'Connor, Timothy, and John Ross Churchill. "Reasons Explanation and Agent Control: In Search of an Integrated Account." *Philosophical Topics* 32 (2004): 241–56.

O'Hanlon, Gerard F. *The Immutability of God in the Theology of Hans Urs von Balthasar.* Cambridge: Cambridge University Press, 2007.

O'Neill, Taylor Patrick. *Grace, Predestination, and the Permission of Sin: A Thomistic Analysis.* Washington, DC: Catholic University of America Press, 2019.

Osborne, Thomas M., Jr. "How Sin Escapes Premotion: The Development of Thomas Aquinas's Thought by Spanish Thomists." Pages 192–213 in *Thomism and Predestination: Principles and Disputations.* Edited by Steven A. Long, Roger W. Nutt, and Thomas Joseph White. Ave Maria, FL: Sapientia Press of Ave Maria University, 2017.

———. *Human Action in Thomas Aquinas, John Duns Scotus, and William of Ockham.* Washington, DC: Catholic University of America Press, 2016.

———. *Love of Self and Love of God in Thirteenth-Century Ethics.* Notre Dame: University of Notre Dame Press, 2005.

———. "Thomist Premotion and Contemporary Philosophy of Religion." *Nova et Vetera* 4 (2006): 607–31.

Pereboom, Derk. *Free Will, Agency, and Meaning in Life.* Oxford: Oxford University Press, 2014.

———. "Libertarianism and Theological Determinism." Pages 112–31 in *Free Will and Theism: Connections, Contingencies, and Concerns.* Edited by Kevin Timpe and Daniel Speak. Oxford: Oxford University Press, 2016.

Perszyk, Ken, ed. *Molinism: The Contemporary Debate*. Oxford: Oxford University Press, 2012.

Pickstock, Catherine. *After Writing: On the Liturgical Cosummation of Philosophy*. Malden, MA: Wiley-Blackwell, 1997.

Pinckaers, Servais. *The Sources of Christian Ethics*. Translated by Mary Thomas Noble. 3rd ed. Washington, DC: Catholic University of America Press, 1995.

Pitstick, Alyssa Lyra. *Light in Darkness: Hans Urs von Balthasar and the Catholic Doctrine of Christ's Descent into Hell*. Grand Rapids: Eerdmans, 2007.

Plantinga, Alvin. *God, Freedom, and Evil*. Grand Rapids: Eerdmans, 1978.

Pohle, Joseph. "Predestination." In *The Catholic Encyclopedia*. Vol. 12. New York: Robert Appleton, 1911. http://www.newadvent.org /cathen/12378a.htm.

Polkinghorne, John, and Michael Welker, eds. *The End of the World and the Ends of God: Science and Theology on Eschatology*. Harrisburg, PA: Trinity Press International, 2000.

Pomplun, Trent. "The Immaculate World: Predestination and Passibility in Contemporary Scotism." *Modern Theology* 30 (2014): 525–51.

Punch, John. *Commentarii theologici quibus Ioannis Duns Scoti quaestiones in libros Sententiarum, tom. III, dist. 7, qu. 3*. Paris: Sumptibus Simeonis Piget, 1661.

Rahner, Karl. *Foundations of Christian Faith: An Introduction to the Idea of Christianity*. Translated by William V. Dych. Rev. ed. New York: Crossroad, 1982.

Rogers, Katherin. *Anselm on Freedom*. Oxford: Oxford University Press, 2008.

Schaff, Philip, ed. *The Nicene and Post-Nicene Fathers*, Series 1. 1886–1889. 14 vols. Repr., Peabody, MA: Hendrickson, 1994.

Schaff, Philip, and Henry Wace, eds. *The Nicene and Post-Nicene Fathers*, Series 2. 1890–1900. 14 vols. Repr., Peabody, MA: Hendrickson, 1994.

Schellenberg, J. L. "The Hiddenness Problem and the Problem of Evil." *Faith and Philosophy* 27 (2010): 45–60.

Schmemann, Alexander. *For the Life of the World: Sacraments and Orthodoxy.* 2nd rev. and enl. ed. Crestwood, NY: St. Vladimir's Seminary Press, 1973.

Schmitz, Fabio. *Causalité divine et péché dans la théologie de saint Thomas d'Aquin.* Paris: L'Harmattan, 2016.

Scotus, John Duns. *God and Creatures: The Quodlibetal Questions.* Translated by Felix Alluntis and Allan B. Wolter. Washington, DC: Catholic University of America Press, 1981.

Shanley, Brian J. "Divine Causation and Human Freedom in Aquinas." *American Catholic Philosophical Quarterly* 77 (1998): 99–122.

Simon, Yves. "On Order in Analogical Sets." *New Scholasticism* 34 (1960): 1–42.

Society of Evangelical Arminians. "A Concise Summary of the Corporate View of Election and Predestination." February 13, 2013. http://evangelicalarminians.org/a-concise-summary-of-the-corporate-view-of-election-and-predestination/.

Stoppard, Tom. *Rosencrantz and Guildenstern Are Dead.* 50th anniversary ed. New York: Grove, 2017.

Stump, Eleonore. *Aquinas.* London: Routledge, 2005.

Suárez, Francisco. *On Creation, Conservation, and Concurrence.* South Bend, IN: St. Augustine's, 2002.

———. *On Efficient Causality: Metaphysical Disputations 17, 18, and 19.* Translated by Alfred J. Freddoso. New Haven: Yale University Press, 1994.

Surin, Kenneth. *Theology and the Problem of Evil.* Eugene, OR: Wipf & Stock, 2004.

Swinburne, Richard. *The Existence of God.* 2nd ed. Oxford: Oxford University Press, 2004.

Tanner, Kathryn. *God and Creation in Christian Theology: Tyranny or Empowerment?* Minneapolis: Fortress, 2005.

———. "Human Freedom, Human Sin, and God the Creator." Pages 111–36 in *The God Who Acts: Philosophical and Theological*

Explorations. Edited by Thomas F. Tracy. University Park: Pennsylvania State University Press, 1992.

Thomas Aquinas. *On Evil*. Edited by Brian Davies. Translated by Richard Regan. Oxford: Oxford University Press, 2003.

———. *Questions disputées sur la verité, Question V: la providence; Question VI: la prédestination*. Introduction and commentary by Jean-Pierre Torrell. Translation by Jean-Pierre Torrell and Denis Chardonnens. Paris: Vrin, 2011.

———. "St. Thomas Aquinas's Works in English." https://isidore.co /aquinas/.

Tilley, Terrence W. *The Evils of Theodicy*. Eugene, OR: Wipf & Stock, 2000.

Timpe, Kevin. *Free Will in Philosophical Theology*. New York: Bloomsbury Academic, 2013.

Timpe, Kevin, and Daniel Speak, eds. *Free Will and Theism: Connections, Contingencies, and Concerns*. Oxford: Oxford University Press, 2016.

Tonstad, Linn Marie. *God and Difference: The Trinity, Sexuality, and the Transformation of Finitude*. New York: Routledge, 2017.

Torre, Michael D. *Do Not Resist the Spirit's Call: Francisco Marín-Sola on Sufficient Grace*. Washington, DC: Catholic University of America Press, 2013.

———. *God's Permission of Sin: Negative or Conditioned Decree? A Defense of the Doctrine of Francisco Marín-Sola, O.P., Based on the Principles of Thomas Aquinas*. Fribourg: Academic Press Fribourg, 2009.

Trakakis, N. N. "Anti-Theodicy." Pages 94–122 in *The Problem of Evil: Eight Views in Dialogue*. Edited by N. N. Trakakis. Oxford: Oxford University Press, 2018.

Turek, Margaret. "'As the Father Has Loved Me' (Jn 15:9): Balthasar's Theo-dramatic Approach to a Theology of God the Father." *Communio* 26 (1999): 295–318.

Turner, Denys. *The Darkness of God: Negativity in Christian Mysticism*. Cambridge: Cambridge University Press, 1998.

————. *Faith, Reason and the Existence of God.* New York: Cambridge University Press, 2004.

Unger, Dominic. "Franciscan Christology: Absolute and Universal Primacy of Christ." *Franciscan Studies* 2 (1942): 428–75.

Velde, Rudi te. "Natura in se ipsa recurva est: Duns Scotus and Aquinas on the Relationship between Nature and Will." Pages 155–69 in *John Duns Scotus: Renewal of Philosophy; Acts of the Third Symposium Organized by the Dutch Society for Medieval Philosophy Medium Aevum (May 23 and 24, 1996).* Edited by Egbert P. Bos. Amsterdam: Rodopi, 1998.

Volf, Miroslav. "Enter into Joy." Pages 256–78 in *The End of the World and the Ends of God: Science and Theology on Eschatology.* Edited by John Polkinghorne and Michael Welker. Harrisburg, PA: Trinity Press International, 2000.

Weil, Simone. *On Science, Necessity and the Love of God: Essays.* London: Oxford University Press, 1968.

Werther, David. "Freedom, Temptation, and Incarnation." Pages 252–64 in *Philosophy and the Christian Worldview: Analysis, Assessment and Development.* Edited by David Werther and Mark D. Linville. London: Bloomsbury Academic, 2012.

Werther, David, and Mark D. Linville, eds. *Philosophy and the Christian Worldview: Analysis, Assessment and Development.* London: Bloomsbury Academic, 2012.

Wiebe, Mark B. *On Evil, Providence, and Freedom: A New Reading of Molina.* DeKalb: Northern Illinois University Press, 2017.

Wierenga, Edward. "The Freedom of God." *Faith and Philosophy* 19 (2002): 425–36.

Wippel, John F. *The Metaphysical Thought of Thomas Aquinas: From Finite Being to Uncreated Being.* Washington, DC: Catholic University of America Press, 2000.

Wittgenstein, Ludwig. *Culture and Value.* Translated by Peter Winch. Chicago: University of Chicago Press, 1984.

————. *Philosophical Investigations.* Translated by G. E. M. Anscombe, P. M. S. Hacker, and Joachim Schulte. Rev. 4th ed. Chichester: Wiley-Blackwell, 2009.

Wolter, Allan. "John Duns Scotus on the Primacy and Personality of Christ." Pages 139–82 in *Franciscan Christology: Selected Texts, Translations, and Introductory Essays*. Edited by Damian McElrath. Saint Bonaventure, NY: Franciscan Institute, 1997.

Wolterstorff, Nicholas. *Inquiring about God*. Vol. 1 of *Selected Essays*. Edited by Terence Cuneo. New York: Cambridge University Press, 2010.

Zimmerman, Dean. "An Anti-Molinist Replies." Pages 163–86 in *Molinism: The Contemporary Debate*. Edited by Ken Perszyk. Oxford: Oxford University Press, 2012.

Zizioulas, John D. *Lectures in Christian Dogmatics*. Edited by Douglas H. Knight. Translated by Katerina Nikolopulu. London: T&T Clark, 2009.

INDEX

Abasciano, Brian, 209n55

Adam: choice of, 20–21n28;
desire to be like God, 106; sin
of, 95, 180–82; struggle against
evil in his self-creation, 171,
172–74

Adams, Marilyn McCord,
27n37, 27n38, 201

adultery, children of, 75–76,
186n26

Alston, William, 137n24

analogy, Thomistic, 135–43,
150–52; distinction between
God's formal features and
attributes, 135–36; distinction
between metaphorical and
analogical terms for God, 139;
distinction between perfections (*res*) and modes (*modus*)
in God's wisdom, 138–43;
as irreducible to univocity,
137n25, 150–51n44; rupture

and the analogical concept
of divine wisdom, 136–39,
151; and Scotus's account of
analogy between God's wisdom and our wisdom, 138–43,
146–47, 150–52

analogy and divine freedom,
Balthasar's account of, 27,
157–66; divine passibility,
158–66; divine passibility
and communion, 161–62;
divine passibility and God's
immutability, 162–63; divine
passibility as metaphor,
158–59, 162–63; fallibility an
essential feature of freedom,
165–66; and God's exemplary
causality, 159–60; and God's
self-creation, 158; grades of
possibility or receptivity in
creatures, 160–61; suprapas-

231

Index

God (beatific knowledge), 98–104; and self-creation, 155–56; Thomas on merit and beatitude, 110–16, 155; three theses in Thomistic account of, 97–104; why we were not created in beatitude from the beginning, 109–20

Bellarmine, Robert, 40–41, 51

Bernanos, Georges, 194n35

Bernard of Clairvaux, 70n47, 99n30, 126n6, 135, 176n8, 177n10, 180n16

biblical criticism, Protestant, 16–17

Black American theodicy, 12

Bonaventure, 188, 191

Burrell, David B., 12, 13, 135–36, 143n33, 150n43

Calvinism, 5, 53, 65, 207, 214

Campbell, Douglas A., 209n55

Catechism of the Catholic Church, 108n42, 204–5n49

Catholic tradition, 17–18, 23, 53; *de auxiliis* controversy of 1607, 23, 41; doctrine of transubstantiation, 75n57; on judgment and God's closing of future choices, 108n42; Reformation-era debates about evil and human freedom, 23

causa sui, 157, 158, 164

chance incompatibilism, 95–96n24

Christian philosophy, 16–17

Christian Platonism, 14–18, 24–25; God's creative agency, 14–15; and God's final causality, 81, 85; God's threefold causality, 24–25; and moderate voluntarism, 85; theodicy and view of evil, 13, 21–22. *See also* Neoplatonism

Christ's self-creation. *See* self-creation in Christ

Chrysostom, John, 20, 207n53, 213n65

Collins, Robin, 201n43

compatibilism: Anglo-American philosophy, 9–10; and incompatibilism, 28, 95–96n24, 125; and predeterminism, 10, 44–45

compatibilist indeterminism, 10–11, 20–21n28, 26, 28, 35, 45–46, 120, 213–14; noncompetitive relationship between God and creatures, 3–5, 10n7, 20, 22–24, 26, 37, 49, 124, 127

concurrence: Bellarmine and, 40–41; Francis de Sales and, 41n10; and God's efficient causality, 38–46, 96–97; Molinist account of, 38–46; noncompetitive, 37; and physical premotion, 41–46; Scotus and the beatific vision, 96–97; Scotus on, 22, 96–97

contingency: Christ's self-

156; and God's exemplary causality, 131–35, 152, 156; and imperfect freedom, 134–35; Irenaeus and optimistic, 131–35, 152, 156; as justifying the possibility of evil, 133. *See also* theodicy

Garrigou-Lagrange, Reginald, 18n21, 47–48n20
German idealism, 158
Gnosticism, 18–21
God's efficient causality, 24–25, 30–31, 33–78, 80; accounting for the occurrence of sin and, 47–56; analogy between final causality and, 80, 81–95; and concurrence, 38–46, 96–97; defining causation itself, 49–50; divine foreknowledge, 35, 63–78, 185–86; God as complete and immediate cause (rejecting the accounts of Molina and Báñez), 36–46; and the malignity of sin, 58–63; Molinism and, 38–46, 63–69, 82; and negation relation, 54–57, 196n37; and negation without premotion, 51–58; and nonacts of the will, 59–60, 83, 86, 105–6, 127n7; and nonconsideration of the rule of right reason, 59, 86, 88–89; and physical premotion, 41–46, 58–59, 90–91n17, 170–71; and predetermin-

ism, 57–58. *See also* divine foreknowledge
God's exemplary causality, 14, 24, 25–28, 121–66; and accounts of freedom that are insufficient, 27–28, 124–31, 166; and analogical participation, 151–52; apophatic approach, 151–52; Balthasar's account of analogy and divine freedom, 27, 157–66; and Christ's exemplary causality, 29, 167, 188–89, 194–95, 199; and divine passibility, 27n38, 158–66; exemplarity and three kinds of resemblance to God, 151–52; Irenaeus's freewill theodicy (and modes of goodness), 131–35, 152, 156; and metaphor, 139, 158–59, 162–63; and noncompetitive relationship between God and creatures, 3–5, 10n7, 20, 22–24, 26, 37, 49, 124, 127; and our self-creation, 152–58, 161; and participated freedom, 27–28, 124–31, 166; Scotus's account of analogy between God's wisdom and our wisdom, 138–43, 146–47, 150–52; Scotus's concept of infinite intensity of divine perfections, 141, 144–50; and Scotus's doctrine of conceptual univocity, 143–44, 146–51; and

Index